The CFO as Business Integrator

The CFO as Business Integrator

CEDRIC READ, HANS-DIETER SCHEUERMANN
AND THE mySAP FINANCIALS TEAM

WILEY

Published by John Wiley & Sons Ltd, The Atrium, Southern Gate, Chichester,
West Sussex PO19 8SQ, England

Telephone (+44) 1243 779777

Email (for orders and customer service enquiries): cs-books@wiley.co.uk
Visit our Home Page on www.wileyeurope.com or www.wiley.com

This publication is designed to provide accurate and authoritative information in regard to the
subject matter covered. It is sold on the understanding that the Publisher is not engaged in rendering
professional services. If professional advice or other expert assistance is required, the services of a
competent professional should be sought.

Other Wiley Editorial Offices

John Wiley & Sons Inc., 111 River Street, Hoboken, NJ 07030, USA

Jossey-Bass, 989 Market Street, San Francisco, CA 94103-1741, USA

Wiley-VCH Verlag GmbH, Boschstr. 12, D-69469 Weinheim, Germany

John Wiley & Sons Australia Ltd, 33 Park Road, Milton, Queensland 4064, Australia

John Wiley & Sons (Asia) Pte Ltd, 2 Clementi Loop #02-01, Jin Xing Distripark, Singapore 129809

John Wiley & Sons Canada Ltd, 22 Worcester Road, Etobicoke, Ontario, Canada M9W 1L1

Wiley also publishes its books in a variety of electronic formats. Some content that appears in print
may not be available in electronic books.

Library of Congress Cataloging-in-Publication Data

Read, Cedric.
    The CFO as business integrator/Cedric Read, Hans-Dieter Scheuermann and the
  mySAP Financials Team.
      p. cm.
  Includes bibliographical references and index.
  ISBN 0-470-85149-X (cased : alk. paper)
    1. Chief financial officers. 2. Business enterprises–Finance. 3. Corporations–Finance.
  I. Scheuermann, Hans-Dieter. II. mySAP Financials Team. III. Title.

HG4027.35 .R43 2003
658.15–dc21   2002191009

British Library Cataloguing in Publication Data

A catalogue record for this book is available from the British Library

ISBN 0-470-85149-X

Typeset in 11/13pt Rotis by Footnote Graphics Limited, Warminster, Wiltshire
Printed in Italy

Preface

The CFO as Business Integrator has a simple, but ambitious goal: to serve as an implementation guide for the CFO's new finance integration agenda. In our many months of researching this book, we've found that executives feel both confused by integration technology and driven to pursue the tantalizing benefits it offers. They want to move from complexity to simplicity, but need a clear integration road map. We believe this book will serve as a trusted, practical companion you can turn to as you shape a fresh new vision for your finance function.

In the first book in this series, *The CFO: Architect of the Corporation's Future*, we found that CFOs were increasingly involved in strategic planning, particularly in building shareholder value. In the second book, *eCFO: Sustaining Value in the New Corporation*, we looked at the enormous impact of e-Business on the finance function. With the growth in importance of intangible assets – brands, intellectual property, and technical expertise – we found the CFO becoming an internal venture capitalist, helping to launch new enterprises, rethinking value propositions, and managing investments as a portfolio of options.

What has changed since these two books appeared? In the aftermath of the dot-com era, the CFO has been left to unravel what we call "systems spaghetti" – a complex and fragmented mix of legacy systems and best-of-breed of Internet software solutions. The result? A huge integration challenge. The Internet has also pushed companies to globalize. The result? Growing complexity.

What else is different since we wrote *eCFO*? Today, we have access to exciting new technologies – advanced ERP systems, exchanges, portals, and middleware – all of which are opening up a rich array of new opportunities for true integration, real knowledge sharing, and faster, better decision support.

We've written this latest book, *The CFO as Business Integrator*, for three reasons: first, to make complex businesses simpler; second, to help you take advantage of integration technology, and third, to show you how to create a finance infrastructure that enables you to leverage your investments and compete more effectively.

The CFO is at the center of the drive for integration – pulling together the critical business processes; planning, supporting, and measuring. Increasingly, companies are doing business with external partners – another integration challenge which quite naturally falls to the CFO. So there are three reasons why we see the CFO as integrator – one, structure; two, process; three, technology. And you could add a fourth – linking the inside world with the outside world.

As CFO, you clearly have a lot on your plate! Integration. Strategy. Risk. Control. Analytics. Competitive intelligence. Value chain economics. Today's finance function is leaner and fitter, but the CFO needs some measure of control over accounting – to hang on to financial strategy and policy and discipline. Stakeholders demand a new level of transparency.

That's why we've chosen the Japanese gate as the icon for this book. It is durable, architecturally elegant, and you can look through it from the outside world to the inside world. Spanning the top of the gate are intangible assets, which generate shareholder value. The left-hand pillar represents the financial supply chain, the right-hand pillar, decision support: the information supply chain. What holds it together? Integration. What does it offer? Transparency! From the inside world to the outside world and back again.

In terms of the route forward, we've put this book together using real-life case studies, best-practice data, and interviews with the CFOs of many of the world's largest and best-run companies. Much of the original research and insights included here are drawn from the mySAP Financials Product Management team, the individual subject matter experts who work closely with companies in a range of industries to develop integration solutions that build on existing systems capabilities and leverage technology investments. The team's continuing dialogue with its customers and commitment to innovation has contributed much to the book's scope and depth.

Once again, we wish to acknowledge and thank the visionary CFOs who generously shared their experience and ideas through their personal introductions to each chapter: Phil Bentley of Centrica, Thomas Buess of Zurich Financial Services, Jim Daley of EDS, Steve Davis of ExxonMobil, Gary Fayard of The Coca-Cola Company, Manfred Gentz of DaimlerChrysler,

Inge Hansen of Statoil, Hiroshi Kanai of the Bridgestone Corporation, Jochen Krautter of Henkel and Wolfgang Reichenberger of Nestlé.

From SAP, we wish to thank the following people for contributing their expertise and experience: Michael Sylvester, Chapter 2; Reiner Wallmeier, Chapter 3; Stephen Burns, Chapter 4; Marcus Wefers, Karsten Oehler, and Sheree Fleming, Chapter 5; Jochen Mayerle, Chapter 6; Markus Kuppe, and Ariane Skutela, Chapter 7; Jürgen Daum, Chapter 8; Kraig Haberer, and Barbara Dörr, Chapter 9. For their support and encouragement, we would also like to thank these SAP executives: Henning Kagermann, Claus Heinrich, Werner Brandt and Werner Sinsig.

We must also give special acknowledgment to our external advisors and many helpful contributors from Atos KPMG Consulting and to the team at John Wiley, especially Rachael Wilkie. Thanks also to our invaluable support team: Karin Abarbanel, Sue Bishop, and Stephanie Eger.

Contents

Contents

CHAPTER 1

From Complexity to Simplicity

ACHIEVING INDUSTRY LEADING RETURNS THROUGH OPERATIONAL EXCELLENCE

Steve Davis, Vice President, Downstream Business Services
ExxonMobil Corporation

ExxonMobil is the largest publicly owned oil company in the world, with a market capitalization of approximately $250 bn. In 2001, it was the most profitable company in the USA, with earnings of $15.3 bn and a return on capital employed of 18%. Steve Davis describes the company's strategic priorities: "Our financial goal focuses on growth in shareholder value; our fundamental business principles are:

- *Ethical behaviour and strong business controls*
- *Unwavering commitment to operations integrity*
- *Disciplined, efficient use of capital*
- *Continuous focus on cost management*
- *Commitment to develop the highest quality, motivated and diverse workforce*
- *Commitment to technology leadership*

Based on the past five years' capital spending patterns, our capital expenditures have exceeded $65 bn, comparing favourably with our peer group competitors. Spending on the replenishment of our resource base and on research to achieve capital productivity is key to our future success."

1

The synergies from integrating the two companies, Exxon and Mobil, have now largely been achieved. There was surprisingly little operational overlap between the two organizations in terms of geography, so employees were able to execute successfully a comprehensive, post-merger integration program with confidence and a sense of personal security. ExxonMobil's management philosophy places a high value on people – it needs to – there are almost 98,000 employees worldwide. Much emphasis is placed on personal development and providing opportunity and challenge across the global organization. ExxonMobil's success in achieving consistently strong financials is also tied to the quality of relationships with their suppliers, their customers and the host governments who partner with ExxonMobil on developing strategic oil and natural gas resources.

Steve goes on to say, "We in the finance function have the current objective of moving our primary role from transaction processing to decision support. I believe we are in a unique position to take on the role of impassionate investor – getting involved at an early stage in deals – how we structure them, how we work with host governments, and also looking at the risks and returns from a shareholder value viewpoint. Finance's responsibility is not getting caught up in the emotion and 'art of the deal', but to focus on the cold realities and the best financial returns for the shareholder. In effect, we are the internal venture capitalist."

At ExxonMobil, finance executives are viewed as advisers on new ventures – 'getting a seat at the table' early enough in the formulation of deals to be proactive and to make a difference, by asking the difficult questions and looking at the business from a holistic viewpoint – not just from an engineering perspective, or perhaps a marketing viewpoint, but across the entire enterprise. As such, flawless execution in their finance function is all about integration, effectively bridging the considerations of all functions. Their strong relationship with the operations and engineering aspects of the business demand a tight collaboration with the finance function.

Steve describes some of the key initiatives for the finance function: "Post-merger, some three years ago, we set out the following initiatives for our short term horizon – these included not only capitalizing on the merger cost synergies from putting together two finance functions, but also business simplification and standardization. For example, we are standardizing our payables process worldwide, using advanced e-Procurement tools. Additionally, we try to harvest numerous 'knock-on' and 'value-added' opportunities. And we continually seek to reduce our internal reporting and consolidation needs – in general, to greatly reduce overall back office requirements.

Looking ahead, we now intend to ramp up our service with value-added advice and to harvest the full benefit of our worldwide SAP ERP investments. In the downstream businesses alone, we have over 35,000 individuals in our ERP user base. In the past two years, we have been working on data conversion, testing and stabilization – we now have a very high percentage of the overall transaction base on the SAP platform and there are still major opportunities for standardization and for gaining the full benefits of our global scale. A significant benefit of our ERP investment is the extension of our shared services delivery model – moving from multiple transaction locations to a much smaller number of large business support centers. The scope of ExxonMobil's shared services initiative ranges from customer services to procurement, general ledger accounting, to HR and IT application support.

Much like others' globalization efforts, we see it more as evolution rather than revolution. We are balancing risk with return and proceeding at a pace of change that is manageable for our organization's resource base and culture. We now have a much larger platform for shared service centers both within our firm and across industries – for example, there is the potential for greater sharing of services between the downstream and upstream businesses – and between industries which are similarly positioned on a global enterprise-wide application such as SAP. Increasingly, we are seeing other companies moving toward broader, global business services models.

What is the savings potential? Typically, in the 15–30% range but this may even be exceeded in certain circumstances. Our shared services initiative has been ongoing for some 2+ years and we expect shared services to be continually optimised. What's our vision? We will know that we have achieved our goal when we are running the shared service centers flawlessly, at improved service levels and at the lowest possible cost to our internal customers. One of the keys is also to install a disciplined set of metrics to gauge service performance and rigorously steward these results."

The successful model for shared services is to effectively balance scale advantage of what ExxonMobil centralizes and what remains at the local *execution level for expertise and business acumen, for example. Some of the activities embedded at the local level are quite often unique to that specific locale. We are striving to make shared service centers more efficient with increasing levels of standardization and extending relationships with external partners where they have relevant expertise, for example with commercial banks. ExxonMobil currently selectively outsources some work on tax, HR benefits and retail engineering services, for example. The intent is to secure efficiencies internally first and, only where it makes economic sense for cost and expertise reasons, to outsource.*

IT plays a critical part in integrating the business through EDI, market places – for example online procurement, online credit management, exchange and contract settlement – as well as through portals. "We have developed a common portal across the organization giving us a consistent look and feel. Our IT integration strategy is in basic two steps:

Step 1: Securing/rationalising our current technology base – through a smaller number of more consistent IT platforms. This involves, for example, standardizing on SAP for supply chain, logisitics, and financials, and on consistent desktop suite applications. We only invest in software where there is a compelling ROI and where the functionality is 'best-of-breed' for our requirements.

Step 2: Fully developing the remaining IT building blocks – this involves standardization on middleware, data warehousing, wireless applications, collaborative tools and, importantly from a finance perspective, analytics. Analytics are tools we use for slicing and dicing our data, taking advantage in our investment in data warehousing and improving our ability to access information, and providing supplementary analyses through flexible management reporting.

What are some of the tangible examples of this integration program for finance? Firstly, internal control: we collaborate over the intranet, sharing lessons learnt from different locations and business controls covering, for example, cash collections and application. We share knowledge on accounting policies and procedures and strive to achieve commonality on the application of such accounting standards across the globe. We have taken a steady and consistent view of the internet – we don't regard e-Business as a new business venture, but as an enabling tool. For example, web-based applications in finance, such as credit assessment and approval, and an internal portal for multipoint-access of data, are able to generate an acceptable ROI, by reducing direct support costs across functions and across geographies."

As far as decision support is concerned, Steve Davis and his finance team continue to raise the bar for operational excellence within their function. They have already invested in processes, systems and data, but there is still more to do. When questioned on the future of the finance function, Steve replied "Finance will be different. We will be focused more on our expert services and efficient delivery of basic transactional services through our large business support centers. Importantly, the finance function is in the advantaged position of influencing decisions affecting the entire enterprise, cutting across all functions and protecting the general interest.

Finance executives should contribute their business views and judgements on critical business decisions. As such, finance professionals should take full advantage of their technical expertise and professional training. At ExxonMobil, we strive to develop finance professionals by giving them operational experience early on in their career to get them much closer to the front line of the business. In an industry like ours, it's important not to specialize too early in your career: be open-minded, explore new situations, have the flexibility to travel and experience diverse cultures. I believe our finance skills enable us to be great integrators – the bridge that cements the real organization of today with the vision of the one for tomorrow."

The challenges facing ExxonMobil today are probably not unlike those you are grappling with at your own company. For large multinationals, the 1990s focused mainly on implementing ERP and achieving some level of global standardization. Investments in technology were justified by the need to replace legacy systems and the race to handle Y2K conversions.

Today's finance world is far different. We have seen the rise and fall of dot-com ventures. We have seen the Internet begin to demonstrate its true transformative powers. And more recently, we have seen the demise of Enron shake investor and shareholder confidence to the core – helping to trigger a serious downturn in the global economy.

Perhaps as never before, the CFO stands at the center of all this turmoil and change – and opportunities they present. It was reliable, sharply focused CFOs who kept their companies on a steady course through the dot-com craze. And it was these same CFOs who have begun to pick up the pieces after the tremendous negative impact of inflated corporate performance. The investing public has said, "We have to trust someone – and we trust the CFO." Sustaining this trust offers both major challenges and rewards.

WHAT ISSUES ARE TODAY'S CFOS GRAPPLING WITH?

In writing this book, we had intense, often lengthy, discussions with CFOs from leading companies all over the world. While their industries, backgrounds, and priorities often differed, three common concerns emerged from these dialogues:

- *Transparency and trust are, and will continue to be, top priorities.* Today, CFOs in every industry are emphasizing professionalism, fiscal discipline, and more rigorous risk management. The drive for *transparency* spurred by new legislation resulting from recent accounting scandals is leading to fresh initiatives for reporting and accounting standards. Keeping the external stakeholder world properly informed about what's happening in the internal corporate world is now seen, more than ever before, as a crucial role for the CFO.

- *The drive for* simplicity *is leading to changes in structure and process.* Reducing businesses' complexity is being viewed as both a critical – and achievable – corporate imperative. Reducing the number of business units, reducing the number of brands, reducing the number of systems – are all examples of how companies are tackling this issue. Our research shows that many CFOs are implementing more shared services, a faster accounts close, and less onerous budgeting processes. There is renewed interest in outsourcing key elements of the finance function.

- *The drive to improve technology* ROI *is reshaping investment decisions.* Many large technology programs that would have easily won approval not too long ago have been put on hold. Investments are being made only if and when there is strong evidence to support quick wins and hard cash benefits.

The CFOs of the world's leading organizations are pushing to gain greater benefits from automation by using a mix of best-of-breed technologies and leveraging existing ERP investment – while keeping an eye on emerging technology tools. Finance's focus is shifting from transaction processing to decision support. Business cases have to be sharper and more compelling.

Technology options and solutions are multiplying more quickly than ever, leaving many companies with a hodgepodge of systems that do not work easily together – what we call "systems spaghetti!". While CFOs are now looking to their CIOs for clearer strategies for integration, they often find themselves forced to lead the way in this area. Why? Mainly because business integration is not just about technology. It is also about reducing complexity, streamlining business processes, and making decision support a reality. True integration: the prize it offers is enormous, but the decisions to achieve it are tough. And more and more often, it is the CFO who must make them!

Reconciling *what customers value* with *what creates value for share-holders* is also a major challenge for the CFO. What's more, linking together shareholder value, customer value, and the value of intangible assets – and embedding this value in your company's financial management processes – requires a major reorientation. The old-world mindset is steeped in traditional accounting based on historically assessing physical assets. The stewardship function of the CFO and his finance staff is, of course, still important. But the new-world management mindset is very different: it is based not on past performance, but on future results that flow from generating sustainable value from intangible assets.

Consider a major oil company's current *finance of the future* vision statement:

". . . We want our finance function . . .

To be a smaller, smarter outfit:
Helping to create new business, managing integration

To eliminate manual transaction processing:
Using the net to integrate and automate processes

To look like a refinery control room:
Monitoring immense flows of transactions, controlling by exception

To use Web-based information portals:
Helping us make more informed decisions at the right time."

So how much progress has been made? How close are the finance teams of leading companies to transforming this type of vision into practice? Most would say that their transaction processing is much more efficient – and that they are well on the road to standardizing ERP worldwide and to implementing shared services. In this chapter we take a closer look at what individual companies are actually doing – their business cases for change and the results so far. The following case studies show that the benefits are coming through from IT investment, but very few companies – even global industry leaders – are satisfied with the quality of their decision-support infrastructure. Consider this case study.

 CASE STUDY
Finance Transformation at United Biscuits

This UK consumer products company embarked on an enterprise-wide change program to fully exploit its quality brand portfolio and to improve profitability. When Ian Cray, the CFO, joined the company, he initiated a finance transformation program. Independent research showed that the finance function did not meet the needs of the company's new business strategy. Ian says: "There was a burning platform for change within the finance team. The organization did not meet the needs of the company's new business strategy and the function was just too expensive. The structure of the finance department was such that our finance staff were not really undertaking value-added activities. There was a lack of clear rules and discipline for consistent performance reporting and the accounting and transaction processes being implemented using SAP had not been re-engineered. Consequently, activities were duplicated and the finance processes were not in line with the rest of the business. At the same time we could not ignore the significant role that finance plays within Corporate Governance. There were clear and consistent imperatives for major change."

Within 12 months, led by its new CFO, the company reduced its finance headcount by approximately one third. Following the successful implementation of shared services, the proportion of finance staff working on transaction processing has reduced and the focus for development is now shifting towards the value adding key decision support areas. The benefits to UB of these improvements are seen to be as follows:

- *Better planning: the budget preparation and approval cycle will be streamlined*

- *Better reporting:*   *reporting will be centralized and consistent*
- *Right first time:*   *transaction error rates will be halved*
- *More responsive:*   *the books are now closed within three days of the month end*
- *More efficient:*   *transaction processing costs will be reduced by a further 40%*

In addition, Ian Cray has set the target of more than doubling the amount of time spent by finance staff on true decision support. The object is for finance to be seen as the "expert partner." The finance change program was designed to be coordinated with other internal change programs and required a disciplined and structured approach. "Planning and implementing the finance change program successfully across the UK and Europe meant that tight project management was absolutely essential" says Bridget Grenville-Cleave, Finance Change Controller. "As well as the executive and management sponsors, we also involved many front-line finance staff in the program." A lot of attention was given to communicating with key stakeholders and tight deadlines were set for achieving tangible results. Eight work streams were organized to tackle two key areas:

- *The core change program – initiatives for reporting, planning, transactions and organization redesign.*
- *The program framework – setting out how the finance transformation program was to be managed and outlining initiatives on four fronts: values, communication, technology, and policy.*

People development was given very high priority. One of the initiatives, for example, focused on a finance development program to upgrade staff capabilities while improving motivation and morale. Surveys measured how successfully the new cultural improvements were bedding in. All initiatives have clear benefits tracking in place. Performance indicators and project milestones are monitored quarterly.

There is still further room for improvement in transaction processing, but Ian Cray's attention is now turning to decision support: "The entire value chain is within the scope of this initiative – accountability for product categories is crucial to us and we are focusing our decision support capabilities on organic growth strategies for our brands and on releasing cost savings from our supply chain. All business decisions are fully evaluated for risk and to optimize return.

I am now looking to my finance people for value-added analysis and insight. We will be sharing techniques, tools, and learning across our organization structure. Our role is changing from 'scorekeepers' to 'business partners.' I believe best practice in finance today is not just about cutting cost to meet a relatively arbitrary benchmark of, say 1% of sales or less. It is much more about finance playing a crucial role in helping the organization as a whole to transform".

UB is under pressure to perform. Finance has taken advantage of a company-wide change program to perform major surgery and speed up its own rate of change. Once the new finance organization is bedded-in, changes will become progressively harder to make because the low-hanging fruit will have already been picked. Companies at the stage UB has now reached are increasingly looking to new technology to drive them to a more advanced stage of development.

In Figure 1.1. we show how a major pharmaceutical company's finance program structured its benefits pyramid – taking advantage of the latest technology for portals, application integration, and *lights-out* transaction processing. The most important thing to note is the pace of the program – the 60-day milestones, for example, and the results expected within, say, 360 days.

The research for this book demonstrates that companies planning carefully structured finance transformation programs with "stretch" targets achieve the best results. Such initiatives tend to fall into three categories.

1. *Cultural change programs.* Companies in this category tend to be inspired by the CEO and his board-level colleagues with a vision for radical organizational transformation. Major cost reduction, rapid change, and an external injection of fresh management talent characterize this type of program. The CFO has to lead by example with a radical overhaul of finance – as in the United Biscuits case study.

2. *ERP programs.* Companies in this category are committed to enterprise-wide business process simplification and standardization using tech-

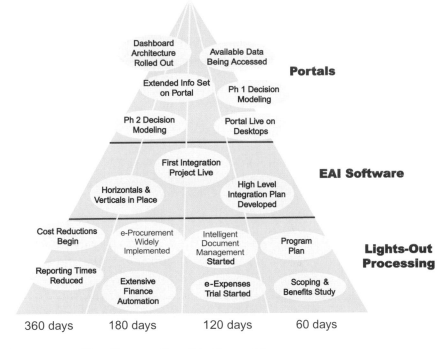

Figure 1.1 *The Finance Benefits Pyramid*

nology. The finance function is a fundamental and integral part of the systems change. Most global companies have either recently installed or are in the process of installing their ERP systems. Improvements in transaction processing are the main benefits. Microsoft, our next case study, is a typical example.

3. *Business partner programs.* Companies in this category do not require radical transformation and typically have already completed their ERP implementation. Such business partner programs are the most challenging because they fundamentally redefine the nature of the finance service and no single systems solution is possible. Evolution, not revolution, is the theme. The CFO has the difficult job of changing the finance skill base and integrating finance with the rest of the business – and coordinating its functions with external business partners. Later in this chapter we use Diageo, a leading-edge consumer products company, to exemplify the depth and breadth of such change.

BEST PRACTICES IN FINANCE: WHAT'S NEXT?

Whatever type of change program you are committed to as CFO, the most pressing issue you face today is how best to harness the power of technology and how far to push for further improvements, without putting your business at risk. The pursuit of efficiency for efficiency's sake must be tempered with growing requirements for control and risk management.

Often, the finance function is seen as the *Trojan horse for change* within a company. As one CFO put it: "Change finance and you change the organization." What he meant by this was that finance can actually be an obstacle to change since traditional accounting and reporting disciplines reflect the old world, rather than the new. The story of how Microsoft began changing its finance function illustrates many common issues and challenges.

CASE STUDY
Finance: The Business Integrator at Microsoft

Microsoft is headquartered in the United States and has regional centers for each continent. Its regional subsidiaries focus on consulting, along with sales and marketing. The company has just three major production sites worldwide. Its subsidiaries adopted a centralized warehouse and distribution model some five years ago. Operations moved away from in-country subsidiary customer service to centralized operation centers which manage the contractual relationship with their customers.

Claude Changarnier, European CFO of Microsoft (EMEA), describes the challenges for the finance function: "Our biggest problem in the past was that we had too many systems. This meant we suffered from too little systems integration and relatively high development and support costs. We were also fairly inflexible and did not have the agility we needed to react quickly. We suffered from business inefficiency – manually intensive business processes, inconsistent business rules, and literally dozens of paper forms per location. We were not best in class."

Microsoft went through a number of stages in restructuring its finance function from the pre-1993 era of scorekeepers, through a program of business-process reengineering and automation in the mid to late 1990s to the present era of full business integration. This evolutionary process is shown in Figure 1.2.

At Microsoft, finance evolved in three phases. Phase 1 involved standard-ization and redesign – developing standardized management accounts and processes, which aligned finance much more closely to the frontline business. Finance roles and responsibilities were more clearly defined.

Phase 2 involved investment in standard platforms. SAP was chosen as its standardized ERP platform on a single database. Consistent worldwide standard views and methods were employed, together with a system of common report-ing. Full advantage was taken by the company of its intranet – especially its Web-based self-service capabilities.

Phase 3 involves the evolution of standard platforms toward best-practice levels that will put Microsoft on a par with other global industry leaders. Its reporting systems need to become more flexible. While the company has a way to go, it is making clear progress – and reaping tangible benefits.

Today, Microsoft has one general ledger, one common chart of accounts. It has standard reporting templates for each functional area, by geography, by

**Post '00
Business
Integration**

**'95 - '00
Process
Automation**

**'93 - '95
Business Process
Reengineering**

**Pre '93:
Scorekeepers**

Figure 1.2 *Microsoft Finance Evolution*

product, and by channel. For accounting, it has standard definitions, taxonomies, and hierarchies. Key financial and operational matrices are available in real time, including:

- *Revenue and inventory by product, customer, location and channel*
- *Organization headcount and people details*
- *Transaction cost detail worldwide*

All financial reports are distributed electronically within four days after the end of the accounting period. There is little IT involvement in report creation or distribution: for all intents and purposes, the processes are seamless.

The cost of Microsoft's finance function today is less than 1% of revenue – employing 1,050 heads out of 50,000 total. Transaction costs have been reduced substantially, for example:

- *Customer order process costs reduced from $60 to $5 of order*
- *Purchase transaction costs reduced from $30 to $5 per invoice*
- *Travel and entertainment expense transaction cost reduced from $21 to $3 per expense report*

The next challenges for finance at Microsoft will be business partnering, analyzing sales productivity, and identifying new revenue opportunities. To support these initiatives, Microsoft's systems investment will focus on business intelligence, business analysis, and data quality management.

As Claude says, "We believe we have achieved our objective of bringing our transaction processing to the best-practice level, mainly through our program of standardization. We have isolated our core processes and aim to minimize the number of information systems we rely upon. Although we have a clear segregation of duties among our sales, marketing, and finance organizations, we want to recruit finance people for the future who want to understand our business as a whole. To meet our next round of challenges we, in finance, need to be business integrators."

What is best practice finance today? The CFOs of companies like Microsoft are striving to push their improvement levels ever higher. They seek finance benchmarking data to calibrate their own progress. However, no one company has implemented every best practice available in every area. In most organizations, there are pockets of best practices.

Quantitative metrics generally cover transaction processing efficiency; usually the results are expressed in terms of finance cost as a percentage of revenues. But this can be very misleading because it is difficult to achieve fair comparisons since definitions of cost and revenue vary from company to company, and industry to industry. Benchmarking data is generally readily available at the finance *process* level – for example, cost-per-purchase-invoice processed.

Qualitative definitions of best practices for transaction processing are more difficult to clarify, and in the decision support area there is definite lack of useful comparative criteria and data collection. What's more, the goal posts are moving! Some of the more commonly used high-level benchmark criteria are set out in Figure 1.3. This figure also compares best practice in finance today with a vision for tomorrow.

Most CFOs see their finance functions on an evolutionary, not a revolutionary, path in their journey toward achieving best-practice objectives. Few companies, for example, can claim to have a truly global shared service center, although many leaders across industries have clearly stated this as a priority.

	World Class	Average
Cost as % of Revenue	Less than 1%	1.5%
Processing Locations	1	More than 3
Systems per Process	1	2 - 3
Budget Cycle	Less than 2 Months	4 - 6 Months
Closing Cycle	Less than 2 Days	8 - 11 Days

Figure 1.3   *Finance Best Practice Today and Tomorrow*

Much of the information and insights you'll find in the chapters that follow focus on how you can stretch your finance function to achieve leading-edge resources and capabilities. Transforming transaction processing from one facet of your finance function into a business in its own right is a target that many companies are taking aim at today. The goal: to generate value from the finance function and higher ROI by fully exploiting new technology tools and processes. Radically improving decision support and extending its reach to every function and employee is another major goal many CFOs are striving for. This means breaking new ground, building new skills, and finding fresh insight.

THE NEW FINANCE VALUE PROPOSITION

Most CFOs interviewed for this book said they wanted the role of the finance function to be that of business partner. However, when asked what this really meant in practice, many CFOs find this new role difficult to describe. This isn't really surprising since decision support, which underpins this concept of business partnership, is an ill-defined and gray area. The term "decision support" can cover anything from strategic investment appraisal, to business planning, to performance management using scorecards, to just simple drill-down for analysis of historical spend. Little wonder that identifying best practices and benchmarks in this critical area is a daunting task!

Different industries have different interpretations as to what best practice in this area means for them. For example in the telecommunications sector, special attention is paid to the analytics for customer lifetime value. In the pharmaceuticals industry, real options valuation (ROV) techniques are used to evaluate R&D portfolio investment. In the financial services sector, customer retention and distribution channel economics are key performance indicators.

All these different approaches can be confusing. But help is on the way. New bodies of learning are emerging around shareholder value and value-based management. Traditional processes, such as budgeting, are being systematically replaced with new processes – for example, dynamic rolling forecasts, ROV, and *cause-and-effect* modelling for linking lead performance indicators. What's more, experience shows that these emerging tools have true cross-industry value. In this case study, the CFO of Diageo's UK subsidiary, Guinness UDV, talks about what's important in the consumer packaged goods industry – but many of the concepts described may prove of value in your own company and industry as well.

CASE STUDY
Search and Spin at Diageo

Diageo is the enterprise that was created out of the Guinness/Grand Met merger in 1997. Today, it is the world's largest branded spirits producer, with brands ranging from Smirnoff vodka and Johnnie Walker whisky to Guinness beer. The merger is seen as a success – synergies have been achieved and the company is achieving impressive year-on-year growth. Ray Joy, the CFO of the UK operation, who has been with the company many years, talks about the post-merger challenges for finance:

"Many consumer goods businesses struggle to make better decisions on how much to invest in their brands. There is nothing to pull readily off the shelf, no magic formula. We introduced an initiative called 'search and spin'. This is a process for searching for ideas and spinning them across the group. We are a global company and our operations vary across the world. One size does not fit all. So we have decided to have our finance function focus on working with our marketing and sales colleagues to determine what creates value and growth.

For example, we have had a lot of success extending our traditional brands into the relatively new ready to drink market. We have achieved this by innovating around the brand in both mature and growing markets with products such as Smirnoff Ice and Archers Apple. Our marketing and finance people work closely together. At a global level, they share knowledge on the relative success of advertising and promotional (A&P) campaigns. We have developed evaluation tools for assessing the effectiveness of advertising and promotional spend and we try to network this information across the organization as much as we can."

Diageo is one of the companies that has abandoned traditional budgeting in favor of a performance management culture based on scorecards with leading indicators. In its case, these indicators measure brand health, equity, and market share. Back-office tasks detracted finance people from focusing on playing their part in growing the business. So transaction processing is being moved into shared service centers, and companies are standardizing their systems on SAP. Culturally and organizationally, Ray believes finance is on a development journey – increasingly focused on managing shareholder value and on delivering performance improvement.

He goes on to say, "As we cut the cost and improve the efficiency of transaction processing, we are investing more of our resources in decision support. Our decision support teams will get bigger and stronger with a broader range of skill. Not all accountants will have the necessary attributes to work with sales and marketing. We, in finance, will still be responsible for leading the evaluation of investments and the control of risk management.

But more and more, our finance executives will have an impact on our commercial decisions. On individual advertising campaigns, for example, we are giving our people opportunities to grow and flourish in ways they haven't had before and we are building a reputation for our leading-edge consumer expertise, so our people are highly sought after by our competitors. Our old systems and processes were not adequate to our needs – we still need to improve in building more infrastructures around our reporting and analytical processes. But I am proud of what we have already achieved in improving our ROI.

Our work has contributed to improved efficiencies in discretionary spend and an overall increase in the net present value of our brands. In 2001, we started a project as part of our global Diageo-wide Brand Building initiative. We established four work streams where our finance people would work more closely with our marketing people:

- *Resource allocation*
- *A&P effectiveness*
- *Econometric modelling*
- *Business process improvement*

This project has had a major impact in terms of the rigor, consistency, and learning shared in our decision support activity. We measure the ROI achieved in terms of brand volume growth, cost savings, and changes in product mix. Finance needs to be close to our innovation pipeline so we can make better-informed trade-offs between short-term trading performance and long-term investment.

Yes, we have got some battle scars from piloting some of our new brands – in some cases, we were too successful! Consumers wanted more than we could make available, leading to frustration. How can you budget on a growth agenda for a brand which can go from zero to tens of millions of cases in a year or so? We challenge our colleagues openly, and it is this learning-based environment which has shaped our growth curve to date."

Companies like Diageo are among the world's best-practice leaders in the fields of performance management and decision support. But even Diageo recognizes that it has more to do to pull together a permanent infra-structure to cross-fertilize its innovations and best practices.

Today, many companies are working their way through the shareholder value-based management (VBM) development cycle. This approach is predicated on a company's financial strategy being expressed in terms of shareholder value improvement. Diageo, for example, expresses its long-term financial goals in terms of total shareholder return (TSR) and moti-vates its management by using peer group shareholder value benchmarks and setting three-year rolling economic profit targets.

The VBM development cycle has gone as far as it can go. Now, it has to be translated into business processes for decision support. Many companies are ready to institutionalize some of their learning into such processes for sharing internally and benchmarking externally. While researching this book, we discovered a number of best practices which, when integrated together, form a decision support process framework that we call *"Plan to Perform."* This dynamic approach is defined and detailed in Figure 1.4.

The process cycle starts with *strategic evaluation* – the appraisal and modeling of strategic initiatives. The second step in the cycle is to under-pin these strategic level processes with *business analytics* – for example, to measure customer lifetime value, business analytics might focus on risk assessment, as well as A&P effectiveness.

The next step is to link strategic initiatives and their supporting analytics to your company's short-term *planning and forecasting*. Typically, these processes are disconnected, resulting in inefficiency and misleading, if not conflicting, messages up and down the organization. Next, short-term planning and forecasting processes need to be aligned with *accounting and consolidation*. Quite often, we find companies with one set of processes and systems for management planning and another for financial reporting. Clearly, this can lead to confusion and unnecessary "work-arounds."

Strategic Evaluation	Business Analytics & Risk	Planning & Forecasting	Accounting & Consolidation	Performance Reporting	Learning & Feedback
▪ Stakeholder Management ▪ Scenario Modeling ▪ Value Calculation ▪ Strategic Initiatives	▪ Customer Analytics ▪ Supply Chain & Cost Analytics ▪ Value at Risk	▪ Medium-Term Plans ▪ Annual Budgets ▪ Target Setting ▪ Rolling Forecasts	▪ Closing Process ▪ Profit Tracking ▪ General Accounting ▪ Statutory Accounts & Reports	▪ Scorecarding & Visualization ▪ KPI Trees ▪ Performance Contract ▪ Incentives	▪ Performance Dialogue ▪ Knowledge Management ▪ Web-Based Training ▪ Problem Management & Resolution

Figure 1.4 *Plan to Perform – Process Definition*

As the "*Plan to Perform*" cycle continues, financial reporting processes are linked to *balanced scorecards* and *performance reporting*. Scorecards are developed for different levels in the enterprise and the two are interconnected. The final stage focuses on *learning and feedback* – the most important part of the cycle. Having a process for a constructive performance dialogue based on key performance indicators that are linked to strategy – that's best practice today!

Reinforcing the learning and feedback processes with infrastructure (process technology and skills) for knowledge management, Web-based training, and online collaborative decision making – that's the best practice for the decision support process of tomorrow!

The implementation issue for most companies is that strategic planning and operational performance management processes are still relatively fragmented and uncoordinated. The next round of process improvements will involve a more holistic approach to process and systems integration.

INTEGRATION: WHAT IT MEANS FOR YOU AS CFO

The theme for this book is the CFO as *business integrator*. The case for greater integration is built on two distinct, but converging, forces:

1. *Transparency.* As a result of the high-profile financial failures at Enron and World.com, the world of the CFO and the finance function has never been under so much scrutiny – or faced so much pressure for change. Although adherence to proper accounting principles and disciplines is obviously part of the answer, it is not all of the picture. Communicating to stakeholders the *value* of your business is still important, but communicating how this *value is changing,* is equally

so. As we noted earlier in this chapter, the *value drivers* of business are changing. These changes must be conveyed not just internally, but *externally* to investors and other stakeholders.

2. *Technology.* Most companies have now invested in ERP and wish to leverage this investment for further benefit. Many CFOs also wish to continue their programs to simplify and standardize *transaction processing.* Many now wish to extend their finance investment into *decision support.* As a result of the technology boom of the last few years, many companies have invested in best-of-breed technology for the Internet – customer relationship management, e-Procurement and supply chain optimization are all examples of such investments. But more and better change lies ahead! New technology is now available to integrate ERP with best-of-breed solutions. Portals, exchanges, and application integration software – all of which we'll discuss in these pages – are all good examples of powerful integrating technologies with tremendous ripple effects.

The shape of the finance function is changing in response to these phenomena. In the book *CFO: Architect of the Corporation's Future,*[1] the role of the CFO was shown to be changing from scorekeeper to strategist. We saw the CFO shaping the future of the corporation using the fundamental economic concepts based on shareholder value. The evolution of finance over the last two decades is traced in Figure 1.5.

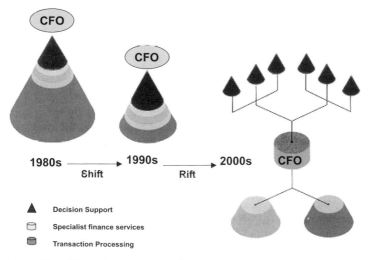

Figure 1.5 *The Changing Shape of Finance*

In Figure 1.5, the finance function of the 1980s is portrayed as a relatively fat pyramid with a heavy emphasis on transaction processing and a light emphasis on decision support. The finance function of the 1990s took advantage of ERP systems and is portrayed as being smaller – with a leaner transaction processing operation and a greater focus on performance management.

Then, in the late 1990s, the Internet made its mark. In the second book in our series, *eCFO: Sustaining Value in the New Corporation*,[2] the CFO was seen as being at the center of a web of relationships – managing the value of the extended enterprise. The finance function was more fragmented, with transaction processing operated remotely in shared services or possibly outsourced. Decision support was embedded in business units. The success of this more fragmented model relied heavily on the ability of the CFO to sustain the integrity of processes and systems. Reporting consistency and data collection and reliability were seen as big issues.

In this new book the themes of integration and consistency are paramount. To symbolize the impact of these issues, we have represented the new finance function using the visual image of the gate to a Japanese shrine. This is intended to symbolize a number of principles the finance function will face in the decade ahead – the *noughties*! These principles are:

- *Transparency*: the gate represents a portal. Stakeholders can use the portal through which to gain insight into the value of the organization. Management can use the portal not only as a tool within its organization, but to gain insight on what's happening in the external environment.

- *Strength*: the *left*-hand pillar of the gate represents the *financial supply chain* which focuses on transaction processing. It is not a fat pyramid anymore, but a lean and robust pillar. It is smaller and more efficient, but remains a vital component of the enterprise – be it insourced or outsourced. The *right*-hand pillar of the gate represents the *information supply chain* which encompasses decision support and reporting – connecting strategy with operational reality. Both pillars now have equal importance to the long-term sustainability and stability of the enterprise.

- *Structural integrity*: the lintel across the gateway is intended to represent the core capabilities and competencies which shape the shareholder value of the enterprise – both now and in the future. These are the *intangibles* – those assets which create cash flow and shareholder value. Most often, these are *soft* assets, such as brands, customers, product innovations, and people. These themes are brought together for the integrated finance function of the future in Figure 1.6.

The integration agenda for today's CFO centers on three critical components: the financial supply chain, the information supply chain (transparent and reliable stakeholder information) and intangible assets. Embracing this agenda will mean changes to finance processes, organizational structure, and employee capabilities. To reap the benefits of achieving this agenda for finance change will require investment in carefully managed and sharply focused integration technology.

However, the mySAP Financials team believe that technology alone will not deliver the results required. Their experience of implementing solutions with finance customers all over the world has shown that such change has to be process-led. This is a recurrent theme throughout this book.

In Chapter 2, we address leveraging your ERP investment, exploring why a lot of companies have ended up with systems spaghetti. Some

Figure 1.6   *The Integrated Finance Function of the Future*

companies, like DaimlerChrysler, have taken an integrated ERP software approach, using SAP, as an essential prerequisite to implementing their strategies for products, services and customers. Other companies have taken more of a best-of-breed approach and have ended up with systems spaghetti. We will describe how such companies will have to prepare themselves to take advantage of the latest integration technologies to promote further collaboration and release untapped benefits. Chapter 3 discusses collaboration specifically for the financial supply chain – how to improve the finance processes for payment, billing, cash management, and in-house banking through further automation. Pioneering these collaborative efforts through the evolution of the finance function and how it is moving from shared services to managed services is explored in Chapter 4.

The chapters which follow explain the latest thinking on the information supply chain. In Chapter 5, on strategic enterprise management (SEM), we show how strategy can be synchronized with performance improvement by upgrading your processes for business planning, budgeting, reporting, and performance measurement. SEM also incorporates risk management.

The new world of analytics, Chapter 6, introduces emerging applications for decision support. This is the missing link between your existing IT investment (in ERP and data warehousing) and your SEM processes. Focusing on transparency, Chapter 7 shows how portals can help improve productivity, promote knowledge sharing, and ensure collaboration, both internally and across the extended enterprise. Since most corporate value today is tied up in intangible assets, Chapter 8 challenges accounting tradition and presents thought-provoking new ideas for managing the value of customers and innovation. It also explores how businesses are beginning to see themselves as value networks and what path leading-edge thinking about value-based management is taking.

The book concludes by bringing together all these best practices for integrating the business – specifically focusing on the *fast close* as a great integrating mechanism for finance processes and systems. The final chapter describes the vision of the mySAP Financials team for the development of the finance function. We end with an epilogue – with a glimpse of the finance function of the future!

CFO CHECKLIST

LEVERAGE YOUR ERP INVESTMENT
Consider the benefits case for your beyond ERP environment. Unravel your systems spaghetti. Rethink, regroup, and recut your finance functions. Design your new "Beyond ERP" architecture.

STREAMLINE THE FINANCIAL SUPPLY CHAIN
Understand the hidden costs of your existing financial supply chain inefficiencies and exceptions. Focus on savings; plan to reduce working capital needs by as much as 25%. Involve your key trading partners in this process. Form multifunctional implementation teams and focus relevant training on cash–flow optimization.

MOVE FROM SHARED TO MANAGED SERVICES
Identify what's noncore – benchmark against leading practices in and even beyond your industry. Take shared services to the next level: expand beyond transaction processing and go global if you can. Consider options for both insourcing and outsourcing. Consider the new market for managed services, business processes, applications management, as well as IT infrastructure and support. Plan for richer, deeper Web–based services.

CONNECT STRATEGY WITH OPERATIONS
Focus your future investment on strategic enterprise management initiatives which create tangible added value. For performance management, strive for a living conversation throughout your company. Translate growth–creating strategies into KPIs (key performance indicators). Integrate risk management with your other SEM components.

CONVERT DATA INTO ACTION WITH ANALYTICS
Go horizontal with analytics across the value chain. Choose your analytics strategy. Leverage investment in customer relationship management (CRM). Apply analytics to the innovation pipeline and product life cycle. Build a proper analytics infrastructure – balance formality with informality.

COLLABORATE VIA THE ENTERPRISE PORTAL
Lead from the top – portal projects need high visibility. Consider the cost of integration of your ERP, exchange structure, and data warehousing resources. Take advantage of prepackaged content. Go for quick wins and then be sure to keep them coming!

MANAGE THE VALUE OF INTANGIBLES
Identify your hidden assets – intangibles! Look for potential missed opportunities for cross-selling and leveraging. Balance the ratio of tangibles to intangibles. Keep an intangibles scorecard. Transform value networks into value centers.

CONSIDER YOUR NEW ROLE AS BUSINESS INTEGRATOR!
Develop global guidelines for enterprise integrity. Encourage transparency – inside out and outside in – for both financial reporting and risk management. Consider the enterprise-wide benefits of a faster close. Look 10 years into the future. For transaction processing, think of finance as a business in its own right. For decision support, focus on the new roles and skills required for long-term value creation.

CHAPTER 2

Leveraging your ERP Investment

PURSUING INTEGRATION AFTER A MAJOR INDUSTRIAL MERGER

Manfred Gentz, CFO
DaimlerChrysler

DaimlerChrysler is one of the largest industrial organizations in the world and a global leader in automotive manufacturing, financing, and marketing. In the late 1990s, Daimler Benz of Germany acquired Chrysler of the United States in what remains one of the largest industrial marriages in history. DaimlerChrysler currently has manufacturing facilities in 37 countries and sells its products in 200 countries around the world.

Manfred Gentz, CFO, describes his company's global ambitions: "Our strategy is based on four pillars. First, there is geographic reach – we aim to be represented in every major region of the world. The second pillar is product range – we have a broad selection of vehicles, from commercial freightliner heavy trucks to the Smartcar. Technology is our third strategic pillar – we believe we have a leading position in the automotive industry based on our continuing investment in cutting-edge technology. Our fourth area of strategic focus is brand development. Brands such as Mercedes Benz are very strong indeed. We try to avoid overlap, investing in individual brands to sustain our market leadership."

As one of the world's biggest transactions, managing DaimlerChrysler's post-merger integration was a formidable challenge. Improving profitability has been a high priority during post-merger integration, particularly in the U.S.-based Chrysler division. But the combined company is now operating smoothly and poised for expansion. Recently, for example, it invested in the Pacific Rim through Hyundai and Mitsubishi.

Building shareholder value is at the top of DaimlerChrysler's strategic agenda and it remains committed to investing in an integrated value chain. Manfred comments on his company's investment policy: "We continue to invest heavily in the Mercedes Benz brand as well as in our people, our technologies, and our relationships with customers and suppliers. We try to maintain a balance between investing in physical infrastructure for manufacturing and investing in intangibles. Bringing the Smartcar to market only took about four years; this is a far quicker time to market than is normal for the automotive industry. However, building a brand takes time and it can be very costly. Investing in brands and technologies ultimately leads to further investment down the value chain in production infrastructure – we cannot neglect our physical asset base."

Manfred comments on DaimlerChrysler's approach to integration and standardization, which is aimed at improving overall performance. "In our experience, what's right for one business is not necessarily right for another. Our predecessor companies each thought their business model was the right one; and of course, when we merged, we found genuine differences. We knew we had to adjust one company's systems to match the other's, but we were challenged as to which way we should go and at what pace.

We started by standardizing processes that supported the consolidation effort so that we could maintain control of the business. We achieved this relatively quickly. It took us longer to find out the special qualities that made Chrysler fundamentally different from Daimler. Below the level of corporate integration there are special processes and systems which are specific to each of our business units rather than standard for the whole group. In pursuing our program of global standardization, we have had to accept valid deviations. It's a question of development. Ten years from now we will have a much higher level of top-down standardization."

Predictably, the newly combined company inherited many legacy systems; since the merger, its policy has been to supplement ERP with best-of-breed resources. DaimlerChrysler is strongly committed to e-Business and has achieved significant strides in the area of e-Procurement. Manfred comments on integrating procurement resources: "It's a mistake to go all out for standardization in a short time. We have made huge progress so far in integrating our processes with our suppliers. Yet while we have achieved savings, they tend to be one-off.

Change is a continuous process of evolution and you have to invest in it. Today, for example, we don't integrate just our first-tier suppliers, but our whole chain of suppliers, right down to the fourth and fifth level – and we still have a long way to go. I am skeptical about the savings potential of industry exchanges like Covisint, but we have to participate; otherwise we would be at a competitive disadvantage. There are still more opportunities to save money on the supply side, but for the future, we see major potential in further integrating our links on the sales side through the distributor network to the end customer. Mercedes Benz has been traditionally strong in wholesale functions, but we are now investing in our retail network within the guidelines of European regulation."

Integrating the physical supply chain processes – from supply through to sales – has generated efficiency improvements for DaimlerChrysler. But there is still potential for improvements in working capital – and the financial supply chain. As Manfred notes: "One of my targets is to reduce working capital and optimize our cash-management processes. The finance function must get involved in operational processes and really understand the drivers behind working capital. We want to better integrate our finance functions throughout the company. We have several projects to address shared services. We started down this road early in Germany by centralizing corporate functions at the headquarters of many of our plants. We launched similar initiatives in our sales organizations and in treasury, specifically in North America, where treasury shared services are fully implemented. We are now implementing programs in Asia, first on a country by country basis and then at a regional level."

For DaimlerChrysler, reducing working capital is a sensitive balance act. It involves achieving benefits for the company without sacrificing valuable customer/supplier relationships. As Manfred points out: "We are working closely with our suppliers, cooperating on engineering and development and on reducing costs in the production process while maintaining our high standards of component functionality and quality. We have to safeguard the interests of our suppliers. We rely on them and they have to earn an adequate return."

Over the last three years, the CFO and his team have achieved success in implementing NACOS (new accounting and costing system) which is based on

SAP's R/3 solution. This is a project for producing financial information for business segments cutting across geographic and legal entities. Timeframes for reporting have also been substantially reduced. To quote Manfred: "We are more or less state of the art as far as European and German company reporting is concerned. In shortening the closing process quality did not suffer – in fact, it has improved with the fast close. Today, our transaction processing is considerably cheaper and more streamlined. Now the finance function needs to concentrate on its increasing role as a business partner.

Two challenges remain for DaimlerChrysler's finance function. First, it must continue its program of process standardization by focusing on selected processes where global standards make sense. For example, the company's management information factory (MIF) initiative will help improve transparency and analytical support. Information provided by MIF also supports the reduction of working capital. The second challenge is to improve DaimlerChrysler's processes for managing risk. As Manfred says: "Controlling risk is not just a technical issue for finance. It involves our whole enterprise: our culture, our behavior, and how our company changes over time."

Since the mid-1990s, companies like DaimlerChrysler, ExxonMobil and Colgate-Palmolive have made a corporate religion out of pursuing total integration across their business operations and geographies – and have profited tremendously from their decision. A deliberate strategy emphasizing process improvement and cost saving lies at the heart of their success. This strategy, coupled with rigorous execution, has produced standout results in a host of critical areas, including data centralization, business process redesign, inventory reduction, on-time delivery, customer service, and cash flow. And there is more to come! For example, when its global integration program is fully operational, Colgate-Palmolive projects total savings in excess of $600 million – an astounding accomplishment.[1]

Although ERP (enterprise resource planning) systems were introduced in the 1990s and eagerly embraced by a wide range of industries, few companies have even begun to move toward what DaimlerChrysler is close to achieving: a fully integrated ERP suite implemented enterprise-wide on a global scale. The rare companies who share DaimlerChrysler's vision and commitment have reaped substantial ongoing advantages:

- Information on customers, suppliers, and business partners

- More accurate data and more efficient data flow to key contact points

- Closer links to customers, improved service and customer satisfaction

- Substantial bottom-line savings across key functions

The fundamental premise behind ERP systems is the management of a company's business processes and information in a single, integrated system, resulting in better coordination, visibility, efficiency, and agility. These systems are classic examples of the network effect, in which value is proportional to how many functions and users are involved and how well the network's disparate parts are connected. The more processes you integrate, the more benefits you reap.

Like DaimlerChrysler, other companies are delayering, standardizing, divesting, connecting, and relentlessly pursuing the holy grail of cost reduction. At the same time, while the benefits of simplification and cost improvement through integration are almost universally accepted, attaining them has proven maddeningly difficult.

As we discussed in Chapter 1, the drive toward integration is being slowed, and, in some cases, even short-circuited, by increasing complexity. Fueling this trend are globalization, industry consolidation, and specialization. We also continue to see robust M&A (merger and acquisition) activity, divestment of noncore functions, a surge in outsourcing – and a greater need for communication, both internally and between businesses.

If this weren't complexity enough, we are confronted with disruptive and accelerating change, the tendency of companies to adopt best-of-breed, but often incompatible, ERP systems –and the ad hoc way in which many e-Business "solutions" have been grafted onto isolated functions rather than organically connected to operating infrastructure. Add all this together and you have a recipe for massive amounts of costly systems *spaghetti*, *not* simplification.

First-generation ERP offerings have proliferated and evolved significantly over the past decade. The huge cost and process improvements we have seen at the more advanced corporations would be impossible without these powerful tools. As companies struggle with increased complexity and ever-expanding IT demands, some challenging problems cry out for a new set of solutions:

- How do you achieve the flexibility needed for changing business models and still maintain integrity?

- How do you sort out your company's systems spaghetti and make true integration a day-to-day reality?

- How do you make ERP changes and still keep the IT landscape manageable?

- How do you reduce costs and improve service with fewer resources?

- How do you take full advantage of the latest integration technology?

Once discrete corporate enterprises now collaborate and communicate more freely than ever before, sharing critical information and processes. To push collaboration to an even higher level, today's dynamic business environment requires a new type of technology platform – one based on smaller, less expensive, independent – and yet totally integrated software applications.

Today's CFOs are on a journey, from disjointed legacy systems, to integrated ERP, to multiple ERPs, to an integrated but open environment. Evolving systems promise not just integration, but flexibility as well. We are moving, not just toward ERP systems that communicate with each other, but toward a more expansive underlying ERP business model, in which traditional organizational borders will open up – and ultimately disappear.

In this chapter, we will explore the changing technology landscape for the CFO, new models for balancing centralization and decentralization, and the exciting advantages that today's evolving ERP systems offer. In this book, this new integrated vision is called Beyond ERP. We will also give specific guidelines on how to evaluate the best strategy for your company in the light of these advances.

WHAT DOES INTEGRATION MEAN FOR THE CFO?

Most companies face an ongoing dilemma – trying to reconcile the conflicting demands of the CEO, on the one hand, for seeking out new commercial opportunities requiring creativity and flexibility, and on the other hand the demands of the CFO for security, structure, and discipline. The CIO has an IT strategy to take advantage of the latest technology – the requirement here is for standardization and manageability. These conflicting pressures are illustrated in Figure 2.1.

Some of the most ambitious and successful business reengineering programs to date have been achieved using ERP software as the application information systems infrastructure supporting the change from rigid, departmentally "stovepiped" organizations into cross-business, process-driven organizations. World-class leaders such as IBM, Kodak, and Chevron have all achieved this kind of dramatic internal restructuring.

Many corporations have generated further benefits by adding new ERP functionality and modules to their original ERP cores. Examples include supply chain planning and optimization at Colgate-Palmolive and Procter & Gamble, e-Procurement at Lockheed Martin and Quaker Oats, enterprise portals at Nestlé and BOC, and product life cycle management at Aventis and Bayer.

In our experience, companies that have deployed ERP most successfully share a common strategic decision: they have adopted ERP as the backbone of their corporate information systems. These corporations typically have stable and mature top management teams who are willing to commit to a clear-cut vision and direction for their corporate information

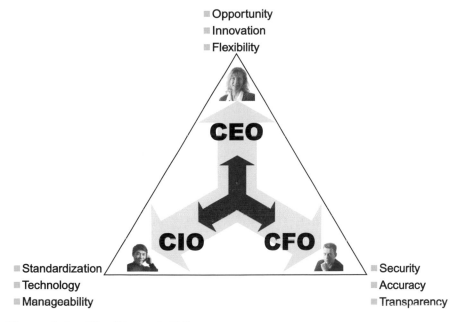

Figure 2.1   *The Strategic Dilemma*

resources. These teams have also stepped up to the plate during execution, directing and controlling the ongoing uptake process across their organizations. In Figure 2.2, we see the way in which such companies have moved from vertically integrated organizations to networked and functionally integrated business structures.

The word "integration" is worth defining at this point. Within the context of business software applications it is often misused, and this can lead to misunderstanding and confusion. When considering information systems, integration typically refers to data integration and process integration (though the growing adoption of "portals" is providing a form of application integration at the user-interface viewing level).

Data integration usually refers to a common data model or common data format, which can be understood or accessed by a number of different applications. For example, a "product" in a customer relationship management (CRM) system is defined in the same format and has the same attributes as a "product" in the manufacturing system.

Standard data formats such as XML (extensible markup language) may ease the communication of a product master record from the CRM system to the manufacturing system (or vice versa), and assist in the transfer of a transaction document (e.g. a customer sales order which refers to a product)

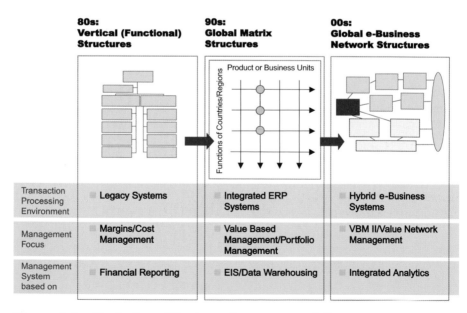

Figure 2.2   *Evolution of Business Structures and Systems*

between the systems. However, this so-called *data integration* does not necessarily tell the receiving system what to do with the customer sales order since there may not be any *process integration.*

Current ERP systems have been designed and built to ensure both data and process integration. There is a common and consistent data model which is used throughout all the ERP applications and components so that a "product" has the same format and attributes for the core ERP component, as it does for the CRM component, the supply chain management (SCM) component, the e-Procurement component, etc.

In addition, ERP is integrated at the process level so that, for instance, a customer sales order generated in the CRM system automatically triggers the following process integration steps: a credit check in accounts receivable, an inventory check in materials management, a manufacturing order for optimized scheduling, and a future cash accrual in the financial system.

The fundamental characteristics of integration and the benefits it delivers are summarized in Table 2.1:

Table 2.1

Integration requires	"Full integration" delivers
Data integration: consistent supplier, product and customer information to present "one version of the truth"	One master record for each supplier, product and customer is available to all users with a different view of the record elements depending upon the user role
Process integration: capture transaction (which can create one or more documents) information once and once only	Information is rolled down or across business processes in real time. Capturing a single piece of information during a transaction may trigger document information flows in multiple processes
Visibility of information down and across business processes	Ability to drill down or through information to give detail to the level of the original transaction and all related documents
Event-driven business process flows	Business processes or workflows can be triggered depending upon the status or value of a given information element

Many companies have profited from the simplification and standard-ization that ERP has brought to their organizations in the form of lower transaction costs, head counts, working capital investment, IT develop-ment and maintenance costs – and greater transparency. At the same time, CFOs and CIOs alike have found themselves struggling to adapt to a painful new reality: the issues that drive corporate IT strategy have shifted dramatically over the last few years.

UNRAVELLING SYSTEM SPAGHETTI

Why do CFOs feel they should be getting more from their ERP investments? Why have new best-of-breed applications muddied the ERP waters? Why do companies still lack the decision support they desperately need? How can CIOs adapt their existing ERP programs to organizational changes, new system requirements, and connectivity with other partners?

Evolving ERP systems must adapt to both internal structural – and external marketplace – changes:

1. *Changes from within* – Operational structure changes require major changes in ERP process and data configuration. Process integration depends on data integration. Changes in management philosophy – such as altering the balance between centralization and decentral-ization – also affect ERP physical installation (instance) and the ERP logical installation (client or company specific, customization, and configuration).

2. *Changes from without* – External organizational repositioning, mergers and acquisitions, divestitures, industry restructuring, shifting regu-latory demands, technological advances, new e-Business initiatives such as connecting directly with suppliers and customers via the Internet, which may involve adapting to entirely new business models.

As a result of all these changes, companies find themselves with *systems spaghetti*. Figure 2.3 offers a visual example of what we call systems and process spaghetti.

However strong the push toward simplification and integration, most companies find it an ongoing struggle to manage scores of systems from different vendors, coordinate their different functional goals and cap-

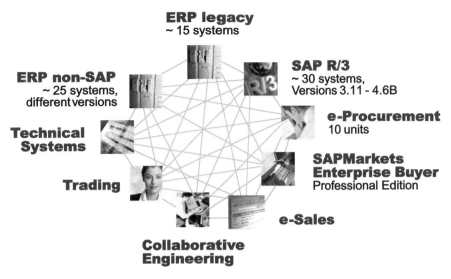

ERP legacy
~ 15 systems

SAP R/3
~ 30 systems,
Versions 3.11 - 4.6B

ERP non-SAP
~ 25 systems,
different versions

e-Procurement
10 units

Technical Systems

SAPMarkets Enterprise Buyer
Professional Edition

Trading

e-Sales

Collaborative Engineering

Figure 2.3   *Today's Landscape inside a company: Systems Spaghetti*

abilities, and adapt their systems quickly enough to meet market and competitive demands.

The following case study based on the experience of a global company shows just how daunting a task it can be to migrate to a more focused integration model. This company's challenge was all the greater because it had recently completed a major merger transaction and found itself saddled with two complex sets of ERP systems – each of them with its own individual mix of quirks, unique advantages, and limitations.

CASE STUDY
Building a New Integration Strategy after a Mega-merger

Prior to the merger, this global chemical company had made a major commitment to installing SAP software in country-based operations throughout the United States, Europe, and Latin America. It had one ERP system for manufacturing and supply, and another for its commercial and financial functions. Elements of the manufacturing and financial systems were intertwined, encompassing close to 200 global business processes configured in SAP R/3 and requiring substantial internal and external staff support.

The company had generated promising first-round synergy savings and was committed to reaching the next level of integration by adopting SAP more broadly for additional functions. At the same time, it had complicated its task by introducing discrete, best-of-breed offerings into its IT mix, inevitably resulting in systems spaghetti. The CFO's and CIO's ongoing challenge involved a twofold goal: expanding the functional reach of core software while reducing organizational, systems, and process complexity. Yet another time-consuming task involved coordinating central management of maintenance, regional support centers, and local country support organizations.

When this company merged with another of similar size, the integration landscape changed dramatically – and not for the better. As noted earlier, the first company was committed to a long-term, phased SAP strategy. In contrast, the acquired company had a consumer goods orientation and its choice of another ERP system was based on markedly different criteria. The acquired company's software was relatively inexpensive but highly standardized. The challenge: merging a global centralized ERP system with the acquired company's decentralized, entrepreneurial approach to systems.

The combined group's board reflected these cultural differences. The board members from the first company remained firmly committed to SAP for manufacturing, and for the time being it was agreed that the strategy of putting SAP into high-priority sites would continue. But this decision was only temporary. The CIO of the combined group, who had previously overseen ERP installation in the acquired company, was less than eager to adopt the more sophisticated solution. At the same time, the combined company's CFO was saying, "We need to start making synergistic savings overall and in our finance function as well."

A number of concerns quickly surfaced:

- New systems requirements generated by the merger: *the need for synergies and savings in cost, maximizing of merged revenue potential – regulatory (manufacturing compliance), information views (portals), technology (e-Procurement), customer/sales synergies (CRM), plus all the cross-functional requirements, e.g. business forecasting, reporting.*

- The core problem: *moving from systems and process spaghetti to an integrated solution in newly formed shared services units. The first company's ERP system was fully integrated for processes and data, so was that of the acquired company. The situation called for* <u>open</u> *integration – unbundling the process and data integration in both ERPs and creating a combined shared services solution which leveraged both companies' ERP investments.*

- Key issues: *mapping the data model or format from one system to the next (or possibly between multiple systems), routing the transfer or data elements from one system to the next (either in batch or real time), implementing an audit system that checks and confirms if and when the data has been transferred successfully, reconciling mismatches between the sending and receiving systems.*

- *Each of these tasks had to be set up and required ongoing maintenance costs. One of the most time-consuming roles of any IT operations support organization is dealing with the interface issues of this nature. (How many IT support professionals have been called out at the weekend because a batch interface job has failed?) From the user perspective, imagine the time involved for the person in marketing who has to try and synchronize product, pricing, and forecast information in different best-of-breed systems?*

As Figure 2.4 illustrates, the combined company's inherited ERP systems had become so complex that they transformed the logistics of post-merger integration into a true IT nightmare.

The CIO's agenda/strategy:

- *Complete integration and achieve maximum synergy*

- *Drive value from IT investments*

- *Optimize supply chain, commercial, and financial processes*

- *Address e-Business developments in the industry*

The integration issues this new company faced were difficult and demanding. In order to continue implementing SAP in manufacturing, a lot of supporting

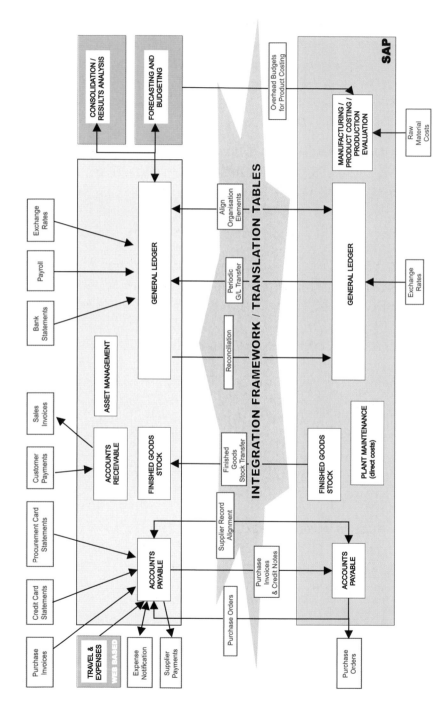

Figure 2.4 *Integrating ERPs for Shared Services*

financial modules also had to be implemented. And in order to connect the two companies' systems, the CIO had to choose one of two major options:

1. *Make the manufacturing component completely self-contained, with its own financials, and have a very simple, but costly, integration interface to allow data to pass from one system to the other; or*

2. *Unravel the systems and get detailed process and data connectivity between them. This would be quite expensive and complex to support, but the systems would function more smoothly.*

The CIO came up with two complimentary solutions:

- **Solution A** *The integration hub – a reduced number of interfaces between the ERPs using the integration middleware. The advantages: reduced complexity, easier maintenance, lower cost, but this treated the symptoms, not the cause. The disadvantages: duplication of applications and data. This would lead to extra configuration and set-up, extra maintenance and extra finance processing.*

- **Solution B** *The unbundling – creating one standard data repository and unbundling the processes in each of the ERPs. The advantages: common data standards and more flexible processes (i.e. the process functionality is separated from the data). This solution would enable the company in the future to adapt to a changing mix of decentralization and centralization in different parts of the world.*

The company chose an integration strategy, which took the advantages of one standard data repository and one integration hub for the separate and varied processes. These processes were standardized in some parts of the world, and customized in other parts of the world where local regulatory complexities were unavoidable.

The complexity and systems spaghetti that the company described above is struggling with is not at all unusual. The types of issues and conflicting opinions reflected in the case study are painfully familiar to any management team involved in a merger or attempting to adapt ERP systems to new marketplaces and to competitive realities. There is no right or wrong answer here, since circumstances between companies naturally differ. However, applying objective criteria can help remove some of the emotion from the decision-making process before project initiatives stall and "analysis paralysis" sets in.

Some principles for the CFO in dealing with systems spaghetti:

- Rationalize your systems landscape – as you standardize and globalize, you rationalize.

- Shift your development initiatives from a number of decentralized projects to a globally coordinated program – direct your company-wide processing and data standards from the corporate center.

- Opt for central governance when managing large projects in the field.

- Utilize global business processes – you cannot implement IT standards, which leverage full benefits, if the business processes themselves lack consistency.

For maximum flexibility and for a more effective ultimate integration, your systems need first to be completely separated and then to have well-defined interfaces. To increase the value of technology investment, clearly map your process and systems architecture, and set definite – and realistic – project timetables and milestones for integration.

BEYOND ERP

Figure 2.5 captures the integration strategy that many companies are aiming to achieve in reconfiguring technology operations: one data repository, one integration hub for separated and varied processes (standardized where appropriate, customized where necessary). Once these changes are firmly in place, you and your corporation will be well on the road to the solution for collaborative community resource planning.

Companies face an increasing need for integration and collaboration.[2] Today, the Internet provides the opportunity for systems to communicate instantly with other systems or individuals. Business processes that were once restricted to intranets and their users are now moving to the Internet.

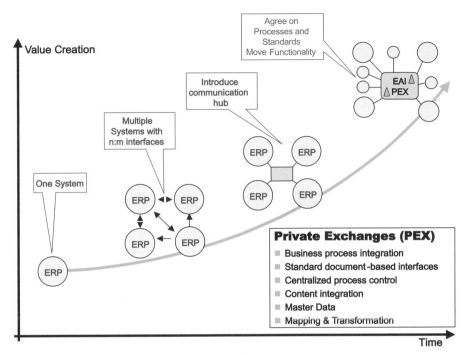

Figure 2.5 *From ERP to Private Exchanges*

Processes like supply chain planning, sourcing, and demand forecasting are automated across enterprises and within continental regions. They can now be implemented across systems at only marginal communication costs. To achieve this, technology components from different vendors need to be integrated and blended into a consistent infrastructure. There is simply no time for comprehensive system upgrades of existing enterprise software or for big replacement strategies in a world of heterogeneous system landscapes.

To capture the next round of efficiency gains, enterprises will be required to deploy collaborative business processes that either cross enterprises or cross functions. Real-time scenarios will replace batch processing. These collaborative processes have significantly more sophisticated requirements for the integration infrastructure than traditional processes.

Exchanges provide an evolutionary path for a company and its business partners to more efficiently automate business processes – using Web services where appropriate, and better leveraging investment in existing ERP and other technologies. The new exchange infrastructure makes it possible to manage diverse, highly heterogeneous components from a multitude of vendors, which run in various technology environments. Exchange-based process integration removes the problems of direct connections by extracting shared collaboration knowledge. Instead of directly coding point-to-point interfaces for each new component, the exchange infrastructure allows instant plug-in of new components. This provides future flexibility for today's fast-changing business world, and most importantly, for the CFO, exchanges reduce integration costs compared with the direct connection alternative.

Figure 2.6 shows the evolution from the original ERP integration through a single centralized data model, to an exponentially growing number of connections in inter-enterprise cooperation landscapes, to collaborative business scenarios using an application integration infrastructure.

Inter-enterprise cooperation and intra-enterprise cooperation based on individual peer-to-peer connections both raise the same problem. In the past, investments in each connection may have been justified by the volume handled and ongoing operational needs. e-Collaboration is different in terms of volume as well as time frame: it requires automated/standardized processes. Collaborative business scenarios must link busi-

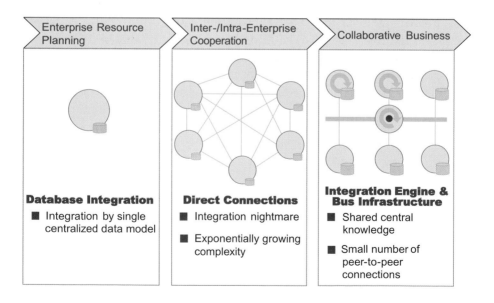

Figure 2.6 *Exchange Infrastructure for Collaboration*

ness partners into one joint process which is linked to related back-end execution functions. This is the return on investment (ROI) benefit you are looking for.

Exchange-based collaboration was pioneered by public exchanges. Private exchanges are becoming more common because some companies in certain industries are reluctant to share exchange technology and processes with their competitors.

Exchanges are of course at the heart of e-Business. During most of the 1990s, the major concerns preoccupying top management were globalization and the integration and coordination of internal shared assets and common business processes. Today, the key drivers behind IT decisions are e-Business initiatives and collaboration with customers, suppliers, and partners.

For many companies, this shift in IT strategy has diverted attention and resources from the implementation and maintenance of ERP systems to projects like e-Procurement. Unfortunately, many of these efforts will fail to deliver the expected benefits because they require tight integration to ERP systems that are not yet fully implemented.

There is enormous market momentum behind these new e-Business application categories. They are imaginative and exciting, and they capitalize on the Internet and other new technologies to enable innovative business models. However, many companies have a tendency to underestimate both the complexity and the cost of real-time interfacing.

Can e-Business applications be deployed without an ERP backbone? Implementation of any form of customer-, supplier- or partner-facing e-Business application designed to facilitate real-time interaction inevitably exposes a company's internal information system to external parties. Ultimately, this requires complex, bi-directional data and process integration between internal and external systems. While there may be some short-term benefit in deploying stand-alone or batch-interface "best-of-breed" systems, real payback comes only from a fully integrated environment. As the volume of Internet-based transactions increases, so does the requirement for a tightly integrated system that manages information for planning, production, inventory, and finance.

New e-Business applications actually *increase* the need for integration. As companies begin to open their systems up to customer, supplier, and partner process activities, the volume and velocity of transactions may surge significantly. Customers will expect a *single point-of-contact* for all products and locations along with real-time access to pricing, availability, delivery options, and order status. An organization concerned about e-Business readiness cannot afford to risk major logistics glitches and customer dissatisfaction by relying on a partial ERP system and/or a mismatched assortment of legacy systems.

REDUCING COMPLEXITY

In your ongoing drive to reduce complexity consider the trade-offs between the need for global standards and the demand for local flexibility. For example, take the pharmaceutical industry, which is undergoing unprecedented change. Like so many industries in transition, it is affected by the following drivers:

- *Increasing globalization* – mergers and acquisitions (up-scaling), changing business relationships, decreasing trade barriers, global competition

- *Changing customer dynamics* – consumerism, managed care, Internet and e-Business technologies

- *Pricing and regulatory pressures* – cost structures, reimbursement changes, intellectual property laws, new legislation

- *Advances in product innovation* – technological and scientific breakthroughs, escalating competition, growing ROI/market expectations, and a constant drive to recruit and retain R&D talent

Given a similar set of forces reshaping *your* industry, what balance between centralization and decentralization is right for your company? The centralized model is based on the vision of an integrated global business – with strategic control, common customers, common products, and *common processes*. The decentralized model is structured as a holding company featuring stand-alone business units with different customer basis, different markets, different channels, different products and *unique processes*. In the pharmaceutical sector,[3] Bristol-Myers Squibb is an example of a more centralized business model; AstraZeneca is an example of a semi-autonomous model, and Johnson & Johnson has a greater degree of decentralization.

Corporate technology models should also follow the business model. The corporate IT model would include one or more copies of the ERP database and associated suite of applications, i.e. the physical *instance/*

instances. Within an *instance/s* there may be more than one copy of a bounded ERP environment – for a group of companies that share common data or trade as an integrated supply chain – known as a *client* or logical system. Within a *client* there may be a number of *organizational units* – legal entities, profit centers, cost centers – which represent a defined company or business unit.

Three alternative corporate IT models are emerging:

1. *Extreme centralization* – one central server supporting global processes and global data standards. A centralized IT model should have a single design, single installation, and mandatory adherence to common standards. In this model there would be one physical *instance*, one *client* with multiple *organizational units*.

2. *A semi-autonomous model* – a single core design (based on templates), multiple installations, some common rules but also local flexibility. In this option the model would have a number of instances. Each *instance* would have its own *client* but these clients would be based on a common design template for global consistency.

3. *Extreme decentralization* – a totally decentralized IT model would have multiple designs, multiple *instances*, a *client* for every instance, and virtually total autonomy.

Many companies have implemented their ERP systems on a decentralized basis and are now trying to standardize and centralize to achieve further efficiencies. However, it is much easier to begin with a centralized model and implement a carefully controlled decentralization strategy over time, than it will ever be to *reintegrate* dispersed systems.

Major factors affecting a company's choice of a centralized or decentralized model include its degree of globalization, internal operating dynamics, and technological sophistication. In a global pharmaceutical company, for example, by opting for a centralized approach to manufacturing, global supply chain integration can have a positive impact on hardware costs, systems management costs, and skill utilization.

In contrast, if the commercial and sales functions within an organization require business-unit independence – a decentralized approach – then country-specific systems may emerge. With this model may come cost disadvantages associated with software upgrades, language and time zone support, and interfaces to legacy and third-party systems.

In Figure 2.7, we show both centralized and decentralized business models with the implications for the associated IT models.

The implications of choosing between this range of options for centralization for your ERP infrastructure are as follows:

- The most centralized IT model is a single "client" on a central database server.

- A degree of decentralization can be introduced and controlled through definition and roll-out of a corporate template or by using a proprietary distributed information management technology.

- The degree of decentralization depends on a combination of factors related to business, geography, and technology.

To summarize, these are your choices:

1. Implement a common global ERP system.

2. Implement a Master Data Client Server.

3. Implement an Enterprise Application Integration hub.

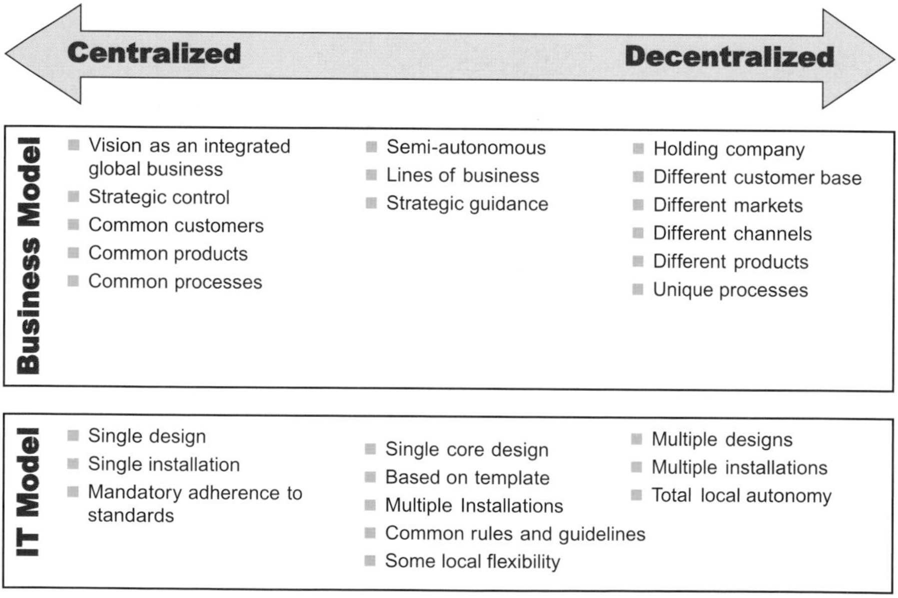

Centralized		**Decentralized**
Business Model		
▪ Vision as an integrated global business ▪ Strategic control ▪ Common customers ▪ Common products ▪ Common processes	▪ Semi-autonomous ▪ Lines of business ▪ Strategic guidance	▪ Holding company ▪ Different customer base ▪ Different markets ▪ Different channels ▪ Different products ▪ Unique processes
IT Model		
▪ Single design ▪ Single installation ▪ Mandatory adherence to standards	▪ Single core design ▪ Based on template ▪ Multiple Installations ▪ Common rules and guidelines ▪ Some local flexibility	▪ Multiple designs ▪ Multiple installations ▪ Total local autonomy

Figure 2.7   *Centralization versus Decentralization*

How do you evaluate the best alternative for your company?

In Figure 2.8, we identify on the vertical axis the criteria for choosing between integration and flexibility. Along the horizontal axis, we identify the three options for centralization. By weighting the criteria and scoring against your chosen organizational style, you can determine the best mix of centralization versus decentralization for your corporate model.

A VISION FOR THE POST ERP ERA

ERP systems and the integration infrastructure have helped overcome IT complexity, but systems spaghetti and limitations remain. The chief limitation is that ERP systems base process integration on data integration. This means that processes work on one version of standardized data. The integration hub facilitates communication among various systems, but the individual ERP instances are still fenced in.

As Figure 2.9 illustrates, the real benefits from ERP systems come with breaking down the boundaries between systems and processes including SRM (supplier relationship management), PLM (product lifecycle management) and SCM (supply chain management), not just linking those systems

Criteria:	Model:					
		Centralized		**Template**		**Decentralized**
5	Degree of Integration	5	= 25	3	= 15	1	= 5
5	Financial Transparency	5	= 25	3	= 15	1	= 5
4	Low Cost	5	= 20	4	= 16	2	= 8
3	Local Business Flexibility	2	= 6	4	= 12	5	= 15
3	Common (Best) Practices	4	= 12	3	= 9	2	= 6
4	Systems Resilience	1	= 4	3	= 12	3	= 12
Score:		92		79		51

Importance: 5 High 1 Low

Capability: 5 High 1 Low

Figure 2.8 *Evaluating the Best Alternative*

together. To break down these boundaries, we need integration at three levels: *people* (through portals); *information* (mapping and routing data through an integration hub/middleware and reporting/analysis in a data warehouse); and most important, *processes* (through an integration hub or exchange infrastructure). By unbundling ERP's processes and regrouping them through an integration hub, we achieve the ultimate integration (along with vital flexibility) – Beyond ERP!

You need the integration outlined in Figure 2.9 to maintain cost effectiveness, efficiency, and strong information flow and distribution. To date, it has been necessary to reintroduce an existing ERP package at each new location and then reconfigure or even dismember it in order to suit the functional needs of that location.

Beyond ERP offers all the applications of ERP today, but it allows you to assemble the packages into smaller units so you can mix and match them as needed and create an open but integrated system that does not require common coding and databases. In short, Beyond ERP offers greater flexibility without sacrificing any of the powerful integration benefits that have made ERP systems so valuable. The idea is to break ERP up into

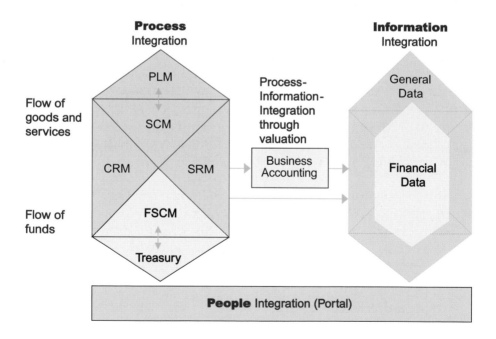

Figure 2.9   *Integration of People, Processes, and Information*

smaller units so that a company can deal with customer payment require-ments without having to install an entire financial accounting package.

Beyond ERP also provides integration among business partners, ven-dors, and customers. Collaboration with partners and communication with customers is hugely important today. One of the real benefits of Beyond ERP is that it takes processes that are collaborative in nature and separates them from back-office accounting processes and lets you put them in the front office or out in the field where they really belong.

Customer payments, for example, aren't about billing, they're about customer relations. Beyond ERP lets you separate this process from your back office and incorporate it into your CRM program. This is important because CRM's function isn't just to track what people have ordered; CRM also involves whether they've received their goods and paid for them. All this information is a vital part of a customer's profile.

Integration is still the name of the game. Only by integrating systems and processes can you achieve the speed, cost reductions, and get the quality and quantity of information you need to manage complexity and support globalization. But integration in tomorrow's marketplace won't be the monolithic kind that we've seen in the past, where you have a giant box or are forced to order a six-course meal when all you want is dessert!

The challenge is to break up into components the very essence of the traditional ERP model – the integration infrastructure, which binds together business processes (both strategic and operational), information, and reporting/analysis. That's what's different about the Beyond ERP model: it is disaggregated into its component parts. Why is this impor-tant? Because CFOs need to unravel their process and technology land-scape in order to reassemble it in a more flexible and efficient way.

In technical terms, this means breaking down a giant ERP program with all its manufacturing, HR, accounting, and other functional pieces into much smaller chunks that are not "hard wired" to one another, but con-nected by an integration hub. Achieving this level of flexibility is essen-tial to supporting innovative initiatives, both internally and externally, such as shared services centers and e-Business ventures.

Let's take the benefits of each of the components of Beyond ERP in turn:

For strategic decision making . . .

- Freedom from transaction processing, for example for offline scenario planning and simulation

- Flexibility to cope with major frequent organizational changes, such as consolidation, intercompany profit elimination
- Ability to cope with managing the value of intangibles, such as R&D
- Pulling together a full picture of events and transactions in real-time

For operational processing . . .

- For collaboration with external partners, for example *my* ERP with *your* ERP, *my* invoice payment with *your* invoice receipt
- For internal collaboration (private exchanges), such as shared services – invoice verification, dispute management, internal billing; collaborative working – business forecasting, activity-based pricing
- For centralizing transaction processing, decentralizing valuation/ reporting or vice versa (centralized accounting shared services, but a decentralized sales and logistics operation)

For information management . . .

- For strategic decision making
- For operational decision making
- For financial and accounting

For integration infrastructure . . .

- Routing (managing the workflow between disparate systems)
- Mapping (matching data between disparate systems)
- Shared master data (sharing data common to disparate systems)

Shared services allow companies to focus on what they do best and concentrate administrative activities in order to reduce costs and enhance efficiency. By breaking up ERP software into component parts, you can deploy only the software you really need at one site without having to implement the rest. Being able to pick and choose allows companies to centralize and minimize administrative work while distributing other functions such as manufacturing.

CASE STUDY

П

Gaining the Flexibility Needed to Create a Shared Services Center

A leading high-tech company was considering creating a shared services center. The company is actually a collection of businesses all across the United States and Canada that were acquired. Not surprisingly, each new business brought its own way of doing things and its own software system into the marriage. Until recently, each company handled its own administrative work, including hiring and training staff.

Since everyone does things differently, staff members were not inter-changeable. Since there are 35 different kinds of software, there are just as many different ways to train people. In addition, there are certain relatively scarce specialist skills (tax expertise, for example) that are very valuable. The company decided that it would like to launch its shared services program with invoice verification in accounts payable because (1) it concerns cash payments and is therefore sensitive; (2) its different companies have widely different procedures and levels of quality; (3) invoice processing involves a great deal of manual entry by a workforce with high turnover, meaning high training costs.

The company was very interested in exploring a potential Beyond ERP environment because it had already embarked on a project linking existing heterogeneous systems with an integration infrastructure and the problems were mounting. The plan was to program its own invoice entry and verifica-tion processes to run on top of 35 different systems via an integration hub. Invoices would be entered at a new shared services center in Florida where they would be verified against delivery data received from the decentralized systems. Once approved, the invoices would be routed back to the decentralized systems to be paid and posted to the general ledgers. Over the next five years, more and more services would be centralized until virtually all of finance and accounting was shared.

The problems encountered in implementing this approach were daunting. Since only one piece of the total purchase-to-pay process was to be shared to start with, the new in-house development would have to be compatible with all the 35 different existing systems: things such as vendor codes, general

ledger (GL) account codes, open item structure, etc – each different in each system – would have to be taken into account. Any change in one of the underlying systems would force a change in the new software, making maintenance a major and permanent headache.

The company's original plan to lay a new shared services template on top of its existing systems proved to be much more difficult and potentially more unstable than expected. Nevertheless, it was still committed to spending $35 million on the pilot because the projected savings approached $90 million. Following the pilot, shared services will likely be expanded to cover financial and management reporting, and possibly sales invoice processing.

This case study is an exercise in simplification and integration. The message: taking advantage of new technology is important, but a do-it-yourself approach doesn't always work. The company described above was going to develop its own vendor invoice processing application using third-party enterprise applications integration (EAI) software. However, the risks and costs were too great, so it looked for a standard package solution to implement the new process. What's really needed here is the ability to process applications in bite-sized chunks. What's also needed is a communications and integration backbone.

These EAI backbones provide a toolbox to build your own integrated solution – use the essential tools that you need (routing, mapping, repository) but don't use the application building tools (you won't be able to support them). Don't be tempted to go it alone and create your own bite-sized chunks. And don't follow a best-of-breed software strategy – it will just add complexity. Select your standardized Beyond ERP components from a software partner with a comprehensive vision of your entire business process landscape.

There are any number of business operations that would benefit from greater ERP flexibility. Dispute management, for example, is another process (like invoice entry and verification) that is typically found in back offices today, in accounts receivable. Here, too, there are a number of advantages to centralizing this activity (in a call center, for example) rather than having it distributed throughout an organization. In Figure 2.10, the development of integration applications from back office to front office to Web-based services is illustrated for the dispute management process.

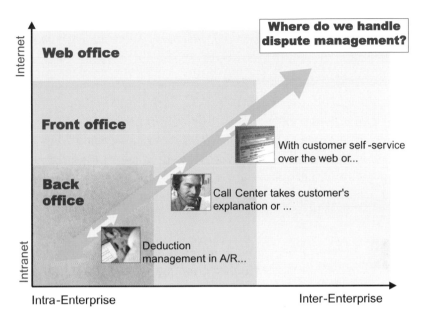

Figure 2.10   *Next Generation Integration*

Regrouping and unbundling finance functions (crossing traditional corporate boundaries) lets you leverage new Beyond ERP technology. Take the case of dispute management. In the traditional ERP system, dispute management is included in accounts receivable functionality. In the Beyond ERP environment, dispute management can be unbundled and regrouped with customer care functionality.

Flexible implementation of processes is the goal. Because processes are independent of recording and valuation, they can be set up wherever needed and can share one back office. Conversely, processes can be centralized into shared service centers and communicate with several back offices.

How do you go about implementing Beyond ERP? Take vendor invoice processing for example.

- *Step 1:* Analyze the old processes, design the new processes.

- *Step 2:* Create an EAI hub – improve communication and connectivity.

- *Step 3:* Implement a new process on the new hub. The ultimate goal – taking all processes and implementing them on the new hub.

Just a quick reminder. What does the EAI hub do? It's a repository – shared master data. It's a mapping service – matching code numbers. It's a routing mechanism – process workflow between systems. What is it? It is a piece of software – a communications backbone. A common infrastructure for internal and external integration.

Just a few tips. Do select EAI middleware. But do not take the existing processes and just stick them together in a home-grown application using middleware. What will happen? The underlying applications will change, forcing changes to the new home-grown application. Maintenance will become a nightmare. Do move toward Beyond ERP. Ensure your underlying applications are process-focused (manageable), independent and interoperable (capable of being linked to other process-focused applications).

The case study which follows focuses on the separation of processes from accounting and data.

CASE STUDY
A Financial Services Firm Unbundles its Finance and Accounting

In this case, a leading European bank's securities trading systems also handled the accounting for the items traded. The problem: the bank wants to apply new accounting standards. If it retained its current IT model, it would have to modify around 80 different systems to make them comply with new regulations. To make matters worse, some of its systems were nearly 30 years old, and though they worked well enough, no one around has any idea how to modify them. This company chose to separate its trading activities, which were decentralized worldwide, from accounting, which were centralized. With centralized accounting, it becomes much easier to implement changes in accounting rules and the trading systems are not affected. In addition, centralization improves consistency and transparency.

For now, the bank has to live with the fact that numerous different methods of calculating interest, for example, are employed, making comparisons unnecessarily difficult.

The key message: it makes great sense to do some things centrally and some things locally; since the ERP system is one big package and works best when everything (processes, data) are bundled, but supporting distributed and changing functions calls for adapting systems to achieve greater flexibility.

MAKING INTEGRATION WORK FOR YOU

Now let us bring everything into one integration framework and see if we can find our way beyond crippling complexity and systems spaghetti.

As CFO, where do you start?

- *Step 1*: Identify your value drivers – decide what's important to you and prioritize your investments. Give a strategic business focus to your Beyond ERP vision, e.g. customer management, R&D/supply chain efficiency, streamlining noncore activities.

- *Step 2*: Shape the new processes – with the newly found freedom of Beyond ERP design what is best, e.g. for the customer care, for innovation/time to market, for maximum cost reduction with the minimum of disruption.

  Traditional functions are rethought, regrouped and recut!

- *Step 3*: Configure your new organization – streamlined, simplified, delayered, focused on value creation, with line-of-sight, shared services, virtual business support over the Web, customer care centers.

- *Step 4*: Design your new integration framework:

  - Map your integration landscape (as-is, to-be)

  - Define your business/technology architecture

  - Select the mix of bundled and unbundled process/information/ reporting, decision-making/infrastructure components

  - Identify the right implementation partner and follow a structured implementation program – with built-in flexibility to take advantage of the ever-advancing technology landscape

CASE STUDY

Realizing an Integration Vision

This is not a real company. It is intended to be representative of most organizations today. Does it resonate with you?

Yesterday . . . we took reports from different systems, we used spreadsheets to type in data, we had reconciliations and errors, this was all too time consuming and expensive!

Today . . . we have invested in data warehouses to automate much of what we did yesterday, overcoming many of the manual and error-prone problems of before, but we have an integration problem – we are treating the symptoms but not the root cause – we have systems which do not speak the same language, therefore we have to create elaborate fixes, e.g. mapping data structures within a data warehouse.

Tomorrow . . . we create an integration infrastructure which allows us to share common data right from the start. We can capitalize on our investment today in both the ERP and data warehouse, but we can reduce the complexity and focus on the value creation – decision support, simulation and analytics instead of data mapping. We now are going to get it right from the start.

What are the steps we need to consider taking right now?

- ***Portals****: starting with the user interface – one face to the user, drawing information from a number of different systems, but to the user it looks the same. Conceal the complexity!*

- ***Processes****: unbundle and reconfigure process infrastructure. Do things right! Go for your shared services, cost reduction, collaboration! Separate the processes from the data.*

- ***Raw data****: store it in the accounting data staging area: separate the data from the processes on the one hand, and separate the data from reporting/decision making on the other. Of course, the data in this staging area will be reconciled, consistent, timely, and accurate. This is the foundation to quality decision making!*

Our goal here: the best of both worlds: detail complexity and reconciled simplicity just through slicing and dicing the general ledger. Just one country or one ERP system is not enough – what we want is the "Full Monty": full access to all data, reconciled.

To get the best of both worlds – the financial world, the management world – raw information is tailored to serve multiple purposes. By inserting an "accounting engine" between processes and data in the staging area, we can achieve multiple valuations (for example in meeting both a variety of national and international fiscal accounting standards) for multiple purposes (for example in financial statement reporting and product profitability). This "accounting engine" (Figure 2.11) is a new concept. It transforms process data into accounting data and, in one stroke, removes many of the multinational CFO's headaches.

In this concept the data in the staging area is now available for use in a variety of applications in the data warehouse with pre-defined data cubes for the general ledger and product profitability applications, which in turn can serve as the source for analytics. What we now have is a logical rather than a physical ERP system, which functions without the disadvantage of traditional system boundaries.

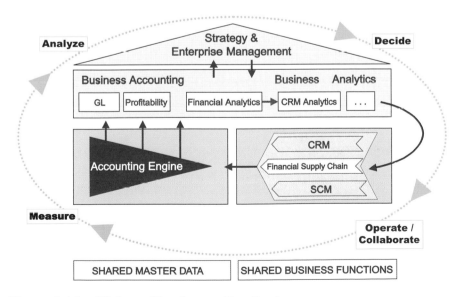

Figure 2.11   *Vision – The Accounting Engine*

CFO CHECKLIST

SQUEEZE MORE OUT OF YOUR ERP INVESTMENT
You have probably achieved 50% of the benefits you originally intended. Go for the other 50%! Jump ahead, formulate a picture of your *Beyond ERP* environment. Target the benefits you want from further transaction processing efficiencies from increased collaboration over the Internet, from improved management information, from further standardization and restructuring.

UNRAVEL YOUR SYSTEMS SPAGHETTI
Honesty is the best policy! Map your existing process and systems landscape (with all its maddening complexity). Do you realize how much this complexity costs you? Take advantage of the integration technologies available and proven on the market today.

RETHINK, REGROUP, AND RECUT YOUR FINANCE FUNCTIONS
Shape new finance processes by taking advantage of all that is good in your existing ones. Take advantage of your newly found freedom with the new generation of ERP design. Do not forget: achieving ROI on any incremental technology investment is an essential discipline.

CONSIDER THE IMPACT OF PRIVATE AND PUBLIC EXCHANGES
Increased collaboration externally with business partners as well as internally across the enterprise should continue to yield you further cost savings and cash generation opportunities. There are many new integration tools. Exchanges for processes. Middleware for data. Portals for information and communication. Take advantage of the latest technical expertise to make the right choices.

SIMPLIFY YOUR PROCESS AND SYSTEM STRATEGIES
Is your organization committed to global standardization? If so, go for it! If not, make considered choices as to which processes, which instances, which installations are to be governed by global

standards and which should be tailored to meet your unique cultural or special local conditions.

DESIGN THE NEW BEYOND ERP ARCHITECTURE

Pull down the boundaries between people, information, and processes. Develop a working Beyond ERP prototype to bring these three resources together. Select as a pilot those parts of the business where quick wins are likely. For example, consider the implementation of an *accounting engine*.

CRAFT A VISION FOR INTEGRATION

Configure your new organization – streamline, simplify, delayer. Focus on value creation. Share services using the new tools for integration. Chart your future integration landscape. Test it. Is it simpler? Is it cheaper? Does it promote collaboration internally and externally?

CHAPTER 3

Streamlining the Financial Supply Chain

CUTTING THE COSTS OF GLOBAL FINANCIAL OPERATIONS

Inge Hansen, Vice President and CFO
Statoil

We call ourselves the "Energy Source." As one of the world's largest net sellers of crude oil, we operate in more than 20 countries worldwide and are the largest supplier of natural gas to Europe. Statoil employs 16,500 staff, having a market capitalization of US$18.5 bn.

What keeps me awake at night? Risk. A major environmental disaster, for example, would be a catastrophe. Fortunately, such risks are rare. Furthermore, we have the business under good control. However, I am always concerned about our trading risk positions. Since we have approximately 2.5 million barrels of oil in a long position every day – we have tight controls to cover this risk.

I think it's the job of the CFO to focus on long-term growth rather than short-term performance. We are a technologically driven company with a unique combination of resources and skills. Skills for dealing with the harsh environment of the North Sea. Skills for enhancing oil recovery, with new technology for drilling "smart" wells and gas/water injection. We have two overriding objectives – to expand our core business internationally and to meet the needs of shareholders. However, I don't see it as my job to tell the investment analysts how to value our company – that's their job. I don't think companies should be slaves of the stock exchange. Rather, we focus on running the business and achieving long-term growth through year-on-year production growth (currently 4% pa) and replenishing our oil and gas reserves. Our stretch targets are set with reference to our benchmark competitors – companies such as TotalFinaElf and ENI. We also strive to improve our return on capital employed (ROCE) and are continuously looking at ways to reduce our cost base.

This year, we have identified working capital as a major cost reduction initiative. We are realizing our vision of having a single, centralized finance function. Our global financial operations began their new centralized implementation with key functional areas such as in-house cash, treasury management, and market risk management. This initiative helped Statoil to centralize data and manage inter-company payment transactions more effectively. It also enables Statoil to streamline payment processes between company units, which helped reduce the volume of physical payment flows throughout the group and optimize how they are applied. We now have a single, centralized, shared services center for performing treasury, banking – we have saved a lot of money by doing this – our in-house bank is faster, more automated and we have reduced the number of external banks we deal with in various countries, along with the interfaces we maintain with those banks. We calculate annual savings to be approx. $3.5 million, on this initiative alone, with a project payback of one and a half years.

Operating units within our group are based in different countries and were going into the international financial markets with opposing currency positions – one might have a surplus in dollars, while another needed to borrow in dollars. Our treasury vision is a "one-stop" shop for banking, financing, and payments. We now have a fully integrated process and systems solution – integrating real-time cash management, cash forecasting, and treasury management/ accounting. We have also integrated our internal bank accounts and centralized payments through our payments factory, recharging for these corporate services as required. All these processes operate on our common ERP platform, which is standard for the whole Statoil group.

Where next? The next phase for development is cash flow forecasting (particularly foreign exchange reporting and control), upgrading our reporting for US GAAP (generally accepted accounting principles), and a group approach to credit risk. We need better processes for internal inter-company netting and financial transparency throughout our supply chain. We have improved our closing process and believe it to be fast enough. We have achieved this because 90% of our business is on one SAP client installation. Reconciliations are now less of a problem – we have more to do in achieving our working capital targets, particularly in the oil trading area, and we have a number of initiatives in hand.

We still have more to do on our "purchase-to-pay" process. Although much of our invoice payment is fully automated (we use intelligent document management software to take out a lot of the manual intervention required), we do have a problem with compliance. We are not comfortable with current purchase order and goods receipt notification disciplines and need to increase the number of invoices backed up by proper purchase order documentation. We need to simplify access to the system, possibly through a portal, to make the "three-way" match for order, receipt, and price.

We are already benefiting from our investment in Trade Ranger – the oil industry trade exchange. In fact, Statoil is currently the most active member of this consortium. We push as much of our procurement through this industry exchange as we can to benefit from global procurement leverage. This, coupled with our drive for corporate shared services, which include procurement, leads to better discipline, lower costs, and opportunities for further streamlining the financial supply chain. Collaboration is a critical success factor for us in this industry; we collaborate with governments, our competitors, our customers – as well as our suppliers. The tighter our physical supply chain, the tighter our financial supply chain and the more effective our collaborative ventures become.

What motivates me most? Just being in this industry. The future is very positive, we can see growth in energy, both supply and demand. We seek to take advantage of this relatively secure position. Exploiting this potential – that's exciting.

How the finance function has changed! Consider the challenges that Statoil's CFO faces today: synchronizing joint-venture operations. Managing risk and options planning. Overseeing e-Procurement. Twenty or even fifteen years ago, the list of a CFO's key responsibilities at a leading company would have been far different. Since the late 1990s, driven largely by the Internet, finance's role has evolved as dramatically as that of any other internal business function – perhaps even more so.

Finance departments have become smaller and physically dispersed. Transaction processing, once a core function, now is often handled by remote shared services groups or outsourced either partially or totally. Decision support, value creation, new business planning, and overseeing systems development and integration – these are the pivotal activities that finance is now engaged in and its performance is measured by.

WHAT IS THE FINANCIAL SUPPLY CHAIN?

Today, the CFO stands at the center of a complex web of internal and external relationships, all of which must be astutely orchestrated and integrated. As integrator, the CFO must also manage all aspects of the financial supply chain (FSC). This chain encompasses all the processes and transactions directly affecting cash flow and working capital. As Figure 3.1 shows, the financial supply chain begins with supplier/buyer selection and extends through the payment process, information reporting and analysis, and cash flow forecasting.[1]

The physical or materials supply chain is a well-established business tool and highly visible in its operation. The FSC, while equally critical to performance, is a relatively recent concept. It is challenging to manage because it depends largely on two intangibles: relationship building and transaction flow. As a result, mastering the dynamics of the FSC represents a new set of demands – and opportunities – for the CFO. For maximum impact and reach, a company's FSC must operate in tandem with internal manufacturing and other supply chains. This is no easy task: its activities must be synchronized and integrated with manufacturing, supplier networks, trading partners, financial institutions, and customer relationship management (CRM) programs.

LEVERAGING THE BENEFITS

Effective FSC management can be an enormous boon to today's CFO. It can positively influence receivables, financial forecasting, and working

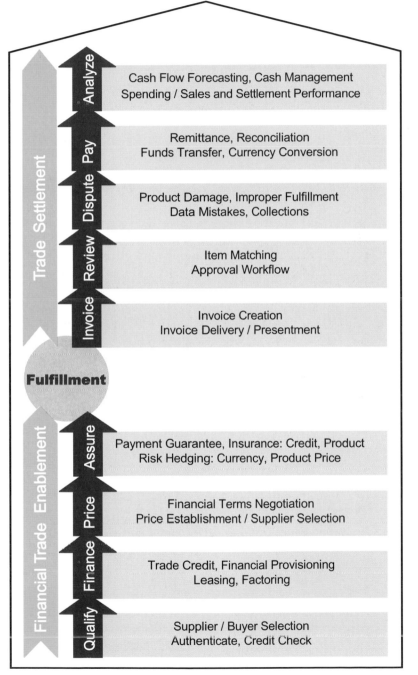

Figure 3.1   *Structure of the Financial Supply Chain*

capital. Among the specific benefits that successful FSC planning offers your company are:

- Improved inventory control and cash flow management

- Working capital reductions of 20% or more

- Lower financing rates on required working capital

- Early warning for commercial transaction problems

- More efficient automated financial systems

By aggressively pursuing FSC solutions, today's CFOs can greatly enhance their ability to create value across their enterprises. According to Killen & Associates, Inc.,[2] better FSC management could save the Fortune 500 nearly $110 bn by improving processing functions and optimizing working capital investment. Until recently, most CFOs have tended to view different financial functions discretely, rather than applying a more cohesive, supply chain perspective to them. However, an integrated approach offers better control of resources and better alignment of the FSC with physical/manufacturing requirements. As CFO, a strong FSC strategy offers you an exciting new set of problem-solving tools. Specifically, it enables you to:

- Obtain more timely and precise data on receivables

- Make more accurate forecasts based on reliable receivables input

- Eliminate costly working capital float

- Secure better terms for working capital

- Drill deeper for detailed financial information

- Resolve payment issues more quickly and efficiently

- Gain a more comprehensive view of trading partners

Armed with these powerful assets, CFOs can forecast earnings more precisely, leverage working capital, and offer better guidance in planning corporate strategy. Equally important, a well-oiled FSC provides speed and customer responsiveness – two critical success factors in today's accelerated market environment. When you contrast the time frame for major transactions in the 1960s with today's turnaround times, it's clear just how important speed is (see Table 3.1).

Table 3.1

	1960s	2000
Order	4–7 days	Today
Deliver	14–21 days	Next day
Invoice	4–7 days	Same day
Payment	45–60 days	45–60 days

Source: Killen & Associates, Inc.

As manufacturing supply chain efficiency has *increased,* the time required to process transactions has steadily and significantly *decreased.* Improving FSC processes still further offers even greater opportunities for quicker transactions through faster payment processing, reducing days sales outstanding (DSOs), and accelerating the flow of information to suppliers, alliance partners, and other external organizations. Along with the need for speed, there's another powerful incentive for enhancing FSC effectiveness and better aligning it with the physical supply chain: reducing excess working capital or non-productive float.

Many financial managers mistakenly believe that sophisticated accounting and ERP systems are synonymous with effective FSC management. But while ERP, EAI (enterprise applications integration), and other technologies provide highly accurate data reporting on internal corporate transactions and processes, most current systems are limited in their ability to share and analyze that data with external partners.

However, a high-performing financial supply chain enables a company to gather and distribute data, not just internally, *but across its network of trading partners.* In a fast-paced business environment, this capability is enormously beneficial; it can, for example, reduce exceptions to almost zero from the current average of 20%.

Today, advanced technology has progressed to the point where FSC processes can provide both improved internal and external capabilities, including:

- Synchronizing financial operations with the physical supply chain
- Providing uniform data, so that trading partners can exchange information without altering the format or structure of their internal data systems

- Tracking financial documents from order entry through reconciliation, including change orders, exceptions, and returns

- Troubleshooting, so that problems such as payment delays due to inconsistent field formats for invoices, can be predicted and preventive measures applied

- Providing proactive intelligence and fostering collaboration among global business partners

Today's FSC systems also provide another hugely valuable benefit: accurate, real-time data on a company's cash flow and credit/liquidity status. This invaluable data enables CFOs to forecast more precisely, identify a full range of risks and options, and plan more successful financial strategies. By operating across both internal and external FSCs, new technology systems enable trading partners to correct time-consuming exceptions and/or errors that create supply chain bottlenecks and impede cash flow. Figure 3.2 illustrates the interactions between buyers and sellers and the role that intermediaries can play in the FSC.[3]

Opportunities exist for cost savings and process effectiveness through the use of external intermediaries for outsourced FSC services. Beyond all these direct advantages, a superior FSC program has a positive ripple effect across a company's core business functions, from operations and customer service to sales and marketing. These indirect, but valuable, benefits include:

- *Upgrading operational efficiency:* all trading partners within supply chain networks can use advanced FSC systems to identify and eliminate inefficiencies caused by problems in their own organizations and their customers' organizations, especially those created by incorrect order entry information. FSC resources enable them to trace delays and exceptions to a specific branch or department, correct mistakes, and make preventive process improvements.

- *Supporting sales, marketing, and logistics:* a strong FSC program can provide powerful analytical tools for sales, supplier management, and other important process areas. Sales and marketing, for instance, can precisely analyze customers based on buying patterns, locale, and credit profiles. Pricing programs can be tailored on a customer-by-customer

Services

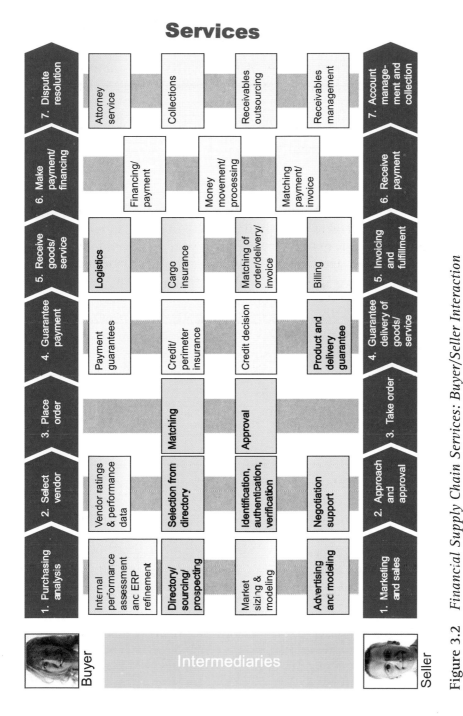

Figure 3.2 *Financial Supply Chain Services: Buyer/Seller Interaction*

basis. FSC systems can monitor sales channel financing and perform-ance.

- *Improving customer service:* a sophisticated FSC system offers a powerful new vehicle for enhancing customer relationships. First, it helps ensure smooth, harmonious payment negotiations between buyers and sellers. Second, it generates the data needed to quickly and factually resolve customer service problems. And finally, it frees employees to focus on relationship building rather than problem solving.

As noted earlier, ERP and other existing software tools were designed for internal use, <u>not</u> to link partners within a network of FSCs. As a result, companies that attempt to share their ERP-based information with that of other trading partners quickly run into a major stumbling block: the difficulties inherent in capturing and reconfiguring data from disparate systems into a spreadsheet format so that it can be jointly reviewed and analyzed. To date, such efforts have proven time-consuming and of limited value, since they do not offer global business partners real-time access to data.

At the moment, cross-company financial supply chain management (FSCM) processes are rarely handled electronically. While classic supply chain management techniques have optimized inventory planning and delivery times, FSC processes haven't kept pace. New FSC management software will fill this gap. It aims to help customers optimize their internal and cross-company cash flows, thereby achieving efficiency levels on a par with physical value chain improvement. These emerging FSC software solutions are being developed in five high-impact areas:

1. In-house cash, bank processes, and relationship management

2. Order-to-cash, electronic bill presentment and payment (EBPP)

3. Purchase-to-Pay

4. Bill consolidation

5. e-Finance and e-Settlement

Each of these five areas are dealt with in more detail in the following sections.

IN-HOUSE CASH AND BANKING

Decision makers in the FSC rely heavily on banks for a broad range of information and services. In the process of interacting with commercial banks, corporate units frequently experience problems – disconnects or costly delays – that impede the flow of information and limit 'real-time' access to financial status.

The services that banks provide "sit" at the strategic point where the functions and operations of a corporate FSC exchange information. Data flows from operating units through the banks to business functions. Executives make decisions at the functional level, which then flow back through the banks to the operating units. Data also flows across banks to and from corporate centers and business units. The major problems occur in this area of interchange.

Global banking continues to be affected by two trends: industry consolidation and the rise of non-bank financial intermediaries. As these trends accelerate, the need for financial market intermediation will diminish. Over the short term, such changes will make securing credit more challenging and put a greater premium on effective bank relationship management.

The disconnects and delays experienced in commercial banking prevent corporate centers' financial executives from "seeing" what is happening in the business units and acting on that information in a timely way. This is an acute problem for members of the FSC that operate many entities, conduct business in many countries, use multiple currencies, initiate multiple payment types, have multiple payment terms, and use multiple banks. Such enterprises incur heavy costs due to float, manual internal processes, lack of visibility (cash position), and banking fees.

According to Killen & Associates, Inc.[4] the key problems such large-scale companies experience include the following:

- *Accounting and the bank cannot stay in sync.* Corporate accounting reports cash based on what it posts – receipts and disbursements. However, banks report cash after transactions have cleared. Accounting's reporting, at a point in time, differs from a bank's report of cash available. A huge discrepancy may exist between the two reports.
- *Not everything expected to clear actually clears.* It can take weeks before the banks provide information on stalled transactions. This lag time introduces inaccuracies and delays.

- *Banks are not organized effectively* to report cash positions to customers. Members of banking groups can have different processes, systems, and communication styles, resulting in fragmentation and costly breakdowns in information accuracy and delivery times.

- *Frequently, a lead bank is looking into a black hole* when it turns to affiliated banks for information, primarily because its internal processes are inefficient since they rely on the phone, Fax, EDI (electronic data interchange), e-mail, and regular mail. It can take lead bankers up to 10 days to find out what disbursements and receipts have been cleared by their affiliate banks. The inability of lead bankers to report this information on a timely basis can throw off reports on available cash by 60%. Some Global 2000 firms generate 60% of their business in markets served by local banks.

- *Difficulty in aggregating cash information.* Even if local banks submit information about cash status on the same day the group lead bank requests it, it would still take a week to make that information meaningful. Banks are insufficiently invested in information technology and modern processes on the commercial side of their business to take headcount out of converting various currencies, entering data into spreadsheets, and performing other processes.

Some bankers are working with enterprises using treasury workstations to provide better, faster reporting on cash positions. While this is a step in the right direction, it does not go far enough. Banking groups need to redefine their role in the FSC in order to smoothly manage bank account balances, cross-border payments, inter-company flows, internal systems and processes, incomplete or faulty settlement instructions, fragmented technologies, and country-to-country differences.

If your company is like most in the new global economy, with a multinational customer base and a growing number of corporate groups, you have probably experienced a sharp rise in the number of intra-group and external payments as well as the number of bank accounts you use – not to mention the considerable costs you incur in making cross-border payments. To gain a competitive edge, it is vital for you to manage payment flows and the related risks efficiently. In-house cash helps you reduce the costs of processing intra-group and external payment transactions, while reducing the number of external bank accounts and international payments.

In-house cash serves as an in-house bank, allowing you to centrally manage subsidiary accounts in any currency. For subsidiaries, in-house cash automates intra-group payment transactions (internal payments), payments made by group companies to external partners (central payments), and incoming payments for subsidiaries from external partners that are initially credited to the head office's house bank accounts (central incoming payments). In-house cash also helps you calculate and debit interest and other charges, grant current account overdrafts, control limits, and generate bank statements for affiliated firms.

The in-house bank and global settlement solution fills the service void between the group headquarters and the business entities, and headquarters and the banks. Sophisticated applications enable new treasury, payment, communication interfacing, reporting, lending, and billing services that unlock cash from inefficient processes. They also enable the corporation to deploy cash more effectively. Figure 3.3 shows the interactions within a group of companies between business units through an in-house bank to external banks. The in-house bank eliminates the need for fixed peer-to-peer interconnections between the entities and other stakeholders.

Improvements in bank processes usually follow three phases of implementation. Phase 1 involves setting up a central payment function. Subsequent phases involve the netting-off of bank interest receivable and payable, and the netting-off of foreign currency exposures.

CASE STUDY
Developing an In-house Cash Solution

The CFO of a global auto manufacturer faced some formidable, but relatively common, challenges. Management wanted systems introduced that would better assess risk and uncertainty while reducing working capital, and cost. Financial process chain synchronization was also a top priority. At the time the CFO began investigating new solutions to these issues, the company's shared service center was handling its in-house payment function.

The company ultimately adopted a highly efficient and integrated three-phase plan for improving its banking processes. The plan's goals were aimed at building an integrated FSC featuring cash management monitoring and integrating treasury activity with ERP financial transactions.

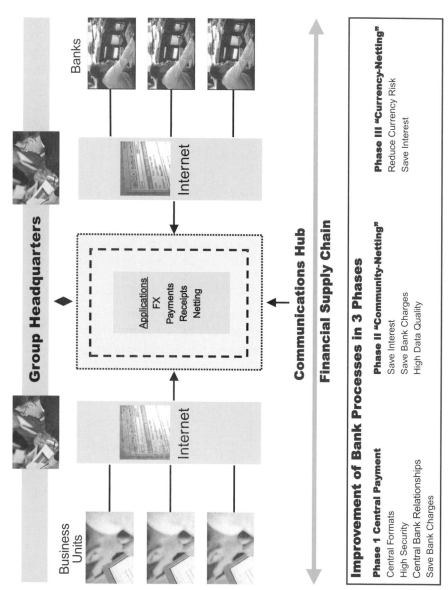

Figure 3.3   *In-house Bank Solution*

Phase 1 of the plan's implementation focused on central payment (a payment hub) and resulted in centralized formats, greater security, unified banking relationships, and significant bank charge savings. Phase 2 focused on community netting (internal bank) and led to interest savings, further bank charge savings, and higher data quality. Phase 3 involved currency netting and focused on the interaction between the USD and the Euro. The results: reduced currency risk and interest savings.

The heart of the company's solution is its in-house cash center. This acts as a service department and is responsible for looking after the financial interests of the group. It also takes on the role of a virtual bank for the group companies. The in-house cash center manages one or several current accounts for each of the company's subsidiaries. For the subsidiaries, the in-house cash center represents an additional bank and can keep their accounts in any currency. Besides keeping the accounts, the in-house cash center provides highly flexible account management functions for calculating and debiting interest and charges, approving account overdrafts, configuring the features and conditions of each account, and generating bank statements for each of the company's subsidiaries.

The in-house cash center controls the automated processes for payment transactions within the group (internal payments), payments made by group companies to external partners (central payments), and incoming payments for subsidiaries from external partners, which are initially credited to the house bank accounts at the head office (central incoming payments).

By managing your internal and external group payments, the in-house cash function can reduce your costs of processing intra-group and external transactions.

The results? You need fewer external bank accounts and make fewer international payments. You also gain considerable savings from optimizing your use of cash reserves. The features of in-house cash[5] give you greater control over payment transactions on both a regional and global level, support corporate group structures, and accommodate changes in those structures due to mergers, spin-offs, or reorganizations.

Not all companies today are able to centralize their payment transaction processes. Your company may be decentralized, with individual group companies processing the payment transactions with their own business partners independently of the parent company. Or you may use a mix of centralized and decentralized models, with payments made through both local banks and headquarters. Whatever your current system, the in-house cash approach offers exciting flexibility. It allows you to centralize your payment processes and benefit from the associated cost savings. The following organizational entities are involved in the individual payment transaction processes:

- Subsidiaries

- In-house cash center and financial accounting in the head office

- House banks used by the head office

- External business partners and their partner banks

The following scenarios highlight the individual payment transaction processes that can be performed by the in-house cash solution.

Automated Intra-group Payment Transactions

The process of clearing payables and receivables between subsidiaries is referred to as internal payment clearing. Example: subsidiary 1 makes a payment to subsidiary 2. To clear its payable items, subsidiary 1 runs the payment program in its own system with the in-house cash center as the paying bank. The in-house cash center receives the payment order and posts the corresponding payment items to the current accounts of subsidiaries 1 and 2. After a predefined time period, the in-house cash center automatically generates and sends bank statements to both subsidiaries. The subsidiary systems import the bank statements and clear the payment items automatically.

Since internal accounts are used to clear the payable items, no cash is physically transferred. The liquid funds remain within the group, no losses are incurred due to delays in value-dating payments or for the cost of external bank transfers.

Automated Outgoing Payments

Central payments are made by the in-house cash center to external business partners to clear amounts payable by the subsidiaries. The in-house cash center makes the payment on behalf of the subsidiaries. The advantages? When payments are made to an external partner, the cash flows only from the bank used by the in-house cash center to the business partner's bank. You can combine several payments from different subsidiaries into a single payment to an external partner. This reduces the total number of transactions and lowers bank-transfer charges, particularly for international transactions.

Automated Incoming Payments

When incoming payments are processed centrally, payments from external business partners are made to the subsidiaries via the in-house cash center. Central processing of incoming payments reduces the number of bank accounts needed within your company without reducing the flexibility of international payment transactions. The incoming liquid funds are instantly available to the in-house cash center, and the payments are automatically credited to the appropriate accounts.

Currency Conversion

Each account in the in-house cash system is managed in the account currency of your choice. The system recognizes any differences that arise when the account currency is translated into the local currency, and posts the gains or losses accordingly. The system also assigns a corresponding reference to all items affected by a currency conversion. As a result, you can identify the items that belong to a particular currency conversion even after the data is transferred to the general ledger.

Summary

The in-house cash solution gives you a flexible software environment for processing worldwide payment transactions. Its automated processes allow you to implement consistent, integrated transaction processes across your entire company, giving you greater control. Because accounts are managed centrally in the in-house cash center, you also have a direct view of all payment transactions in your group and of the liquid funds available in the accounts of your subsidiaries. You can control liquidity optimally, since you can avoid situations where one subsidiary has to borrow money while another has spare funds to invest. This feature enables you to maximize overall interest revenue and minimize interest costs.

Centralizing external and intra-group payment transactions reduces the number and volume of external transactions, which, in turn, cuts your transaction charges and, in the case of intra-group payments, avoids losses from delays in value-dating payments. It also reduces your overall currency risk, since you have lower foreign currency positions, and lets you optimize the structure of your external bank accounts. Above all, the automated in-house cash processes let you handle payment transactions between subsidiaries much more efficiently.

Many CFOs have implemented their ERP systems and now want to fully mine their benefits. Their *physical* supply chain has been improved – transaction processing costs are lower, working capital is reduced, and supply chain speed has improved. In the case studies that follow, we show how two companies are pushing to generate added benefits by further automating their order-to-cash process, which focuses on customer relationships, and their purchase–to-pay process, which concentrates on vendor relationships. In both instances, these companies are building on the foundation of their existing ERP implementations to improve their overall *financial* supply *chain*.

ORDER-TO-CASH/ELECTRONIC BILL PRESENTMENT AND PAYMENT

CASE STUDY
Building an Integrated Order-to-Cash System

One global chemicals company headquartered in Europe had regional customer service hubs in Germany, the USA, and Singapore. Worldwide it had 3,000 customers; each year, it processed approximately 100,000 customer orders and a similar number of sales invoices. Sales executives in the field and customer relationship coordinators in each of the hub locations were the main contact points with customers.

The company's first-time order commitment was achieved in only 70% of cases. To improve this track record, better stock availability and credit authorization processes were needed. Also, all invoices required some touching by hand, resulting in many invoicing errors. Benefits were sought in the following areas:

- *Pricing – provisional prices were often quoted and then had to be adjusted.*

- *Rebates and commissions adjusted to customer invoiced amounts were a continuous problem.*

- *Disputed items – communication between internal credit control, customer relationship coordinators, and sales executives was often poorly coordinated.*

In addition, the company was in the process of joining a new chemical industry exchange with a view to reducing costs and encouraging new business. This required linking up with 19 other industry partners. The company had also begun setting up its own private website called the Customer Lounge. The site allowed customers to quickly see the status of their orders, place new orders, share documentation, view their sales ledger account. The ERP was connected to provide an integrated online system.

The next step was to further automate the order-to-cash process. This process encompassed qualification of the order, credit management and agreement of terms through execution of the order, handling exceptions, managing returns and queries.

Improving billing and collection processes offered further improvement opportunities. The automation of the order-to-cash process resulted in the following features:

- *Qualification and sales: online credit checking, factoring and financing; use of mobile device for transmission of orders and their validation; mobile access to relevant end-to-end account data.*

- *Order fulfillment: automated data entry; customer self-service for order status.*

- *Returns and queries: automated routing of queries; self-service query support; reporting on returns and queries processing.*

- *Billing: electronic presentment of invoice over the Web; customer managed billing; electronic customer payment facilities.*

- *Collection: autoposting; customer viewing of sales ledger postings; online dispute resolution.*

The company also integrated its ERP resources with a number of best-of-breed systems as shown in Figure 3.4. The SAP ERP system was supplemented with SAP Biller Direct (electronic billing presentment and payment) functionality. A CRM package was used for customer relationship management and was integrated with both SAP and specialist software for intelligent e-mail handling, credit checking, and accounts receivable workbench. All information was collected for viewing through the company's portal.

Significant improvements were achieved in net cash inflow, reduction in accounts receivable outstanding, and customer relations. Customers now receive more responsive service through mobile access, more accurate invoices, and faster information access via the Customer Lounge. Real-time cash flow forecasting is now possible on a global basis.

Like the chemical firm described above, companies in every industry are pushing the technology envelope in order to achieve greater process efficiencies and cost savings. Among the broad benefits they are seeking:

- Using browser-based applications to reduce total costs of ownership, increase control, and leverage scalable solutions

- Using applications hosting where possible to reduce ownership costs

- Eliminating manual transaction processing and reducing order errors

- Hiring fewer but more skilled staff to investigate exceptions rather than input data

- Implementing regional shared service centers

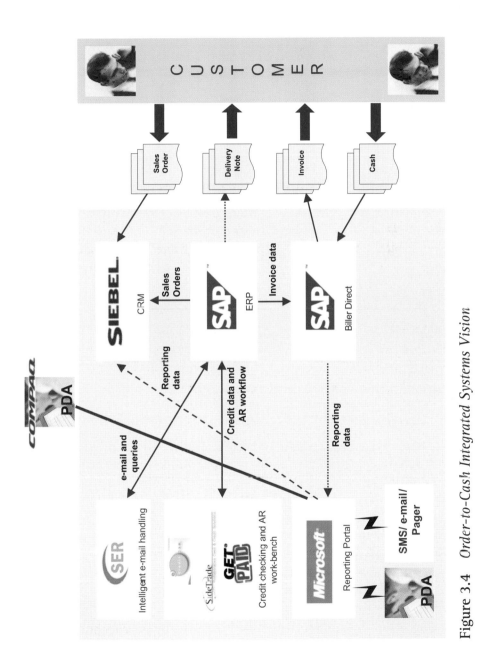

Figure 3.4   *Order-to-Cash Integrated Systems Vision*

Along with these broad benefits, there are some very specific advantages to fully automating and integrating key financial processes. Let's take a closer look.

Benefits of automating the credit process:

- Provides instant confirmation and faster decision making
- Collects and processes data so you can proceed confidently with transactions
- Frees staff to focus on higher-risk opportunities
- Better manages credit risk; consistent credit policy supports better risk assessment across a company's entire portfolio
- Works with multiple finance partners based on risk profiles which can increase sales
- Increases ability to meet customer expectations quickly

Benefits of automating invoice generation and query handling:

- Accelerates dispute resolution and reduces days sales outstanding (DSOs)
- Enables non-EDI customers to trade electronically
- Integrates data into accounts receivable system, eliminate re-keying of information
- Offers ability to review invoice requests online, modify and approve them, and use the system for cash forecasting and reporting
- Offers ability to review, query and request credit notes on outstanding invoices

Benefits of automating the collections process:

- Enables credit controllers to provide better, quicker service to customers
- Puts accounts receivable information and payment trends at credit controllers' fingertips

- Frees staff to talk with clients, resolve problems, and reduce overdue accounts
- Reduces cost of administrative operations

According to a recent Gartner Group, Inc. study, the number of companies sending out business invoices via the Web nearly tripled by the end of 2002 to 26%, up from 9%. By the end of 2004, this is expected to rise to 35%. Business-to-business electronic invoice presentment will dramatically reduce the current 41-day average time to collect payments, allowing companies to reduce debt and invest cash more quickly. Other major benefits of EBPP include:

- Significantly reduced billing and payment transaction costs
- Improved cash flow projections
- Simplified payment, settlement, and reconciliation processes
- Reduced float
- Increased customer loyalty
- Huge cross- and up-selling potential
- Better customer relationship management

"Three times more companies sell products or services over the Internet than invoice customers using Internet channels," said Avivah Litan, research director at Gartner in an article published in February 2001. "The primary challenges will be convincing buyers to give up their checks in order to take advantage of Internet payment benefits."

EBPP offers a host of far-ranging business-process advantages that promise to dramatically reshape billing and payment processes:

- *Improved payment services* – automatic application of payments to accounts receivable, online payment guarantees, and multi-currency payment management will all be possible with EBPP. Currently, sellers receive one payment for every three invoices sent through traditional channels.
- *Reduced billing costs* – according to the Gartner study, companies expect to lower the typical cost of producing a paper invoice from $5

to $1.65 for an electronic invoice by reducing labor, postage, paper and equipment costs. The cost of manually resolving an invoice dispute is also expected to decrease from $20 per call to $10 per dispute that is handled electronically. Other more significant savings come from streamlining accounts payable and receivable system processes, and ultimately reducing inventory.

- *Links with shipping and logistical systems* – linking EBPP with logistical systems will automatically trigger payment once buyers receive their goods.

- *Improved financing services* – more than 60% of the companies surveyed finance sales using the open account method, so automation that leverages trading partner relationships is bound to be very widely accepted.

- *Improved customer bill review and payment processes* – surveyed companies estimate that 11% of their customers face significant challenges in handling and paying paper invoices, while 46% experience modest challenges.

- *Integration with billing systems* – the second major barrier inhibiting billers from adopting EBPP after lack of customer adoption is the need to integrate with legacy billing systems. Payers are also reluctant to adopt EBPP without tight integration of their accounts payable systems with new EBPP applications.

- *Document exchange and reconciliation* – EBPP systems will enable buyers and sellers to exchange and easily track documents related to a sale. Buyers will also be able to review and reconcile the document information. This capability will proactively prevent disputes, leading to sellers being paid in full more quickly.

- *Integration with c-Procurement* – 30% of companies surveyed use e-Procurement systems, but just 3% have linked them to EBPP systems or strategies. According to Gartner, a fully integrated and automated supply chain is important to maximize e-Business returns.

- *Customer authentication services* – of the surveyed companies selling on the Internet, 57% make use of user IDs and passwords to authenticate customers, while just 14% have implemented digital certificate authentication technology. However, less than 1% of all B-to-B trans-actions are secured by using digital certificates.

Credit institutions and other financial intermediaries are striving for closer customer contact and want to offer their customers electronic bill display as well as classic services such as electronic banking. Service providers responsible for aggregating bills are called "consolidators."

As Figure 3.5 indicates, EBPP also offers great flexibility because there are several different ways in which systems can be modeled for optimal efficiency and speed. In contrast to EDI connections that require expens-ive point-to-point channels, consolidators work according to the network principle behind electronic purchasing platforms. Via the consolidator, a "many-to-one" relationship arises between vendors and the customer.

This application supports the "thick consolidator" as well as the "thin consolidator" model. In the "thick consolidator" model, the biller sends all bill information to the consolidator. In the "thin consolidator" model the consolidator receives only the final amount (subject to tax on sales/purchases). The customer is re-directed to the vendor's website for detailed bill data. The biller provides the consolidator with a URL (uniform resource locator) for this purpose. The company can also carry out personalized advertising (one-to-one marketing) in this way.

CASE STUDY
EBPP in the Utility Industry

Utilities have the right customer and billing characteristics to take advantage of EBPP. One electricity utility had millions of customers and was diversifying into new market segments such as gas. Opportunities existed for cross-selling and up-selling using the customer accounting databases. Also, there were opportunities to streamline work order management processes – supported by the engineers – with those in the finance department. The strategy of becoming a multi-utility was fast becoming a reality. New customer billing systems were implemented, which provided consolidation and convergent billing facilities – enabling the utility to tie many orders to one invoice. The company was rapidly moving towards its technology vision, too. The electricity and gas meter readers, for example, were connected using their handheld remote meter reading devices

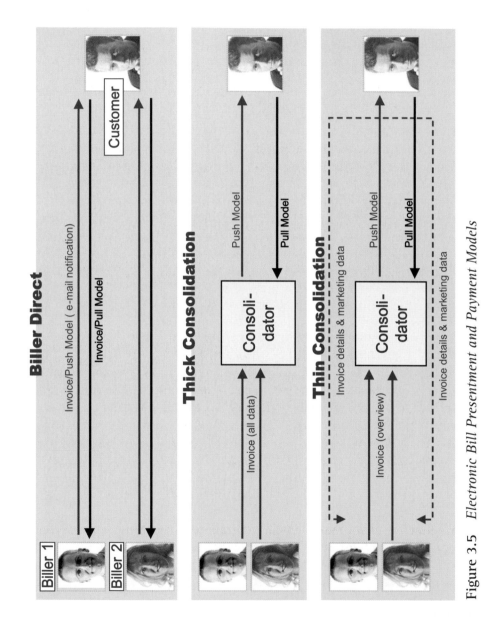

Figure 3.5   *Electronic Bill Presentment and Payment Models*

to the mainframe over the Internet. This saved transaction costs and improved cash flow. Additionally, the call centers – the first point of oral contact with the consumers – provided a one-stop shop for processing customer enquiries; these call centers were linked using customer relationship management software to a customer data warehouse, which not only was linked to the billing system, but also incoming and outgoing e-mail. Workflow software was installed to manage the credit control processes – coordinating dispute management and providing online dispute resolution. The integration between finance and engineering also meant that the call center could bring together automatically a truly cross-functional service for the customer, eliminating unnecessary internal and external communications traffic.

Mailing invoices to customers requires numerous individual steps for both you and your customers; your company must print and mail invoices and your customers have to collect and check them. All this costs more than you think. In fact, invoices sent by mail can cost up to $15 each! And by slimming your invoicing process, you can reduce costs by as much as 70%. With EBPP, convoluted processes not only disappear, the interaction between the invoice issuer and recipient significantly improves. For example, better communication makes it easier to deal with payment shortfalls and to provide high-quality customer service.

For companies with a large customer base, it is very important to be able to process and check the credit lines of customers at a central point. New applications make it possible to create a central credit control area in distributed systems. Previously, large groups with different product lines, investments, and distribution channels had no access to a central credit management.

An effective credit management program reduces arrears and prevents potential nonpayment where delivery has taken place. Prerequisites for a company-wide credit policy are integration in all distribution channels, automated real-time decisions, and access to internal and external credit information for all employees. Additional functions are the classification of customers according to creditworthiness or risk groups, or the integration of variable and dynamic content – for example, credit memos, credit insurance, guarantees, or use of payment cards.

PURCHASE-TO-PAY

The purchase-to-pay process – making purchases, receiving goods and services, processing invoices and credit notes, creating and distributing payments through to maintaining the purchase ledger – provides great opportunities for benefiting from a combination of ERP, best-of-breed and the linkage between the two made possible through EDI.

To achieve these kinds of benefits, firms are increasingly using EAI (enterprise application integration) technology to integrate legacy and best-of-breed solutions. Many companies are moving away from the standardization *one-vendor one-system* approach to a number of *best-of-breed* applications to provide increased functionality and access to data from multiple ERP systems. The following purchase-to-pay case study shows what can be achieved.

CASE STUDY
Streamlining the Purchase-to-Pay Cycle

The CFO of a major oil company was tasked with the following change agenda for his corporate finance function:

- *Velocity – increasing the speed of finance processes*

- *Visibility – improving finance's ability to provide accurate information*

- *Value – achieving some quick wins*

Detailed analysis of the company's "purchase-to-pay" cycle showed that the processing of invoices and credit notes offered greatest potential for clerical cost reduction. An intelligent document management solution was chosen for integration with the company's e-Procurement and ERP systems. This enabled an electronic image of the invoice to go through the three-way automatic match inside the ERP (the clearance of the invoice against order, price and delivery). The intelligent document management software recognized invoice data and processed it automatically using preset control parameters. Accuracy improved and is expected to increase over time as the system learns from its mistakes and control reports reject invoice data that falls outside preset guidelines. Overall, the benefits achieved through the purchase-to-pay process using intelligent document management proved significant:

- *A highly automated process with embedded business rules and logic.*

- *A scalable solution was rolled out quickly across the enterprise.*

- *Eliminated data entry; clerical effort is required only for exception management.*

- *Transparent end-to-end processing allowed bottlenecks to be identified and quickly reengineered.*

- *Working capital and compliance costs are reduced through indirect tax reclaim.*

The business case provided a quick payback: transaction costs per invoice were cut from an average of $3.20 to 50c. The company processed approximately 2.5 million invoices per annum and total savings amounted to $6.7 million.

The intelligent document management solutions referred to in Figure 3.6 enabled automatic recognition, validation and posting of manual invoices to the payables ledger.

SIMPLIFYING BILLING AND PAYMENT: BILL CONSOLIDATION

Biller consolidator software has been developed for service providers (consolidators) who collect invoices from various business partners and summarize those invoices for "partner" customers. In contrast to using electronic data interchange (EDI), which required expensive point-to-point connections, consolidators can operate through networks that have already proved successful for electronic purchasing.

Biller consolidator functionality can greatly simplify billing and payment processes and help those involved to reduce transaction costs. The exchange of information can reduce the average number of days sale outstanding (DSO) and thereby improve the cash flow of the billers. The

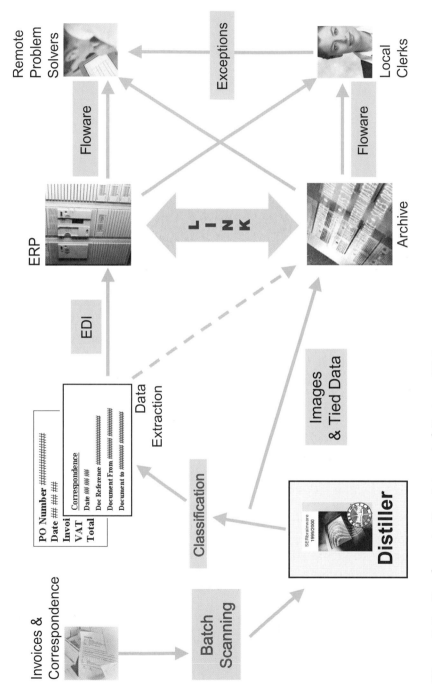

Figure 3.6   *Purchase-to-Pay Integrated Systems Vision*

application can shorten the time needed for customers to review and pay bills – which, together with one-to-one marketing capabilities, can improve customer relationship management. Customers can integrate invoice data with their accounts receivable system and eliminate re-keying of information. Even non-EDI customers can exchange invoice and payment information electronically.

The biller consolidator supports an open network that consists of the consolidator, the business service provider (BSP), and the customer service provider (CSP). The consolidator does not appear externally to the biller or the customer. The BSP and CSP represent the direct interface. They take care of the interests of the biller and the customer and integrate those interests with the consolidator's system. The BSP receives invoices electronically and forwards them to the consolidator.

The CSP is primarily responsible for presenting the invoices the customer receives from the consolidator. It informs the customer about the status of an invoice – whether it is open or released. Figure 3.7 below illustrates the roles in the Biller Consolidator.

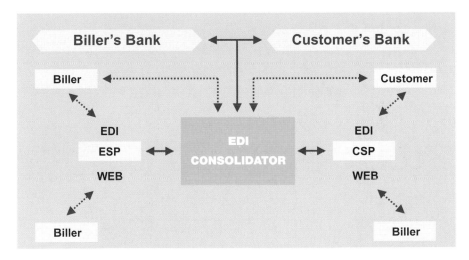

Figure 3.7 *Roles in the Biller Consolidator*

e-FINANCING AND e-SETTLEMENT: A PROMISING NEW TOOL

Traditional financing, payment, and settlement processes typically account for most of the costs of a finance function, and they tie up large amounts of working capital. e-Settlement with Orbian,[6] an integrated supplier settlement and trade finance mechanism, is an option for reducing the cost of financing and settlement. Let's take a closer look at how one company used this innovative solution to reap tremendous savings.

 CASE STUDY
Reducing Working Capital Costs

The Stanley Works was established 156 years ago in New Britain, Connecticut, USA and boasts one of the world's most recognized and trusted brand names for tools, hardware, doors and home décor products for professionals, industry, and consumers.

Stanley's offers over 50,000 different products and sales in 2000 exceeded $2.75 bn. Its global presence is firmly established, with 114 manufacturing and distribution facilities covering every major region of the world. Stanley products are sold globally through distributors and retailers, including thousands of retailers in the USA alone.

Due to the scale of their business and complex sales and distribution logistics, Stanley's FSC was facing mounting pressures on several fronts. Management was focusing aggressively on working capital targets and on generating the best possible return on its working capital investments. This internal pressure was intensified by Wall Street's relentless scrutiny of working capital utilization. At the same time, a concerted drive to outsource components and products was pushing working capital expenditures upward. Equally critical, Stanley's suppliers faced problems of their own in funding their supply chains and were looking for better payment terms.

Several key concerns had to be addressed: how to avoid the higher cost of goods and capital – and how to reduce lost discounts and limit supply chain disruption. In response, Stanley chose to implement Orbian, a unique new electronic financing and settlement solution that enables businesses to trade on better terms and benefit from reduced working capital requirements. A coventure of Citigroup, DCE, and SAP, Orbian gives both buyers and suppliers the opportunity to access additional working capital at a lower cost than traditional financing methods.

Stanley's main goal in implementing Orbian was to address the increasing pressure of working capital on their supply chain. Their customers were paying later, their vendors wanted payment sooner, management was looking to drive ROCE (return on capital employed) through initiatives such as production outsourcing, and analysts were pressing them to generate improved results from their working capital investments.

Orbian allowed Stanley to stretch their payment terms with their vendors, thus extending their DPOs (days payable outstanding) to be closer to their DSOs (days sales outstanding), and reducing the need for working capital and for borrowing. At the same time it offers supply chain benefits, since even though actual payment terms are longer, it allows the suppliers to instantly liquidate their entire Stanley receivables (irrespective of terms) at a low cost, reducing their DSOs and generating incremental free cash flow.

Along with these substantial benefits, SAP was able to seamlessly integrate the Orbian settlement, posting, and reconciliation processes into its payable (and receivable) processes within mySAP Financials. This allowed Stanley to significantly accelerate their systems improvement schedule and to focus on business implementation rather than technical implementation. Overall, Stanley anticipate savings of $20 million as a direct result of their reduced working capital requirements.

Commercial trading transactions have long been subject to uncertainty regarding the settlement of indebtedness. Trading inefficiencies and delayed payment of invoices are a global problem. For example, European settlement periods tend to be 50–60 days, and in southern Europe, suppliers often fund their customers for more than 120 days. Similar trading problems exist in the United States.

The integration of the Orbian finance and settlement service offers a straightforward way to solve these problems. Orbian provides a way to improve flexibility in negotiating invoice settlement terms with suppliers, while allowing suppliers immediate access to the value of those invoices. This reduces working capital requirements and improves the certainty and timing of settlements to suppliers. Orbian ensures that the incoming settlement is made to the supplier. And because Orbian is integrated with ERP, invoices can be settled easily. Supplier settlements are handled the same way as bank transfers or settlement by check.

As shown in Figure 3.8, buyers use Orbian to settle with their suppliers for goods and services. The buyer posts outgoing invoices with the payment method specified as "Orbian" and with an agreed-upon settlement date. The open item is then paid using the normal payment program, and the solution creates a payment file that can be uploaded to Orbian over the Web. Both the buyer and supplier receive daily Orbian statements and process them like normal bank statements. The required postings and clearings are executed when Orbian automatically processes statements.

The supplier receives a settlement from Orbian in the form of an Orbian credit, which has a specified maturity date, value, and currency. This is effectively an obligation from Orbian to settle the specified amount on the maturity date. The supplier can use this Orbian credit in one of three ways. It can:

- Convert all or part of the Orbian credit into cash before its maturity date

- Settle obligations with its own suppliers using the Orbian credit

- Wait to receive the full cash value of the Orbian credit on its maturity date

Recent implementation experience shows that companies who have succeeded with e-Settlement systems of this nature have had to overcome initial reluctance by vendors to participate. By creating a sales pitch to vendors and starting with an initial target list, CFOs should champion the initiative.

THE FUTURE: INTEGRATION AND COLLABORATION

Electronic Data Interchange (EDI) has proven limited in its application and expensive as well. Today, Extensible Markup Language (XML) is leading the way to Internet-supported collaboration. Basically, the idea behind XML is to separate content, structure, and layout. XML has given the Internet community a common language to exchange and share information and data. A common standard is a prerequisite for data exchange – increasingly all business messaging is done in XML. With

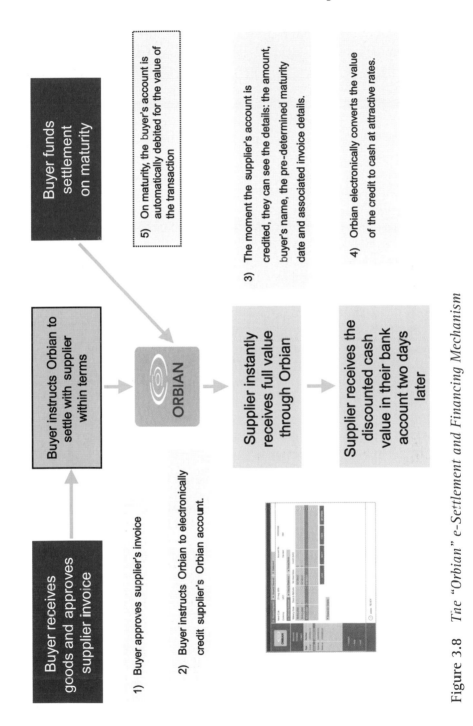

Figure 3.8 *The "Orbian" e-Settlement and Financing Mechanism*

the help of XML, a common grammar of the language can be defined. Still the words and the semantics need to be agreed upon. XML allows companies to structure the information they exchange with other companies or marketplaces.

Increasingly, the format of commonly used business documents such as a sales order or a procurement request is defined and available in XML. Now enterprises can instantly implement collaborative business scenarios such as buying and selling or demand and supply planning. XML enables a direct, seamless information exchange between two entities using widely available, inexpensive Internet technology – eliminating the need for intermediaries.

A procurement request, for example, can directly flow into a seller's planning system and be answered by order acknowledgment documents sent to the buyer. Thus, XML helps companies move beyond their traditional business boundaries and unleash the ultimate power of the Internet: customers, employees, suppliers, and business partners are networked together and working as one successful entity.

Exchange-based collaboration was pioneered by public and private exchanges. In the future, exchanges will prove to be the most effective way to streamline and standardize processes across organizational boundaries while cutting costs through higher efficiency. Three principles guide the evolution of this new approach:

1. Management of heterogeneity: multiple vendors systems and legacy systems within and across organizations

2. Non-disruptive implementation so that companies can follow an evolutionary path to solve their integration challenges

3. A high level of openness, flexibility, and performance

Putting these principles to work in reshaping the FSC poses a host of challenges, but the rewards will prove enormous: true internal and intra-company collaboration, real knowledge sharing across corporate boundaries, tremendous cost savings in logistics planning and working capital, and better customer service. Figure 3.9 illustrates how an exchange can cut down on the number of process and data connections between external business partners and internal business functions.

Companies face an increasing need for integration and collaboration. Today, the Internet provides the opportunity for systems to communicate instantly with other systems or individuals. Business processes that were once restricted to intranets and their users are now moving to the Internet to become part of a network of Web services.

Processes like supply chain planning, sourcing, and demand forecasting are automated across enterprises and within regions. They can now be implemented across systems at only marginal communication costs. To achieve this, components from different vendors need to be integrated and blended into a consistent infrastructure because there is simply no time for comprehensive system upgrades of existing enterprise software or ambitious replacement strategies in a world of heterogeneous system landscapes.

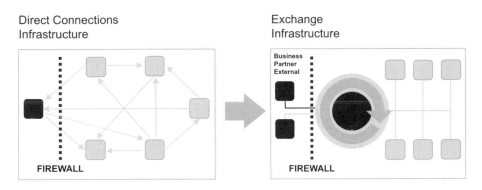

Figure 3.9 *The Concept of Exchange-based Integration*

CFO CHECKLIST

ASSESS ENTERPRISE READINESS
Form a team composed of finance, order fulfillment, logistics, and IT. The team should help the departments involved to understand the hidden costs of current FSC inefficiencies and exceptions.

LET THE NUMBERS SPEAK
Calculate potential savings. Demonstrate the degree to which physical and financial supply chains are out of sync and resulting inaccuracies in accounting processes. Focus on results: plan to reduce working capital needs by as much as 20–25%.

BUILD CORPORATE CONSENSUS
Start with the CEO. Because optimizing the FSC crosses all supply chain boundaries within the company, turf issues are likely to arise. Top-down support and enthusiasm will help keep the effort on track.

SOLICIT PARTICIPATION OF KEY TRADING PARTNERS
Involving partners in the planning phase creates ownership in the new approach. Prior to implementation, educate all trading partners on the need to adopt this approach and the benefits of an optimized FSC.

RATE SUPPLIERS OF FSC SOLUTIONS
Evaluate potential suppliers on their ability to understand your detailed process and data issues. Consider as well their ability to provide non-invasive and highly interoperable systems that can help you work with your customers and suppliers. In addition, when seeking an outsourced solution, find providers who are neutral and will earn the trust of all parties in the supply chain.

CREATE A VALUE ANALYSIS PROGRAM
Announce savings in working capital and transactions processing on a monthly or quarterly basis. Demonstrate progress toward

specific FSC KPIs. Continually reinforce the benefits for new personnel and trading partners.

DEVELOP FSC TRAINING
Anticipate changes to different people's jobs within the enterprise. Develop appropriate training to help people understand how they can use FSC information to better interpret the company's cash flow. Demonstrate how optimizing the FSC can provide the basis for non-emotional, fact-based payment negotiations.

CHAPTER 4

Moving from *"Shared"* to *"Managed"* Services

SHARING THE BENEFITS OF SCALE AND EXPERTISE
Jim Daley, CFO
EDS

EDS is one of the world's leading managed services and outsourcing companies. In the years after General Motors (GM) acquired EDS, the company's workforce zoomed from 13,000 to more than 30,000. GM catapulted EDS into the manufacturing market and extended its reach to countries outside the United States. In this period EDS developed systems management and systems integration relationships with a variety of customers, deepening its expertise in a widening range of industries and regions. GM divested EDS in 1996 and since then, EDS has broadened its offerings into new areas, such as consulting and business process outsourcing. Today, the company employs 140,000, with a revenue base of $21 bn.

As Jim Daley, the CFO, comments, "We know the issues our customers face with their support infrastructure because we experience these issues ourselves. Our customers today are looking not only to reduce costs, but also to maximize shareholder value from their internal support services. The real driver behind the growth of this market is technology: from the early mainframes to electronic data interchange to client server, and now the Web. The shift to Web applications is particularly dramatic. We have a declared strategy for Web services, both inside EDS and externally. It focuses, not just on creating websites, but on mission-critical business processes, too. The shakeout in the Web hosting market has really helped us. Unlike new entrants, we don't suffer from weaknesses in security and reliability since we specialize in large-scale infrastructure: today, we host some 45,000 servers! We have a number of Web applications, such as e-Procurement. Our sheer scale enables us to negotiate, for example, excellent rates and skills when procuring services through a specialized website for the outside IT contractor market. We call this website "Easytemp" – it is a global procurement function listing all our qualified contractors. This cuts administration costs for both EDS and its customers.

The EDS business model is predicated on substantial investment in mainframe technology. The big outsourcers, like us, have the capability to help their customers make shifts in technology without incurring big spikes in cost. For example, we have invested in solutions for customers such as computer-aided design, integrated with the supply chain – a software solution used by both GM and McDonald Douglas, which is integrated with the enterprise resource planning (ERP). Most of our work involves building solutions for customers. Quite often, we are invited to share the expertise built up with one customer across their industry sector.

Following our period of rapid growth, we were left with a relatively inefficient organization – we had 48 strategic business units and lots of internal competition! When I started this job, we needed to improve our financials and I brought with me some of my experience gained at PwC (Pricewaterhouse Coopers) in managing a global business – sharing synergies across geographic and cultural barriers. One of the first things we did was to form a new e-Solutions unit. We now only have four lines of business, down from 48. We have changed our compensation system to promote cross-selling. But most importantly, we have worked hard to capture knowledge across the organization with new processes and systems. This helps us achieve productivity gains and leverage our collective intellectual property. So now, as we grow, our cost base remains fairly stable and we can deliver the performance improvements our shareholders require.

So what's the future of outsourcing? It must be strong, if the value proposition is there for the customer and if services can be provided of a better *quality at a lower cost. What differentiates success in this industry is ability to execute. This, coupled with our installed infrastructure, represents our competitive advantage. More and more, we are being asked to build total solutions. I believe the market is moving from just one integrated solution to a series of independent, best-of-breed solutions, which our customers can access remotely. Traditionally, we have serviced customers independently on a contract-by-contract basis. Increasingly, we have been encouraged to share these services across customer contracts, where customer confidentiality allows.*

Some companies exploit their shared service operations by marketing their expertise externally to others – turning these into profit-generating propositions. We have seen examples of companies like GM spinning off EDS, Philips doing the same with Origin, and American Airlines selling Sabre. These businesses benefit from sharing expertise: in designing state-of-the-art business processes, in building robust solutions, in maintaining applications and in operating physical infrastructure. Massive partnership opportunities are likely to emerge between players like us, our customers, and technology vendors."

Companies like Procter and Gamble (P&G) have implemented shared services centers (SSCs) for finance and already brought their cost benchmarks up to the standard of the professional outsourcers. P&G based their North American shared services in Costa Rica; its center there provides the required level of service at a fraction of its former cost. Like EDS, P&G's CFO says, "It's all about execution!" Everyone who has launched a shared services program agrees.

But many CFOs who have made a concerted effort to implement well, aren't sure how successful they have been – or how much further to push their programs. Then there is outsourcing – the elephant in the middle of the room! CFOs constantly ask us: Are there really huge benefits to outsourcing? Wouldn't we be better off investing in a home-grown center, rather than giving up control? What's new, better, faster, cheaper? P&G have achieved their economies without having to outsource. Now they are prepared to joint-venture with others to exploit their finance services expertise still further.

In this chapter, we will examine the evolution of shared services to outsourcing, with emphasis on the impact of new technologies and Web-based exchanges. The world is changing, and a new managed services market is evolving with it – combining the benefits of shared services, business process outsourcing, managed infrastructure services, and applications management. Finally, we will look at the impact of Web services and what they mean for you as CFO.

WHY MOVE TO SHARED SERVICES?

Cost, certainly – access to less costly resources or better processes. Change, inevitably – outsiders are invariably needed to help drive through change. Up-to-date skills in a risk-free environment. And the commercial flexibility to cut fixed costs as business conditions change. And of course, there's the core competency issue. Many companies go down the shared services route so that they can concentrate on their core business and avoid the distraction of new technology.

Shared services are not about steady state service delivery; they <u>are</u> about constant evolution, spanning many years. As such, they represent one of the most challenging and unique environments in which to operate. Change comes quickly and in many forms as you navigate your way to powerful results. Along the way, the most common pitfalls you'll face are:

1. People do not understand the pressure to change

2. Executives are not equipped to manage the process of change

3. Lack of a coherent vision undermines long-term benefits

4. Underestimating the enormous communication required

5. Too narrow a focus, obscuring obstacles from executive line-of-sight.

6. Long-term goal shifts focus away from short-term wins

7. Changes are not assimilated into the corporate culture

8. Victory is declared too soon

In helping companies make the shift to shared services, we have found that implementation usually follows one of three paths:

1. Shared services are implemented within a *country* or a single business unit.

2. Others go *regional* – processes are shared for all business units across a continental theatre.

3. Some companies are even more adventurous – they go *global*, establishing a single shared services center for all business units in all regional locations.

As companies fine-tune their approaches, feedback about what works and what does not is accumulating. Today, some trends are emerging:

Shared Services Centers Are Increasing in Scope

- Economies of scale are being achieved by bringing more countries and business units into the fold.

- More processes are included such as IT, finance, human resource management, procurement, and customer relationship management (CRM).

Shared Services Centers Are Shrinking in Size

- Better technology, less human intervention, and greater speed are close to making "lights-out processing" a reality.

- Collaborative relationships are increasing as process specialists move beyond corporate boundaries.

Businesses Are Being Pushed toward Greater Flexibility

- Companies are being driven to quickly decide whether to perform services internally or to outsource them.

- Companies have to move faster to absorb new acquisitions and handle disposals.

Businesses Are Working Hard to Drive Down Investment and Operating Costs

- Using new technology to process transactions in lowest cost locations.

- Partnering with suppliers, customers, and possibly competitors to share non-strategic support services.

As shown in Figure 4.1, when it comes to both structure and operations, shared services offer the benefits of both worlds – centralization and decentralization.

Many companies have realized the benefits of shared services, but this has taken time. Initially, reductions in the fixed cost base were the objective – through staff reduction or redeployment, lower software purchasing and licensing costs, and lower systems support costs. Next, reengineering and productivity enhancement led to the elimination of non-value added processes – resulting in fewer errors, less rework, and more timely and accurate information.

Value creation and continuous improvement are the ultimate prizes. Business performance is enhanced through greater leverage with sup-

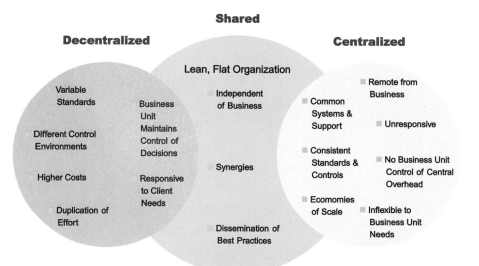

Figure 4.1 *Shared Services Combine Centralized and Decentralized Benefits*

pliers and customers, as well as improved reporting and decision support. Bristol Myers Squibb's European Financial Service Center is a case in point.

CASE STUDY
Launching a European Financial Shared Services Program

Bristol Myers Squibb (BMS) is a diversified healthcare company with sales of approximately $20 bn and 44,000 employees worldwide. Its products range from pharmaceuticals to consumer goods. In the mid 1990s BMS embarked on a shared services program for Europe.

The mission: develop, drive, and deliver world-class business services, which enable BMS to achieve and maintain superior competitive advantage and fuel growth. The major goals: significantly reduce transaction costs and implement best practices. The drivers for change: top line growth, Y2K, and the need to harmonize processes and reduce financial consolidation and reporting time frames.

The company started with benchmarking transaction processes for functions such as accounts payable, payroll, and travel and entertainment accounting. The scope of productivity initiatives included strategic sourcing, demand management, financial services, and order-to-cash. The selected approach was to reengineer the processes first set up as regional shared service centers using a common global model, and then to move to a common IT system – a single instance of SAP.

A shared services global team was created to form a global integration approach with regional teams for Europe, North America, Latin America, and Asia Pacific. The regional teams worked to a global charter.

The European shared services operating plan included:

1. *A multilingual support service*

2. *Customer-driven service level agreements*

3. *The use of enabling technologies such as SAP and document imaging.*

The European teams focused on transaction processing, continuous improvement, and value-adding services. Finance was refocused on supporting the businesses – reducing transactional workload and concentrating on enhanced analytical support.

The accounting changes included setting up various statutory charts of accounts, accommodating local GAAP postings, calculating multiple VAT rates, and dealing with other specific country differences. The SAP solution was designed to manage this complexity. A special ledger accommodated statutory reporting and different document type codes, allowing the books to be kept in local GAAP.

Perhaps the biggest challenges in implementing SAP were change management – the acceptance of global standard processes, and changes in cultural philosophy. These challenges included the elimination of direct invoices, the importance of users coding requisitions and the loss of country-specific systems. During the implementation, the ability to respond to changing needs with ongoing support was a priority. Also critical to success was training as the user base grew. The development of expert users and an effective help desk was crucial.

Today, the BMS European financial shared service currently employs only 103 people with multilingual capabilities (seven languages), and is approaching its fifth full year of operations. It serves over eight markets, including over 60 legal entities and supports over 6,000 European users.

The current plan is to increase the scope of the shared services center by adding new services and including small-market implementations. Meeting the changing needs of the BMS business units is still a high priority. Coping with system upgrades and new technology requires huge flexibility. Staff training and retention are still big issues.

As BMS has learned, successful implementation requires integrating many different components – often too many! Business processes have to be matched with people and cultural issues, as well as systems and technology. Organizational structures and interfaces have to be well thought through and internal customer requirements must be met.

Like everyone else, the managers of internal shared services face constant pressure to do more with less. Intelligently automated shared services can relieve that pressure and boost profitability. One of the big lessons learned: shared service delivery is often hampered by lack of synchronization. The answer? More delivery automation.

Most companies start by installing automation software to handle financial transactions, but HR is also ripe for automation. Bringing catalogue management or even sourcing elements into the shared services environment can also produce big benefits. However, conflicting priorities when outsourcing shared services can slow down the automation process if organizational responsibilities for *who does what* are segregated.

Providing services that people need and are willing to pay for, at a cost, quality, and timeliness competitive with alternatives, is the only way to survive. Companies cannot cut costs by outsourcing or centralizing shared services unless they have an automation platform that improves service delivery. With a dedicated software platform, companies are finding that they can:

1. Improve coordination on many different levels

2. Realize direct and indirect savings

3. Enhance customer satisfaction by managing expectations and meeting commitments

SHARED SERVICES TODAY

Accounts payable and accounts receivable still top the list of services provided.[1] The general rule of thumb is that homogeneous, cross-business processes are suitable for shared services. Right now, SSCs tend to handle processes that don't demand complex customer interaction. The norm is rule-based, high-volume, non-critical transaction processing.

In a recent survey, the top five services performed were:

1. Accounts payable

2. Accounts receivable

3. Travel expenses

4. General ledger and consolidation

5. Payroll and benefits

Other results from the same survey:

The top four reasons for establishing an SSC (%):

1. Reduction in general and administrative costs	83
2. Better service quality, accuracy, and timeliness	53
3. Standardization of business processes	48
4. Optimization of working capital	42

Top criteria when selecting a site (%):

1. Labor: availability of skilled people, new skills	74
2. Communications/infrastructure: telecommunications, transport, etc.	48
3. Proximity to customers	36
4. Proximity to corporate/regional headquarters	25
5. Office space: availability, cost, etc.	23
6. Labor costs	20

Top five success factors (%):

1. Senior management commitment	85
2. Finding the right people to lead and work in the unit	44
3. Early successes (quick wins) to build momentum	32
4. Clear communication of goals to all employees	28
5. Emphasis on effectively managing the change	25

Those in the planning stage should consider that shared services projects need to be designed and implemented as holistic change programs to achieve full cost benefits. This means the following:

- *Standard technology,* such as a single instance ERP system, delivers platform scalability, reduced software costs, reduced licence fees, reduced maintenance costs, and reduced support costs. Lack of standardization results in duplication.

- *Best practice processes*, for example in the areas of order-to-cash, purchase-to-pay and account-to-report, provide significant product-ivity gains and reduce operating costs.

- *Strong service culture*, uses service level agreements and other tools to improve service quality thus reducing rework and employee turnover.

Many organizations are cutting corners in at least one of these areas. Beware! Ignoring any of these factors could jeopardize the overall suc-cess of the SSC initiative. When companies adopt a holistic approach, 30–40% savings are very achievable.

PHYSICAL VERSUS VIRTUAL SSCS: THE LIGHTS ARE STILL ON!

Why consider virtual SSCs? "Lights-out" processing! Ultimately, com-panies want to achieve maximum automation in their back-office pro-cesses. With integrated supplier, customer, and internal systems, and with data entry becoming the responsibility of customers, suppliers or line employees, we move to a very different environment indeed.

Virtual SSCs represent one of the steps down the path to lights-out processing. Nevertheless, there are serious pros and cons to taking this approach (see Table 4.1).

Financial transactions still account for the majority of services pro-vided by SSCs. However, IT, HR, legal, and facilities transactions are increasingly being processed in SSCs. Non-financial services provided by an SSC typically include: compensation and benefits, IT operations and development, procurement – strategy/negotiations and order processing.

An SSC represents a big step toward providing lowest cost services to business units. Before making this move, companies often simplify or standardize relevant processes within the units. Flying in the face of conventional wisdom, a few companies have begun sharing frontline, marketing, and other services. For instance, Hewlett-Packard's European Customer Support Center provides multilingual telephone assistance to 19 countries.

Each step brings more benefits.[2] But each step also means more

Table 4.1

Advantages	Disadvantages
No staff upheaval, people remain in existing locations	Difficult to share and implement best practice ideas
No requirement to find or build physical SSC	Difficult to implement and maintain standard processes
No loss of knowledge built up with existing staff	Remaining Finance & Admin staff will have too wide a span of control
No problems with obtaining local language skills	No labor arbitrage
No cost or effort of hiring and training staff for the SSC	High cost of maintaining finance management in all countries or sites
No large change programme diverting focus of senior management	Difficult to achieve service culture in existing local sites
	Standard technology does not always lead to standard processes

change and more barriers to overcome. As Figure 4.2 indicates, making this shift requires a high tolerance for change and puts a premium on adaptability.

Step 1: Simplify – Do things better, country by country This approach involves basic business-process reengineering within each country and subsidiary to eliminate non-value adding activities and develop local solutions to improve performance. Some corporations achieve cost savings in excess of 30% just by simplifying.

Step 2: Standardize – Do things consistently in all countries Implement common systems and use consistent charts of account for operating units across national borders. Best practices in any one unit should be extended to others. Beyond cutting costs and complexity, you gain an enormous benefit: the ability to compare data across companies in different countries.

Step 3: Share services – Bring together resources and processes to achieve economies of scale Here, processes are moved from the business units to

Cost Reduction Versus Base

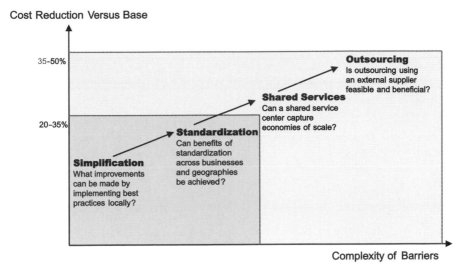

Figure 4.2   *An Escalator of Change to World-class Performance*

a dedicated center that provides services on a national, regional, or even global basis. Going beyond the practice of using a single data center, this approach brings together people and facilities. Reorganization eliminates many duplicated costs. The center both exploits economies of scale and frees business units to refocus on higher value-adding tasks. As the CFO of a US-based multinational said: "We can streamline the process dramatically and remove big chunks of cost by having heavy mechanization. We get higher quality transactions with fewer errors. It's a home run!"

Step 4: Outsource – Use an external service provider   Certain processes may be best managed by third-party outsourcers who combine minimal cost with maximum service. Now widely used for IT and facilities management, outsourcing is often extended to other noncore business processes.

TO OUTSOURCE – OR NOT TO OUTSOURCE?

In the United States, more than 75% of the Fortune 500 have initiatives under way to outsource a broad range of business-support services. But outsourcing generally works well only for carefully selected non-core processes. One Japanese finance director regards his staff as the "brains" for the CEO and senior management, and says he "could not conceive of outsourcing their services." We find that companies often hesitate to run the risks associated with outsourcing. They fear losing control or getting locked into using a single supplier, particularly for critical functional areas such as finance.

In deciding whether to outsource processes internally or externally, consider five issues:

- Does company culture incline you to keep direct control over key services?

- How rapidly do you want to move? Implementation may be achieved in a shorter time frame using an external supplier, especially if other initiatives compete for internal resources.

- Can your team make the change itself? Honestly appraise your track record in internal reengineering and restructuring. Have you delivered winning results on time and within budget?

- How do people feel about each alternative and its implications for the company's growth and their own career paths? Could external outsourcing cause industrial relations problems?

- Can your systems be segregated easily to permit external outsourcing?

The logical progression shown in Figure 4.2 scarcely suggests the full power of sharing services. The center must do more than drive down costs. What differentiates shared services from merely consolidating functions is the internal supplier–customer relationship that develops between the center and the business units it serves. In the most successful programs, the SSC handles activities on behalf of the business units both more efficiently and in ways that better meet their needs. The center actively manages the supplier–customer relationship. It aligns its competencies with the expectations of internal customers who offer continuous performance feedback.

CASE STUDY
Outsourcing the Finance Function

When Safeway, a leading UK supermarket chain, decided to outsource its finance function, it represented a huge cultural and operational shift. The objectives of the program are the same as those when it started six years ago: decision support to enhance shareholder value; improving business perform-ance; financial stewardship of resources; and acting as the financial conscience of the management.

According to Simon Laffin, the CFO: "In the past, finance was viewed nega-tively by other functions. It was seen as a policeman, an obstacle, a less-than-useful resource isolated from the mainstream business. The new finance team operates very differently. The routine transaction processing and financial accounting was outsourced to PwC. It also outsourced its business controls (internal audit). That left the in-house finance team to focus, in addition to core functions such as planning, treasury and tax on Financial Support Teams (FSTs). These teams support, and are indeed, co-located with the other divisions."

The company charted a careful, two-stage strategy. In Stage 1, it focused on business controls – a combination of external audit and outsourced internal audit. This "communication web" tying together outsourcers, in-house resources, and external service providers makes the business secure.

When satisfied that this approach was working, Safeway advanced to Stage 2: fully outsourcing transaction processing. Achieving scale is a big issue for the number four player in its market. To date, they have achieved considerable savings, more than 20%. Outsourced services include accounts receivable, accounts payable, payroll – and routine banking and credit card processing.

Simon Laffin goes on to say, "Making these changes has allowed us to focus our remaining resources on the job of decision support and gathering insightful information. Our skills mix has changed. We are now very analytical and commercial (not policemen!). We serve ten million external customers a week; we try to avoid too much information, too much analysis, which is of too little value. We rely more on the informed judgments of our retailing experts, focused on sales and margin management, store operations, and customer-led competitive strategies, which are conceived and executed within relatively short time frames – within a matter of weeks rather than months. Two hours is a lifetime for our CEO!"

When outsourcing works well, it works wonders! Firms can typically reap cost reductions of 10–30%, along with improved service.[3] No wonder the outsourcing industry has doubled in size in less than five years! What's more, outsourcing is expected to continue growing as firms outsource, not just information technology, but entire business processes.

Consider the case of BP. It outsourced parts of its human resource function to Exult. Today, PwC handles its downstream finance and accounting processes for Europe, as well as its upstream processes for most of the Americas. Accenture handles finance and accounting for BP's downstream operations in the US, as well as its upstream operations in the North Sea. The SAP financials module in Aberdeen, Scotland, is shared by six North Sea oil companies for upstream finance and accounting operations. BP also outsources logistics, engineering, and some production.

Outsourcing, however, runs counter to a parallel business trend: the tight integration of a firm's enterprise solutions. It is integration that delivers the business benefits so often promised by enterprise solutions, including increased productivity, efficiency, customer satisfaction, and responsiveness. When data, applications, and processes are handled by different firms, then achieving integration can prove difficult.

One government agency, for example, had outsourced to so many vendors that integration became nearly impossible. To integrate data, they often had to resort to batch processing interfaces, which undermined responsiveness to changes in business conditions. Coordinating their vendors became so difficult that the agency recently closed down its existing vendor arrangements to pursue a new more focused strategy. Not a happy situation!

Not all outsourcing arrangements pose significant integration challenges. Firms that choose to host their own applications on someone else's servers, for example, can integrate them fairly smoothly into their existing portfolio of applications. Explains one manager: "It's still the same system. The fact that parts of it physically reside outside our firewall in different locations doesn't make much difference."

ConocoPhillips, for example, one of the oil firms participating with BP in their shared services group in Aberdeen, decided to maintain ownership of its own software to avoid potential integration problems. The outsourcing staff is now directly linked to Conoco's SAP R/3 Financials module in order to perform Conoco's financial processes. The outsourcer is also required to maintain Conoco's standards and upgrade schedules.

Most outsourcing arrangements require sharing a common application platform to achieve efficiency gains. This demands that vendors change their customers' existing applications. At a minimum, a provider will change a firm's system to meet the vendor's own operating standards. Most often, a provider will want to use its own system, thereby spreading systems costs over multiple firms. In this case, interfaces need to be built for each outsourcing vendor to connect its system to a firm's system. Differences in customization of functions, set-ups of data structures, and upgrade versions between firms may cause significant integration problems.

In addition to integration challenges at the applications level, outsourcing also creates challenges between vendors at a process level. Some processes outsourced to third parties, like procurement and benefits management, have little interaction with one another. But other processes, such as payroll and accounting, require tighter integration with one another.

When outsourcing to multiple vendors, firms should carefully consider technical, organizational, and integration issues:

- *Technical issues*: firms should standardize their applications and processes as much as possible before outsourcing them. The more customization there is, the harder it is to achieve the cost efficiencies and to integrate applications and processes distributed among multiple vendors. Make a conscious decision to choose only those vendors that can support the same type of enterprise solutions you already have. If the majority of your enterprise solutions are from SAP and you want to outsource finance, then choose a vendor that can support the SAP finance module.

- *Organizational issues*: carefully review your current operations to ensure the integration of applications and processes across multiple firms. Vendors might be encouraged to work with one another to exchange process maps, for example, or in defining middleware connections for application integration. Be aware, however, that vendors are often wary of working together for fear of giving away their secrets. In addition, it can be difficult to clearly define and delegate responsibilities when they fall in the gray areas of connectivity and integration. All too often, one vendor blames another for an unforeseen problem, but no one takes responsibility for fixing it.

To help ensure that multiple vendors work together to promote your enterprise solutions, carefully structure their contracts up-front and provide incentives. Although it is tempting to outline detailed responsibilities for each vendor, it is precisely this approach that can lead to trouble. When unforeseen tasks inevitably arise that are not part of the original contract, they may be neglected. Clearly but broadly outline roles and responsibilities rather than detailing specific steps.

- *Integration issues*: BP, for example, achieves data and application-level integration for financial data by employing an integration hub. Each application inputs its business results in a standard format to the hub, where a consolidation tool integrates them. Having installed the technology to integrate its various best-of-breed applications, it was a simple step for BP to use it to integrate applications from the outside as well.

  Another new integration tool combines the capabilities of enterprise application integration (EAI) with workflow software to integrate applications at both data and process levels. Called "business process integration technologies," they promise real-time orchestration of processes between firms and modeling, monitoring, and optimizing processes that cross firm boundaries.

- *Multiple vendor issues*: in general, the fewer vendors you have, the easier it is to integrate them. Strive to outsource highly related processes to a single vendor. Finding the right one may not be easy. Even today, the industry is awash with highly fragmented specialist vendors offering leading-edge practices for individual processes.

Cost reduction is still cited as a major driver for outsourcing, yet 75% of large-scale outsourcing agreements do not appear to yield savings. Outsourcing can typically cost 10–15% more than a large-scale internal service center. What benefit does outsourcing offer? Mainly, increased focus on core competencies. CFOs can concentrate on building world-class capabilities and accelerating the benefits of reengineering.

An external outsourcing solution makes sense in these four circumstances: your primary intent is strategic change, not just cost-focused; you have already captured internal economies of scale; you do not have and cannot build competitive internal resources; and finally, your organization is ready to give up internal control of support functions.

Companies that benefit most from outsourcing start with standardized IT programs and leverage best practices already in place. Then they tightly manage the outsourcing process from beginning to end by pursuing the following approach:

- Defining service items or offerings: a detailed analysis of scope with clearly defined responsibilities is critical (including a profile of baseline business).

- Establishing service level agreements: these support robust processes and attain mutual agreement concerning criteria that are controllable and measurable.

- Structuring an agreement that is flexible enough to reflect changes in transaction volumes and performance measures (including quality, and opportunities for partnering).

- Partnering with a provider that offers full value on several fronts, including best practices and process improvements.

- Understanding that with outsourcing you are paying for services instead of internally dedicated employees.

- Communicating desired objectives and benefits of outsourcing to both internal and external stakeholders.

- Demonstrating a sense of urgency and moving quickly to drive value. Build a performance dashboard and reporting tools.

Add Web-enabled technology into the mix and you will not only reap further improvements in service quality, but also create a seamless end-to-end transaction environment. Take full advantage of technology, shared services, and outsourcing to achieve your process vision of having your outsourcer(s) handle most of the activity in buying (purchase-to-pay), selling (order-to-cash), and accounting/reporting. The Internet links customers, suppliers, and a partner bank: the outsourcer does the rest.

EVOLVING TECHNOLOGY: WHAT'S NEW, FASTER, BETTER

Like most fields, shared services is struggling with fragmentation. There is a confusing array of new technologies for which standards are still evolving. XML and its relationship with its predecessor EDI is a big issue for the CFO because it is the medium through which financial information is transported via the Internet. Systems development, trading relationships, accounting transparency and security – as well as reporting – are all affected.

What's our advice? Ensure that your ERP backbone is capable of supporting the front runners in XML standards as they emerge. EDI has always been, and always will be, dynamic. When industry standards and tools change, EDI changes with them. Whether we call these interchanges EDI (electronic data interchange) or DDI (direct data interchange), we are still talking about interchanging the same documents and automating the same critical processes.

The future of data interchange is phenomenal! The marriage of XML and EDI is an excellent short-term solution to the barriers imposed by the exclusive use of EDI. Merging these two powerful technologies opens a window of opportunity to increase trading partner relationships via the Internet. The Web allows companies to further benefit from e-Business infrastructure by creating an electronic link for trading partners without EDI capability.

The original goals of EDI – to automate cost savings and eliminate errors – are still important. However, the stakes are getting higher! The need to recognize the long-term value and future potential of an e-Business infrastructure is also paramount for success.

The challenges facing companies transitioning to XML-based e-Business: the linking, the synchronization, and the standards differences between the two types of infrastructures. A new approach to B2B integration architecture that can automate linking and synchronizing XML and EDI is known as EIM (enterprise integration modeling). This leverages a repository-based model (much like a thesaurus) to automatically identify matches between business trading partners' business content regardless of whether it is in EDI or XML format.

Following rapidly on from the introduction of XML is a new technology – Web services. Web services are applications that can communicate with each other and exchange data without human intervention. They are based on the XML Internet programming language.

Web services provide applications over the web and enable many users to access the same web service at once. For CFOs and finance functions this technology should assist in achieving shared services and out-sourcing since it provides the opportunity for scale, the advantage of leading-edge applications and new solutions. To use web services you will need to clarify issues such as service definition, service access and standardization, as well as data security. Web services should lead to a greater openness in your IT infrastructure. The full potential of web services is discussed later in this chapter.

You may be asking, "How does our company fit into e-Business?" When businesses move into e-Commerce, they are typically automating the supply chain through multiple trading partners – and linking internal and external business systems. The Web expands the benefits of e-Commerce by creating an electronic link for trading partners, letting them trade documents and expand their global reach.

You may already have many of these pieces in place. The trick is to find your way through the EDI evolution process. Knowing where you are at today and where you want to be is key. If you currently have an EDI package, upgrades to e-Commerce capability may be available already.

EDI is always evolving. Building an execution strategy may seem overwhelming. But the payoff is tremendous! As pieces fall into place, the scope of what you are accomplishing for your company will shine through. Keep your focus on the long-term growth of your company. Ultimately, the scalability of your solution will help you recover costs and maximize your business growth.

CASE STUDY
Restructuring the B2B Integration Equation[4]

Inside Osram Sylvania, a multi-million dollar enterprise resource planning system from SAP delivers accurate, critical data in real-time to those who need it. But try to share that data with trading partners, and what happens? Delays of up to 24 hours and inaccurate data in one in five transactions.

The culprit: the slow, cumbersome, error-prone technology known as electronic data interchange. At stake is Osram Sylvania's ability to reliably exchange order, inventory, and other key business data with customers and suppliers. The stakes are growing as one of its target markets – automotive – grapples with an economic slowdown.

That's why Osram Sylvania has set up a new system for sharing business data with its trading partners. The system uses XML, a flexible way to create common information formats and share both format and data via the Web, intranets, and other means. The technology should let the $2 bn lighting products unit of Osram exchange the same up-to-the-minute data with partners that is available internally. It may also let Osram Sylvania finally realize a greater return on its ERP investment. "The main attraction for us is the fact that we can make our ERP system a true competitive advantage," says CIO Mehrdad Laghaeian.

Osram Sylvania's system-to-system integration project entered the planning stage a year ago and is now in the implementation phase, but the uncertain economic climate has given it a strong boost. "It's weird, but perhaps the economic slowdown is exactly what the doctor ordered for this project to take off," Laghaeian says.

Today, manufacturers are scrambling to respond to changing market conditions and to coordinate their production plans with partners. Despite this, business-to-business integration initiatives are among the IT projects being spared; in some cases, such projects are even gaining higher priority. Companies are adopting emerging technologies and languages such as XML and e-Marketplaces as alternatives to proprietary EDI networks or to processes that still require fax, mail, and phone calls. Such improvements in the way companies share information about orders, inventory levels, and production plans could help partners quickly send signals about demand throughout the supply chain and respond nimbly to changing market conditions.

APPLICATIONS MANAGEMENT AND MANAGED SERVICES

As we have seen so far in this chapter, CFOs typically start first with shared services and then consider the merits of outsourcing their finance function. Recently, however, a new industry has grown up in parallel called managed services – and this, in turn, has recently been extended into applications management services. Some suppliers now offer one integrated solution for outsourcing all of these three services – processes, IT infrastructure, and applications.

But first let's consider what these terms mean. *Applications management* can be defined as the ongoing management, maintenance, enhancement, and support of an organization's business systems throughout their life cycle. *Managed services* is the provision of external support for the infrastructure, the hardware, and the software that support the company's applications. Do you have a mix of legacy or current software applications that consume your IT resources? If so, read on!

What type of company outsources their applications management? Those who face a pressing need for solid, cost-effective IT operations – and growing pressure to improve margins. But perhaps the most important factor is the increasing focus within a company on its core competencies.

A survey by Gartner in 2001 showed that 36% of global enterprises anticipate adopting a *virtual organization* structure. While growth in the outsourcing market for legacy applications management will slow, strong growth is forecast in outsourced management of ERP and e-Business applications. However, not all companies have a successful experience. Some are disillusioned with this more holistic outsourcing model, usually due to a mismatch of customer and supplier needs.

In structuring an outsourcing deal, be clear about those elements of the solution development life cycle you are covering – from design to build to run. Contrast the differences between a pure support and maintenance agreement, which is trying to *do the same thing in a better way,* with an outsourcing agreement focused on *doing the same thing in a new way* (transformation). Then contrast these two approaches with the ultimate goal: creating business partnerships designed to *do new things in the best way.* In Figure 4.3, we set out on the vertical axes these three different approaches, compared on the horizontal axes with commensurate pricing structures for charging and risk/reward.

When considering the right supplier, review in detail their abilities to cover the full solution life cycle and their competencies. For example, the *design* offer might include consulting and change management. The *build* offer may include package implementations, customer solutions and application integration, migrations, and upgrades. The *run* offer encompasses applications support, application maintenance, operational support, and help desk.

At the heart of a successful managed services deal is a *services delivery model.* This model should ensure that the service provided by your sup-

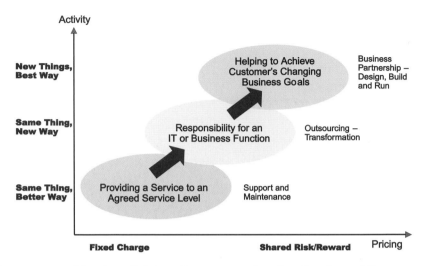

Figure 4.3 *Varying Pricing Structures for Applications Management Contracts*

plier is delivered with quality and consistency to meet the performance measures defined in the service level agreements (SLAs). An SLA for applications management is segmented according to progressive service levels:

- *Preventive* – activities to improve applications or make service improvements

- *Corrective* – responding to incidents, reestablishing live running and making permanent fixes if appropriate and agreed

- *Adaptive* – changing an application to fit different hardware or software

- *Supportive* – enhancing an application to reflect changing business requirements

- *Competitive* – driving through business change and innovation

The anchor point of operational delivery is the *service specification*, a document equally as important as the contract. The service specification is a core component of the service management approach. Every unit operates a service specification and every member of the unit leadership

126

team needs to understand the content, structure, and change control mechanisms for that unit's specification. The service specification plays a major role in both establishing the operational unit and reflecting changes in the demand.

The service specification consists of the following: the *service definition*, setting out the proposed services so they can be used to set target performance, articulate volumes, and operate with a business, rather than technical, perspective. The *service measurement* approach, which measures performance against targets set out in the service definition; the *service charging* approach, whereby operational costs of service delivery are linked to the service specification itself. This helps the client to make better value judgements about the costs and benefits of service at a more granular level.

Here are some questions you need to answer when entering into an application management services contract:

- What is your application budget?
- What is the current workload – availability, interfaces, number of users, etc.?
- What is the volatility – requests for change, etc.?
- What is the hardware/software package, and to what standards?
- What is your current headcount – type, skill, location, etc?
- Is there any other third-party involvement?
- What metrics are used to gauge performance?

In three short case studies,[5] we illustrate how three companies defined their business needs and service proposition for outsourcing, together with the benefits they have achieved.

CASE STUDIES
1. A UK Bank Seeks New Capabilities

This bank faced growing demand from its customers for products over the Internet. Additional resources were required to develop and implement specific new systems. Specifically, it chose to outsource its UK life policy and invest-

ment systems, together with the system for pensions. The bank established service definitions for production support, systems enhancements, and system development – particularly for investment products over the Web – and application consultancy and training. The infrastructure comprised a UK mainframe, which was supported remotely by a number of programming languages. The service level agreement (SLA) was geared to "response and resolution" according to business criticality, and included out-of-hours support.

The key benefits included accelerated product development – access to the required IT skills and organizational flexibility. Substantial cost savings were achieved through the reduced use of contractors, economies of scale, and office space reduction. Systems performance and resilience improved, mainly as a result of operating larger-scale systems and working to the SLA standards. Generally management overhead was reduced and employee morale improved.

2. A Global Electronics Group Seeks to Reduce Costs

The challenge: cost-effective support of legacy systems to centralize by moving to a standardized platform. The objectives: to reduce maintenance effort, facilitate application enhancement, and eventually, replace the system totally. The application: the global financial system, comprising general ledger, accounts payable, and accounts receivable.

The services needed were defined as follows:

- *First and second line support*

- *System enhancements and upgrades with global rollout*

- *System development*

- *Application consultancy and training*

- *Vendor management*

The infrastructure outsourced was based on three mainframe installations in Europe, the Far East, and the United States. The company was successful in achieving standard business processes across different countries and in pro-

viding cost-effective global support. The benefits enabled the company to focus on strategy and new product development.

3. A Global Chemical Company Improves Support

This company wanted to migrate to a new ERP on a worldwide basis. However, its old applications needed to be supported during the transition. This required specialist knowledge, product management, and best practice support. The application was its critical proprietary ERP system, currently used in 26 countries for production, sales, distribution, manufacturing, and finance. It was critical to manage supply and demand across countries while interfacing with shop-floor systems.

The managed services external provider defined its mandate as global production support, product management, system enhancements, and application training. The service level agreement was amended to include minor upgrades and rewarded the supplier based on the achievement of clearly defined targets. Conversely, the supplier was penalized if it failed to meet milestones and deadlines.

The company achieved its objectives, releasing staff to focus on the new systems implementation and reducing management overhead. The scene was set for a standardized global implementation based on SAP R/3.

As these case studies suggest, there is a range of ways in which companies can manage their service initiatives. Applications management and managed services contracts can be priced according to four different methods:

1. *Resource based (time and materials)*: the client buys a predetermined level of resource support from the supplier. This is most typically used for development services. The disadvantage: service quality can be uneven because service agreements are optional.

2. *Service based (fixed price)*: services are based on defined service levels, governed by an SLA. The SLA will typically contain penalties for missed service levels and the supplier faces penalty risks if it fails to meet the service levels set out in the SLA.

3. *Transaction based (unit pricing)*: suppliers are paid on the throughput of their clients' business – for example, per ticket sold or per credit card transaction. Usually, there is a baseline for service revenue plus a marginal per-transaction revenue.

4. *Open book (cost plus)*: suppliers are paid through a management fee over and above an agreed cost level. This is a good way to combine both resource- and service-based deals. However, this approach can lead to cost disputes.

EVOLVING EXCHANGES: HUGE PROMISE AND TOUGH REALITY

Exchanges play a growing role in the world of shared services, out-sourcing, and managed services. Finance processes are heavily involved in their success. The CFO needs to reconsider the feasibility of exchanges in streamlining business processes in the light of experience so far. Exchanges promise cost savings and growth opportunities. The reality is that many have already failed and many others are struggling. But there is much to learn from the success stories.

Business-to-business (B2B) exchanges are online marketplaces for businesses to buy and sell goods and services from other businesses. Automated B2B transactions are not an entirely new concept. In the early 1990s, large organizations began using automated systems to streamline transactions with business partners. General Electric's Aircraft Engines division, for example, had a system by which a customer could order a part, initiate the shipping process, be invoiced, and pay, all within 45 minutes!

These automated systems, however, needed dedicated, expensive data communication facilities and required significant investments in large, complex software. It took the Internet to bring down the cost and technology barriers.

Today, things are moving even faster. New digital marketplaces (DMPs), or Web-based trading communities, have been announced in every major industry. However, a shakeout has already begun. Even so, the benefits of connecting businesses through Internet exchanges are clear and some DMPs will continue to survive.

DMPs can be defined as business-to-business, Internet-based inter-mediaries that connect supply chains in various vertical industries or across industries, introducing new efficiencies and ways of buying, selling, and brokering products and services. *Public DMPs* allow buyers and sellers to engage with other buyers and sellers – on a real-time basis. *Private DMPs*, by contrast, let trusted trading partners who regularly do business together create efficient Web-based trading networks to reduce supply chain costs.

B2B exchanges are designed in three ways:

- *Public exchanges*, such as Commerce One, are run by a third party and are open to all companies that meet the standards defined by the exchange.

- *Private marketplaces* are run by a single company for its key suppliers. Wal-Mart and Dell Computer Corp. are two companies that sponsor their own exchanges.

- *Consortia* are typically formed by a group of leading vendors in a particular industry, such as Transora – for consumer package goods companies and retailers.

Although public and private exchanges have proliferated, few have realized their promise of seamless integration of the supply chain. This is making it difficult for companies to determine which type of DMP they should embrace, or how to employ the DMP within their IT plan or day-to-day operations. As Figure 4.4 highlights, the road to exchange growth and progress continues to evolve, hand in hand with companies' plans for B2B integration.

The larger exchanges require significant up-front investment – private exchanges are delivering returns, but for public and the larger industry exchanges, the jury is still out. Positive market statistics still abound, but are often overly optimistic. Despite recent consolidation, DMPs represent a growing portion of B2B transactions over the Internet. Industry research predicts that electronic market transactions will account for 53% of the $2.7 trillion that researchers expect companies to spend in B2B electronic commerce by 2004.

Public exchanges often have simple goals. They want to streamline participants' purchasing and procurement processes by building a com-

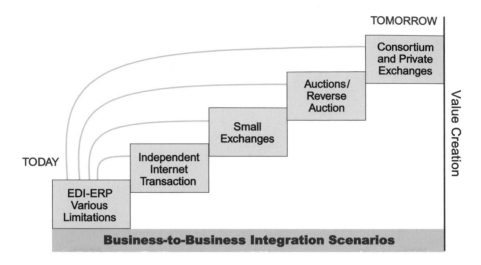

Figure 4.4 *Evolution of Exchange Technology*

mon information technology platform. They should never favor buyers or suppliers but also have to be profitable in their own right.

Industry-specific exchanges, on the other hand, offer more value to suppliers and buyers and are designed to improve the overall performance. They offer a strategic tool for a company's buy-side, allowing it to reach a more fragmented community of trading partners that it does business with only intermittently.

CASE STUDY

An Innovative Niche Player[6] Transforms an Industry Exchange

TexYard was formed in early 2000 with the objective of bringing European clothing retailers closer to their suppliers via the Internet. Brent Dennison, CEO, wants to provide a "faster and cheaper" approach for his clients (6–8% procurement savings). When TexYard was launched, there were already some big players in this space: WorldWideRetailExchange and GlobalNetXchange. However, TexYard's original investors believed there was room for a niche *player offering customized solutions rather than off-the-shelf packages. Just recently, the American e-Commerce company, Internet Capital Group, agreed to invest $4.5 million to expand TexYard's reach.*

TexYard brings buyers and suppliers together to make the process of apparel sourcing easier, faster, and more efficient. Buyers can put their complete sourcing process online, obtain the best possible price, and accelerate their time to market. They can also use a comprehensive database to find new suppliers from around the world. Suppliers can gain access to major European retailers, expand their customer base, and increase new business opportunities.

TexYard accommodates both forward auctions, in which buyers bid increasingly higher prices, and reverse auctions, in which buyers and sellers bid progressively lower prices. The exchange also allows buyers to define full details of an upcoming production contract – from technical specifications and quality measures through to shipping and delivery instructions – and get bids on these contracts. The TexYard team developed an application that provides what is, perhaps, the most sophisticated procurement process ever created by a trading exchange.

The project was managed and developed by a global team in five locations with 35 members, including a project manager, 6 business and systems analysts, 2 XML developers, 25 application programmers, and a production support professional. As a result, the exchange got to market early with relatively low development costs. It has been successful in attracting customers and suppliers, and recently obtained a new round of financing.

In Brent Dennison's view, a "marketplace is software," nothing more, nothing less. It is just a private trading network between retailers and suppliers. Brent's biggest challenge now is to "scale up."

The landscape is littered with the hundreds of failed B2B exchanges. Even for the survivors, demonstrating success is not easy. Yet several B2B exchanges, such as TexYard, are still operating after several years.

Although public exchanges have attempted to persuade their members to collaborate more closely, they have found that creating communal relationships with anonymous or infrequent business partners can be difficult. This is proving to be the point at which private exchanges demonstrate advantages over public ones.

Private exchanges are by nature more collaborative because the players are known, trusted partners who consistently do business with each other. They often share information, for example, by designing collaboratively and tying inventories closely together. In addition, they may work in partnership to improve delivery cycles or quality management.

Companies that operate their own private exchanges are likely to invite partners to join. Partners understand each others' operations and product specifications and can create efficiencies across the supply chain by sharing inventory information and manufacturing requirements. As relationships develop, some companies will invite suppliers to join. On the private side, developing a network with a select group of partners entails a thorough examination of a company's business processes to determine where the cost-takeout opportunities across the supply chain actually exist. This can involve change management issues as well as technical integration concerns. Security, while also an issue, is not as predominant a concern as it is with public exchanges since partners are known and trusted.

Whether to join a public or private exchange is not always a clear choice. Both public and private DMPs face their share of challenges. In addition, in order to achieve significant benefits from connecting to either a public or private exchange, companies will need to integrate the exchange with their back-end systems. This integration can be a sizeable task.

The automotive industry provides a good example of what can be achieved through a consortia-based industry exchange. Current predicted savings by Goldman Sachs from automotive B2B activities could range as high as $2,000 per vehicle. Performance improvements from such an exchange flow from the following activities:

- *Automating the procurement process*: the reduction in paperwork can bring cost-per-purchase order from approximately $100 to $20.

- *Auctions*: online auctions have the potential to reduce prices, as large numbers of suppliers compete for contracts.

- *Collaborative planning*: major savings can be achieved if plants across company supply chains can view each other's inventory levels and production schedules.

- *Collaborative design*: designers from different companies can work in tandem. Time to market is faster and efficiencies can be built into product design earlier and more cost effectively.

B2B exchanges in the automotive industry can improve the relationship between buyer and seller. Covisint is the premier industry exchange for the automotive industry.

CASE STUDY
Pushing Exchange Benefits to a New Level[7]

Ford, General Motors, and DaimlerChrysler formed the Covisint exchange in early 2000. Later that year, it was extended to include automotive companies in Europe and Japan. Covisint provides access to the global automotive industry via a common technological infrastructure based on a leveraged systems investment.

Covisint's objectives include the strategic sourcing of products and services, new standards for the exchange of information in the global automotive industry, and connectivity between members through systems applications and portals. Figure 4.5 shows the various parties involved in the exchange, with examples of their connectivity.

As part of the exchange, Covisint also hosts online auctions, electronic parts catalogues, and provides applications for sharing inventory, manufacturing schedules, and automotive designs online. The central hub where trading partners of all sizes come together to do business is a single business environment using the same tools and user interfaces. The industry operating system leverages customers' existing legacy systems and uses common standards to deliver mission-critical information with the goal of improving communications across the entire automotive supply chain.

All industry participants can communicate securely via the Internet-based, Covisint-hosted portal by using a Web browser. A tailored content-management tool provides the ability for customers to manage their own content creation, editing, and publishing.

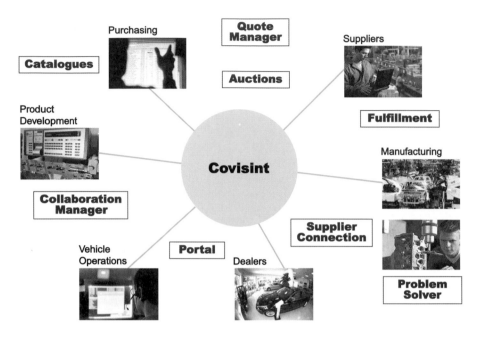

Figure 4.5 *Covisint – Exchange Connectivity in the Auto Industry*

In 2001, Covisint had 1,400 online bidding events, aggregating $51 bn. One event alone was valued at $3.5 bn. In the first quarter of 2002, there were 600 events adding up to $4.5 bn. Covisint estimates that over $100 bn worth of electronic RFQ (request for quote) applications covering a number of years into the future have been distributed through this exchange. Some 7,000 companies participate. Critical mass is the key to survival: Covisint is probably 20 times bigger than most other exchanges.

Covisint is still very much in its infancy. Its history has not been plain sailing. During the initial phase of development, it turned to vast numbers of management consultants; the burn rate was too high and there was little revenue coming through what was an unproven business model. There were technical issues to be resolved between partners, there was little organizational structure, and it needed a culture of its own. During the second phase of development, a cohesive leadership team was brought on, the business model began to take shape, costs were cut, and a permanent staff was installed. Stability emerged.

In the third phase – which is ongoing – volumes have increased and the revenues are coming through. However, there is still much to be done in terms of delivering profitable results and accountability for performance. Two strategic business units are currently being formed – one focused on customer retention and the other on customer acquisition and revenue generation.

Covisint's relative success is an exception. Many industry exchanges were formed because early Internet entrepreneurs saw low barriers to entry. These entrepreneurs were not necessarily familiar with the industries they were trying to serve. For Covisint and the automotive industry, the business processes haven't really changed – they have been e-Enabled. There are patterns of social interaction that are deeply embedded in the systems of procurement, which differ by company history, by country precedent, and law. They are not easily overturned by some wonderfully convergent vision. Their role in influencing the adoption of a new technology is often underestimated.

B2B will be "evolutionary" rather than "revolutionary." What is the future of B2B exchanges? General Electric's Jack Welch was right when he said that in the near future we will not be using the term "e-Business" because all business will be e-Business. We will soon see the emergence of the real-time organization in which every bit of information, from time cards to financial statements, is updated instantaneously. The benefits should be enormous!

THE POTENTIAL FOR WEB SERVICES

So far in this chapter, we have covered shared services, outsourcing, managed services, applications management, and exchanges. All these have major implications for the CFO, the structure of the finance function, and its supporting processes. The rate of structural change is escalating as the impact of the Internet gains momentum. One new phenomenon to emerge recently has been Web services. This new development is likely to change the way business works.

So what are Web services? Web services are a way of connecting business processes – both within and between organizations – more quickly, flexibly, and cost-effectively. In technical terms, Web services are a set of common emerging IT standards that, when "wrapped around" a business application, allow it to integrate with any other application that also has a Web services "wrapper."

Web services allow applications of any type to connect to each other irrespective of the technology platform of the individual applications. This means, for example, that any Web services-enabled enterprise resource planning (ERP) system (running on, say, Windows NT) can be "plugged in" to any other system such as a Web services-enabled financial system (running on Unix, for example). This is a major breakthrough!

Vendors are almost unanimously backing Web services and are committed to building common standards into their products and services. By 2004, 95% of all major IT vendors will have added Web services standards to their applications. According to a Gartner Group finding,[8] *by 2005, the aggressive use of Web services will drive a 30% efficiency increase for IT development projects.*

Corporate IT programmers currently spend around 65% of their time building tailor-made bridges between applications to allow them to communicate with each other, according to another Gartner estimate. Web services' *raison d'être* is to minimize the need to build proprietary bridges. They provide a versatile tool for solving the majority of your IT integration problems, opening the door to a more flexible, agile, and cost-effective business infrastructure.

In summary, Web services allow companies to:

- Adapt their internal business processes more quickly and efficiently

- Outsource noncore processes to third parties, "renting" services, such as credit checking, and staff training as and when they are required

- Enhance their relationships with existing partners, customers, and suppliers, through the deeper integration of business processes and systems

- Expand their customer base more easily, connecting instantly with external order systems and other processes, whatever they may be

Don't be fooled by the technocentric terminology – Web services do not simply make life easier for your IT department. Their biggest value lies in the business benefits they bring. Figure 4.6 shows how Web services can connect the extended enterprise through new Web applications.

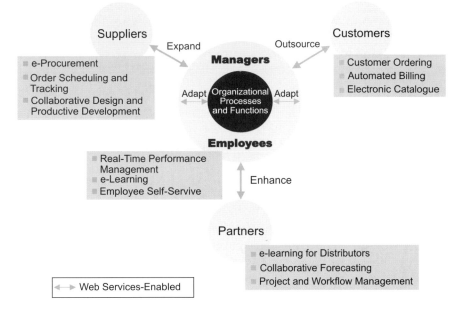

Figure 4.6 *Extended Enterprise: Potential Web Applications*

Web services are not, of course, a "silver bullet" solution for increased agility. Integration always takes place on two levels: the *technical* level, which connects processes, and the *business semantics* level, which determines precisely how data is interpreted and manipulated between those processes. Web services alone offer a solution to the technical integration, but not the business integration. They must, therefore, be deployed in tandem with effective change management and robust business process design.

Nevertheless, Web services will make it easier to enhance, adapt, and replace your internal and external business processes – and your business relationships – more quickly and flexibly than ever before. Cost reduction is another huge benefit. Web services not only cut the cost of the integration process, they also allow you to make deeper savings from integration itself by:

- *Reducing integration costs*: by reducing the need to build bespoke bridges between business applications, Web services will cut integration time, saving organizations money. Web services, however, are a common set of standards that almost every major vendor is backing. Every piece of your business and IT infrastructure will therefore become quicker, easier, and therefore more cost-effective to connect.

- *Increasing business process efficiency*: because Web services make integration easier, they allow organizations to take integration further than ever before. And further integration means improved efficiency. The automation of internal processes (such as expenses claims) and external processes (such as company credit checking) can dramatically reduce administration costs.

- *New outsourcing opportunities:* Web services make it easier for organizations to "rent" business processes from third parties, unlocking the cost savings and other benefits offered by the outsourcing model in areas where outsourcing has simply not been viable before. As the market for Web services-enabled applications provided by third parties develops (buoyed by increasing broadband penetration and the resolution of security and data privacy issues), outsourcing will become a realistic possibility for businesses that have previously balked at the obstacles. For example, the settlement functions of investment banks could be outsourced once Web services make it possible to assemble a credible service provider.

At present, your company's infrastructure is probably built like a 1960s car. It is made up of lots of different components; all customized to work with your particular make and model. It just has not been possible to replace your commercial equivalent of a Rover gearbox with one made by BMW. However, the automotive industry has matured to the point where many key components are made to standard specifications, allowing a particular vehicle to be built from parts sources from many different vendors. Similarly, Web services allow you to take your car-like IT infrastructure, and adapt, enhance, upgrade, and transform it using universally compatible components.

Now is the time to use Web services in small-scale e-Business projects intended to improve operational effectiveness. Imagine, for example, a corporate training company. Using Web services technology, its payroll, payment processing and other financial systems could be handed over to one firm, its HR processes to another, its training content development to another, and so on.

IT applications are still focused on finance systems, HR systems, customer relationship management systems, and so on. In contrast, Web services will allow a new breed of horizontal applications to emerge. Called "cross applications," they deliver adaptable cross-functional business processes.

Take the merger and acquisition process. It requires services from a wide range of sources, internal and external. This is exactly where Web services-based cross applications excel. They accumulate information, transactions data, and services from different sources and present them consistently only to those charged with managing the merger or acquisition.

But how will end-users – be they employees, partners, or customers – actually grab hold of and use Web services-enabled business processes? The answer is through a 'portal' – a personalized Web interface on the user's desktop, mobile phone or any other Web-connected device. Employees, for example, will personalize their portal to provide instant links to marketing databases, invoicing systems, and other business applications they need to do their jobs better and faster.

What will the Web services future look like? Here, three industry scenarios provide an exciting glimpse of what's to come.

Public sector: *Public agencies tend to operate in fragmented cultural and technical "silos". Different government departments, for example, often have incompatible legacy systems where data is stored in different, incompatible ways. Web services will provide for the fast and cost-effective integration of these silos. This will open the door to closer collaboration between departments, reduced duplication of data gathering, and improved services for citizens.*

Imagine the future: a single directory of public sector services covering national government, local government, health, justice, and agencies. People will be able to select just the services or data they need and have it delivered via a personalized portal.

Financial services: *A basic issue lies at the root of the financial services sector's IT problems: ageing heritage systems find it hard or impossible to talk to each other. The challenge is to integrate these so that, in the case of retail banks and insurance companies, customers are presented with a single face, or in the case of investment banks, goals such as straight-through processing can be achieved.*

Web services offer a neat solution. They "wrap" each system with a set of common standards, so they can speak to each other. Data can be mapped, integrated, extracted, or consolidated seamlessly, enhancing customer relationships and increasing the ability to analyze data for marketing and real-time cross-selling. Imagine the future: a single financial portal where all your financial affairs can be viewed and managed on a single screen, irrespective of the provider!

Pharmaceuticals: *Here, R&D and marketing functions will benefit significantly from Web services. The availability of information – the analysis of a patient's blood or the competitive sales analysis of compounds - is profoundly important. Today, such information must be analyzed by teams of highly skilled information experts who spend a large proportion of their time resolving the issues of data compatibility.*

Web services are going to make many of the issues surrounding data capture (from automated lab systems, clinical data capture systems, enterprise resource planning (ERP) systems, and external organizations) much easier to overcome. Imagine the future: pharmaceutical research collected from hundreds of different sources around the world, instantly and automatically delivered, processed, sliced, and diced, in any way that users want it!

While all these options are intriguing, getting there from here won't be easy. There are six major barriers facing companies looking to implement Web services:

1. *Risk.* The greatest value of Web services lies in their flexibility and openness. But at present, these are also the root of their greatest weakness. Security, reliability, trust, and privacy remain pressing issues for firms using Web services to connect with external business processes. Standards for encrypting XML, creating digital signatures, and related security measures are being developed. But other risk and reliability issues, such as the structure and content of service level agreements, also must be addressed.

2. *Accountability.* Responsibility and accountability are the flip sides of risk. A single business process may include Web services from a

number of different sources. This means that new, inter-organizational methods of accountability must be created.

3. *Further integration standards.* If Web services are to truly become the universal "collaboration glue" of business, then they need to address the interoperability issue. Solutions are emerging. For example, a standard called the "Web Services Choreography Interface" (WSCI), co-developed by SAP, SUN Microsystems and others, enables Web services to interact in ways that meet the needs of complex, real-world business processes.

4. *The commercial and legal framework.* Web services providers need to explore different charging mechanisms – just as Internet service providers have done. It is also important to consider where legal owner-ship of intellectual capital, customer data, liabilities, and so on, lies in the chain of loosely coupled Web services. A tight legal framework will be needed to protect companies, customers, and suppliers.

5. *The user experience.* The effectiveness of business applications employing Web services technology will depend on how well they serve users' needs. Issues like the design of portals – the "front end" of Web services – are of paramount importance.

6. *Comprehensive integration.* Web services technology alone will not serve the needs of employees, customers, partners, and suppliers. What is needed is a consistent and unified user interface. Remember, Web services technology can lay bare bad business infrastructures, as well as improve good ones.

How will Web services develop?

Business–to–business As companies become comfortable with using Web services technology, they will begin to connect with partners and customers. B2B Web services will include:

- Integration between buyers' sales systems and smaller customers' order systems – imitating the EDI networks that currently connect larger customers

- Rented applications providing companies with remote access to data-base management, CRM, HR and other business functions as needed

- Collaborative business processes that run seamlessly across multiple enterprises – creating the long-awaited "eco-system," and challenging traditional business models, as competition surges between value chains rather than individual companies

Business-to-consumer Unresolved security issues make widespread adoption of business-to-consumer Web services impractical today. However, once businesses are Web services-enabled, both internally and between themselves, the delivery of customer-facing Web services is next. Business-to-consumer Web services will include:

- Rented software and other applications, which will be delivered to consumers via the Internet – video games, home movie editing suites, personal finance management services and so on

- Music, film and other forms of entertainment, which will be ordered and accessed from a single "portal" site

- Lifestyle propositions developed using an aggregated range of Web services – offering services from home insurance to online shopping

MAKING IT HAPPEN

What can you, as CFO, do today? Assess your infrastructure's readiness for Web services. Develop a blueprint for internal Web services. Review lessons learned:

- *Think* about how Web services' ability to increase business agility and reduce costs could benefit your business. Which of your business processes most need greater flexibility? Where could Web services be deployed to reduce costs? How can greater agility boost productivity and sales?

- *Talk* to your CIO and your IT team. Find out how much of your existing IT activity could immediately embrace Web services standards, how much of your infrastructure can be upgraded to these standards, and when obsolete parts of the infrastructure can be replaced.

- *Implement* discrete internal Web services. Start experimenting with real Web services right now! Begin with discrete, noncore, internal business processes. Choose an internal process that has a good potential ROI, such as filing expense claims. Bring that service online and integrate it into your existing IT infrastructure. Strategic, tactical, technical, and cultural lessons learned today will prove invaluable tomorrow.

As we'll see from the following scenarios, leading companies from many industries are already reaping exciting benefits from Web services.

Web Service Scenarios

Dell uses a Web service to publish an updated manufacturing schedule for each of its plants every two hours, supercharging the responsiveness of its entire supply chain. Dell is going to extend the system to provide links to all of its key supply chain partners in order to coordinate demand forecasts, share real-time inventory data, and track deliveries – all with no investment needed from the partners!

Ford pulls real-time information from rail and truck carriers, combines it with data from its own systems, and delivers a Web service to dealers that tracks expected arrival of vehicles in transit.

Tesco, the UK headquartered supermarket chain, uses Web services technology to link its own customer-facing online ordering system into its partners' systems for electrical and other non-grocery goods. This lets Tesco use its website to sell a wide range of products supplied by third parties without the need for rekeying of orders.

Build a business-focused strategy. Implement It *inside* your business first with employees (B2E) – where security, reliability, and other variables can be controlled and risks minimized. Then use Web services to connect to business partners (B2B). As quality and security standards are established, use Web services to connect to new partners and suppliers, and to deliver new kinds of services to customers (B2C).

Let's speculate with 10 predictions for the future:

1. The standards underpinning Web services will hold up.

2. The financial services, travel, energy, and public sectors will be among the first to fully exploit Web services.

3. The US will not take its traditional lead over Europe in technological innovation. Right now, they are neck and neck.

4. There will be a shift in the balance of power between technology vendors and customers. Customers will come out on top!

5. Software will be sold as a service, radically changing the traditional vendor business model.

6. Web services will become so commonplace that they will be seen as the natural building block of technology and business architectures.

7. Security issues, particularly in terms of authentication, personal privacy and data ownership, will move up the corporate agenda, as Web services promote more extensive sharing of data.

8. Web services will inevitably lead to greater connectivity – within businesses, across supply chains, and with customers. As more functions are carried out online, users will be increasingly bandwidth-hungry.

9. As Web services make it easier to share information within and between businesses, demand for improved knowledge management, data storage, and data retrieval systems will rise.

10. As Web services mature, they will generate exciting new business models, including the long-heralded "virtual organization."

Here is how one industry – financial services – will look as the future unfolds.

Financial services is a fast-paced industry. Market dynamics change frequently with new or revised regulations, customer capriciousness, and the volatility of capital markets. Financial institutions are constantly trying to outdo one another with the introduction of novel products and services. Many firms expand by entering new geographic and product segments through mergers and acquisitions. Web services is an emerging technology that has the potential to offer financial institutions new ways to serve their customers. Web services let firms creatively configure existing offerings into new bundles of products and services.

Let's consider specifically wholesale banks, which have a very complex IT environment with a diverse number of systems used to offer, deliver, and manage banking products and services. Mid-sized banks could have well over 100 applications and large banks could have in excess of 1,000 applications running at any one time. Figure 4.7 lays out for illustrative purposes an overview of the functions of a wholesale bank, its underlying processes and systems, and the typical interactions with third parties. It's complex!

Customers and partners connect to a bank's systems in various configurations. For instance, a customer's corporate treasury system must connect to a bank's cash management, risk management, global trade, and payment processing systems. In contrast, the customer's general ledger system may only need to deal with a bank's payment processing system. A bank typically must build new, hard-wired connections to big

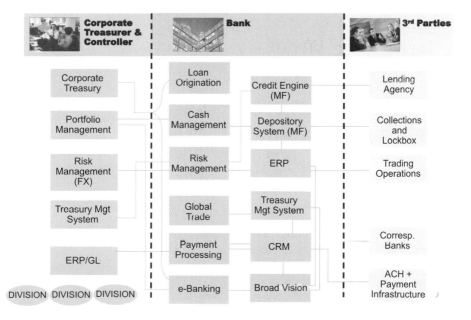

Figure 4.7   *Web Services Example: Wholesale Bank Applications*

customers and partners as they come on board. Smaller customers and partners are seldom catered to.

⛩ FUTURISTIC CASE STUDY
Bringing New Web Services to a Wholesale Bank[9]

*This bank wanted to identify those applications that would benefit most from a Web services implementation. It selected a treasury management system (TMS). Potentially, the TMS is accessed by dozens of disparate internal systems, such as cash management, risk management, and payment processing - as well as external sources, such as a partner correspondent bank. Given the current security limitations of Web services, this bank preferred to move forward with the **internal** deployment of treasury-related Web services before exposing this sensitive data to **external** customers and partners via the Web.*

The first step was to determine the information or functions that were most conducive to being delivered by Web services, including positioning monitoring, foreign exchange and interest rate data, and activity reporting. These services lent themselves to Web exposure because they involved common activities, typically synchronous calls, and frequent access by multiple sources. It developed the relevant Web services. The benefits to the internal IT environment were immediate and tangible. With the Web services interfaces in place, other internal systems could easily access the TMS functions. For example, the administrator of a cash management system was able to connect his system to the TMS without any knowledge of its underlying code.

In the future, new internal systems can also easily connect to the TMS without being hard coded or requiring customer interface capabilities. Since connections are made using Web services, modification can take place within the TMS or any connecting systems without affecting the Web service interface itself.

The second step would be to extend the services externally. Web services were seen to greatly reduce the complexity of the bank's integration with its customers and partners. As the Web services market matures, the bank will want to encapsulate robust features for external communications (such as security, reliability, and guaranteed delivery). The bank could then safely expose its Web systems externally. Corporate customers and partners will in the future be able to gain more up-to-date information and greater flexibility and control over their banking activities. The bank should be able to provide this higher level of service at less cost. In addition, it will no longer need to customize interfaces every time a new customer or partner comes on board.

As in banking, so in other industries. Building your Web service capabilities is a must. The question is not why, but how. Spending the time upfront to plan carefully, understand what your company really needs, and then do your homework in scoping out implementation requirements will increase the likelihood of success. Remember, it's not just the destination, it's the journey!

CFO CHECKLIST

SHARPEN YOUR FOCUS ON THE VALUE-CREATING CORE OF YOUR BUSINESS
Identify what's non-core – benchmark against leading practice; frame a separate business proposition for the packaging and future development of your support services.

DEVELOP A GLOBAL STRATEGY FOR SHARED SERVICES
What is the potential for taking your present shared services to the next level? Expand the scope beyond transaction processing. Revisit the barriers that have held change in check. Go global if you can.

FRAME A VISION FOR VIRTUAL FINANCE
Reevaluate the opportunities provided by the latest technologies and languages – such as XML – for moving your shared services to a *virtual* environment.

RESEARCH THE EXTERNAL MARKET FOR MANAGED SERVICES
Consider options for both insourcing and outsourcing. What solution fits best your corporate culture? Choose a managed services partner who best meets your longer-term requirements. Visualize a holistic solution – business processes, applications management, *as well as* IT infrastructure and support.

CONSIDER THE RELATIVE MERITS OF PUBLIC AND PRIVATE EXCHANGES
No one size fits all – tailor your choice to your own business model and culture. The jury is still out on exchanges; proceed with caution. Your procurement – or sourcing – will probably have the strongest business case for your first move into exchanges.

EXPAND THE ROLE OF YOUR INDUSTRY EXCHANGE
Explore the potential of new exchange services for supply chain management, collaborative engineering, and knowledge sharing. Consider the impact on the finance function and associated processes for payments, collections, cash, and banking.

PLAN FOR WEB SERVICES
Evaluate the Web services potential for reducing the cost and improving the effectiveness of your business processes and their interconnectivity inside and outside the organization. Determine your infrastructure's readiness for Web services; develop a blueprint for implementing discrete internal Web services first.

CHAPTER 5

Connecting Strategy with Operations

MANAGING GLOBAL COMPLEXITY
Wolfgang Reichenberger, CFO
Nestlé

Wolfgang Reichenberger communicates regularly with Nestlé's finance community across the world using the corporate intranet. To quote one of his recent communications: "While there remain vast differences between our company, as global as it may be, and the Nestlé communities around the world, we have to increase our efforts to explain why we set targets linked to shareholder value, why superior performance is essential, and why financial measures are the best (but admittedly not the only) tools for allocating scarce resources. We cannot take it for granted that everybody within our company – and even less so outside – understands that the consistent and socially responsible application of economic principles is the best way to improve general standards of living."

Nestlé's market capital is approximately $100 bn. Today, Nestlé has over $10 bn of intangible assets on its balance sheet alone. The Nestlé brand covers approximately 40% of the products it sells. It uses brand valuation techniques for external transactions and benchmarking. Nestlé has a very sophisticated method of planning and reporting by geography. It can aggregate information for each geographic zone, each market, and each sales office – quickly and reliably. Recently, it adopted more of a top-down approach to planning.

Wolfgang comments: "I see my role as the CFO more as an internal venture capitalist – financing the good ideas, evaluating the risks and opportunities. Our internal venture capital company – Life Ventures – allocates resources – and as chairman of that company, I work very closely with my colleagues in R&D – aiming for economic success and accountability, not pure research for the sake of research."

Nestlé has enjoyed double-digit shareholder value increases over the last 10 years or so and is driven predominantly by growth and comprehensive performance criteria, rather than purely by accounting measures. Although shareholder value is important to Nestlé, it does not sacrifice long-term growth purely to report short-term improvement in results. "We believe we have the confidence of our shareholders as they have seen the longer-term benefits come through."

One of the biggest issues Nestlé faces is how to report information by product globally and by customer as well. This horizontal approach contradicts the vertical geographically based approach. "Unlike some of our American competitors," notes Wolfgang, "we want to keep a local image of the product characteristics our customers value – what they can see, touch, feel, and taste. Consumers don't necessarily behave globally – they often relate best to local products. Other companies adopt a 'one size fits all' approach – there is nothing wrong with that, it's just that we prefer to address customer needs from a local market viewpoint. Nevertheless, we want the benefits of global scale and we want to market our product groups on a global basis. We want the best of both worlds."

Nestlé is a complex company, it has many different product categories with many geographic variations – for example, chocolate in France is very different from chocolate in neighbouring Switzerland. Ice cream taste and flavors also vary greatly, it has to try to manage these complexities. Nestlé is aligning its global supply chains and making efficiency improvements in its back-office operations. It is also reducing complexity in the way it manages its IT resources – the way it pays bills, does its accounting, and manages global logistics. Shared services opportunities are also high on the agenda.

"Project Globe is an initiative designed to help us act as a global company, rather than as a series of national companies. It will allow us to manage our

inherent complexity. Where appropriate, we behave as a horizontal global product/market organization – for example, in servicing customers such as Wal-Mart. Project Globe involves the worldwide rollout of SAP, our ERP implementation. Once the rollout is complete, we should be able to monitor profitability by customer and by product on a global basis. Globe should lead to greater global standardization, data cleansing, and to global effeciencies in purchasing and supply.

At headquarters, we have become much clearer and more precise in setting the targets that we want our businesses to achieve. These top-down targets are tougher than before – and a stretch. These stretch targets are set based on external benchmarks, which we believe are achievable, but only with high levels of performance. We, in Vevey, assist our businesses worldwide in achieving their stretch targets – by, for example, providing guidance on how to reduce overhead, how to distribute product more efficiently, how to achieve growth (for example, through trade promotion and spend improvements).

We also try to reduce duplication and excessive detail in the planning and budgeting processes. We used to have regular budget revisions during the year. Now, we've cut down on the amount of detail submitted to headquarters on in-country products; we try to avoid great armies of accountants consolidating detailed data. We would like to rely more on forecasts, possibly an 18-month rolling forecast. This would eliminate seasonal distortions in our projections and allow better comparisons in our annual reporting cycle."

Nestlé uses key performance indicators (KPIs) – non-financial as well as financial measures. These are particularly useful for balancing capital investment and capacity worldwide. It has created eight strategic business units (SBUs) to coordinate products on a global basis. The primary tasks of these SBUs are market planning and research; they do not participate in local financial target setting and measurement for the short term. The global SBUs take a longer strategic view and focus on longer term financial and non-financial KPIs – for example, return on invested capital in five years and market share and quality measures.

"In addition to revamping our planning we have actions to improve our performance: we recently launched our Project FitNes – an internally driven program designed to increase white-collar productivity, reduce overhead, and

improve administrative processing. We wish to maintain our reputation of being best-of-breed within our competitor peer group in achieving year-on-year earnings growth of 4%. Having said that, we have more to do to improve our working capital and capital investment productivity."

Nestlé is a vast organization employing more than 230,000 people. Keeping employees abreast of developments and informed about the progress of strategic initiatives is always going to be tough. Wolfgang places a high priority on measuring the progress of strategic initiatives at the corporate center in Vevey. For initiatives such as earnings growth, FitNes and Target 2004, targets are set globally, then split into different geographic zones. Wolfgang tracks the benefits against predetermined milestones. He works hard to avoid making this an accounting exercise – and to keep Nestlé's employees focused on achieving results.

As far as the performances of the finance function itself is concerned Wolfgang comments: "We must have one of the world's biggest finance functions. Our mantra in finance: driving superior performance and being more proactive. What, exactly, does this mean? Driving functional excellence, setting standards, and developing KPIs for risk management and decision support. Our priorities in finance? Playing our part in developing the global business approach, implementing, for example, the Globe template, and monitoring the business case for ERP benefits. These benefits include purchasing reductions, lower IT costs, shared services, lower supply chain costs, and increased efficiencies. We are making considerable progress in our quest for a world class finance function. We are honest enough to admit that we don't have all the answers; we are always searching for better tools and techniques."

Nestlé is not alone. CFOs the world over are preoccupied with maximizing shareholder value. Pure financial information cut by geographic segments is not enough. The challenge is to provide the CEO and corporate Board of Directors with information on strategic initiatives – linking plans for improving performance with what's actually happening. In short, connecting strategy with operational reality.

INTRODUCING STRATEGIC ENTERPRISE MANAGEMENT (SEM)

The components of SEM are not new: performance management, business planning and risk, consolidation, and reporting. What's new is the drive to coordinate all these business components with the goal of fully integrating strategic and operational decision-making. And then, integrating these processes with the systems and information flows. Few companies effectively link strategic objectives to resource allocation and performance management. As a result, operational decisions consistently fall short in delivering on strategic objectives. Yet this close linkage between strategy and operations is precisely what is needed to achieve superior investment return.

What's the real problem? Quite simply, most companies have failed to recognize the biggest challenge they face: ensuring that people *throughout their organization* make shareholder value central to their decision-making. The right information systems architecture is critical in making this happen.

As a divisional manager at one multinational company observed: *"The CFO is really hooked on this shareholder value thing. Out here in operations, where it counts, it means nothing. It simply hasn't been translated into terms that we relate to. We haven't got a clue how to put it into practice."*[1] Setting targets alone – even when soundly based on shareholder value principles – won't deliver the results desired. Translating those principles into operational imperatives and obtaining buy-in are critical.

To succeed, value-based management must add transparency to the decision-making process: it must let employees at all levels see the likely impact of their decisions on the value of the business – not just major strategic decisions like mergers and acquisitions, but operational decisions, too. What will be the impact on shareholder value, for example, of reducing manufacturing lead time? Of reconfiguring the supply chain? Of rationalizing the product range? By expressing shareholder value in terms that everyone can understand, you can forge direct links between shareholder value, corporate strategy, and operations.

Your objective must be to combine historic and predictive views with financial *and* nonfinancial business drivers. You must motivate employees at all levels to pursue the overriding objective of improving shareholder value. To operationalize value-based management, take four essential steps:

1. Understand what drives value

2. Find where value is created or destroyed

3. Establish value as the criteria for decision-making

4. Embed value management in your culture

SEM provides a framework which allows companies to value their strategies. One proven approach: start with the key performance indicators (KPIs) on your balanced scorecard and cascade them throughout the enterprise. Use these KPIs as targets for business planning and as a basis for both strategic and operational budgets. Simulate different scenarios for decision-making purposes by linking KPIs together and assessing their impact on shareholder value. Take into account where things can go wrong – the key risk areas.

Most CFOs have in place accounting consolidation and routine reporting processes. They have established budgeting disciplines which, although cumbersome, provide a measure of control. They have strategic plans, which are updated from time to time, but not always consistently.

There are also mechanisms in place for identifying and monitoring risk. However, as with Nestlé, rapid change is undermining the benefits of these basic tools. Most financials are still constructed based on a stable, predictable geographic model. However, organizations are beginning to adopt a product/market focus, which is far more dynamic. CIOs have established IT strategies for standardizing transaction processes using an ERP system. But the CFO has two main areas of dissatisfaction:

1. The strategic planning and operational control processes are disconnected. Consequently, the budgets take too long to prepare and are too detailed – they reflect an outdated business model. Furthermore, if something major goes wrong, the finance function is expected to detect it first, but can't. The impact of a major quality problem, such as a product recall, the collapse of a developing economy and its currency, or a manufacturing failure – are all examples of life-threatening risks to the business, which are not easily monitored.

2. Although the ERP-based IT strategy has achieved many benefits through the integration of transaction processing, a *best-of-breed* (non-integrated) approach to financial management applications has been adopted for strategic planning, budgeting, forecasting, accounts

consolidation, and performance tracking. The result? A hodgepodge of applications which don't link together.

The strategic processes involved in SEM are integrated with those for operational execution in Figure 5.1. The strategic and operational cycles together constitute the performance management framework. They are brought together through the translation of the vision into KPI targets.

Where should the CFO begin when implementing SEM? With the business case. Very few CFOs develop a business case for the major overhaul of their traditional decision support infrastructure. In fact, most CFOs interviewed for this book do not know the cost of their management information. Have you considered the full cost of the wasted time of your directors (and your managers and staff) spent in trying to secure the right information for making decisions? Add to this huge time cost of the planning and reporting processes carried out by the finance function and others. Add to this the relevant proportion of your IT and systems infrastructure.

The CFO should have little difficulty in proposing an alternative SEM-based approach with a strong, *hard* case based on improved management productivity and lower overall cost. The *softer* benefits – such as quicker time-to-market, targeted marketing investment, improved supply chain – may be more subjective, but based on shareholder value creation, should be similarly overwhelming.

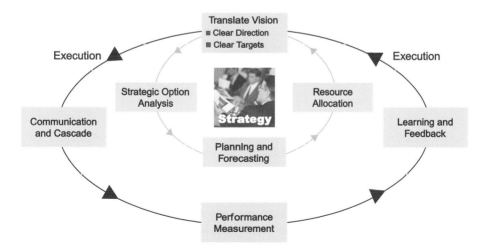

Figure 5.1   *Strategy Meets Operations*

TRACKING CORPORATE PERFORMANCE

Many CFOs ask where they should start implementing SEM. Performance management – the development of scorecards with appropriate KPIs for each layer in the organization – is a good place to start. It's where you can achieve visibility and quick wins.

Performance management should bring about sustainable change. Focus on what needs to be done – not what has happened. Performance management should also direct resources where they're needed most – to the targets of each business unit and on material issues/priorities. Getting the right information at the right time with flexible access is no easy task.

Best practice performance management involves the selection and implementation of scalable tools and processes – tools that are flexible enough to accommodate a wide range of metrics and visualizations.

In summary, performance management should help your company:

- Create a line of sight between strategy and operational activities by linking strategic objectives with activities and performance

- Create transparency between short-term decision-making and how it affects long-term value creation

- Ensure it has the capability to deliver against performance targets

- Reduce nonvalue-added effort by focusing on "what we should be doing" rather than on "why something happened" – from lagging to leading indicators

- Move to a "living conversation" throughout the company supported by real-time, event-driven information

- Share information across functions to foster broader accountability for results

One way to achieve these goals is to adopt the ***enterprise dashboard***. An effective performance dashboard uses fewer, more relevant metrics to focus time and effort on optimizing performance. These alert-driven metrics highlight opportunities, risks, and actions to be taken as early as possible. An illustration of a performance dashboard for a global petrochemical company is shown in Figure 5.2.

This figure illustrates a dashboard for an oil field with *drill-downs* into scorecards for operations and "people" indicators. Different levels of the organization need to focus on different information. In an oil company, the corporate level requires financial information – total shareholder return, and information on reserves replacement, asset acquisitions and disposals. At an investment portfolio level, information is required on over/underperforming assets, benchmarks, and capital allocation. At an operational unit level, information is required on major projects, for example wells coming on line and maintenance programs. In addition, information on health, safety, and environment is important at all levels. The key is to have touch points in the information, which provide a common language for target setting and review.

Dashboard developments need to be business-benefits driven. Quotes from one company after a successful performance dashboard implementation:

"We can highlight the major issues and respond to problems before they become severe."

"Information that is business-critical can reach anyone, real-time."

"We can communicate without traditional organizational boundaries, accessing the information we want, when we want it."

Increasingly, dashboards containing KPIs are being developed by companies anxious to improve their performance management process. Best-practice experience shows most effective dashboards have the following characteristics:

- *Visualization*: information is presented in an insightful way, creating transparency across the enterprise around key priorities, goals, and performance.

- *Drill-down capability*: visualizations can be structured so that the user has access to key issues at every level.

- *Tracking and document management*: performance of key initiatives and projects can be managed through comprehensive document management facilities.

- *Alerts*: protocols for metrics can be set up so that selected personnel can be alerted to movements outside defined boundaries. As the dashboard is integrated over the Internet – and the corporate intranet –

Performance Dashboard

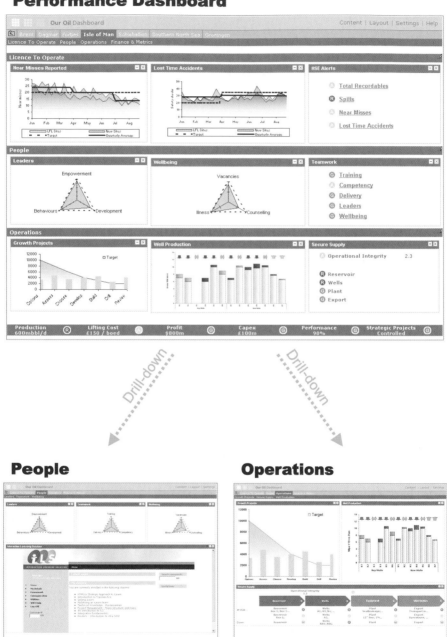

Figure 5.2 *Performance Dashboard for a Global Petrochemical Company*

with e-mail, discussion forums, and document management systems, alerts can trigger on-screen traffic light indicators.

- *Customizable*: the dashboard can be customized to suit the needs of individual users who may select their content from a standard set of predefined core metrics, supplemented by their own locally based indicators.

- *External search and report capabilities*: data capture and representation are not confined to information gathered from internal systems. Data feeds can be established via external Web pages.

- *Open technology*: the data rendered as visualizations in the dashboard can be sourced from all open data systems.

The case study which follows sets out the challenges faced by a multinational oil company in introducing dashboard applications. It includes three real-life examples of the benefits achieved in practice.

CASE STUDY
Implementing a New Approach to Performance Management

This company wanted a step-change in performance. There was a big gap between the corporate management team and the operational managers in business units. What was needed was improved line-of-sight between the corporate directors and the business unit managers. The corporate strategy unit was focused on theoretical concepts and on supporting the Board. The annual budgeting process was carried out by business units and did not reflect corporate strategy. Different information was used to manage the performance of the company at different levels.

A dashboard approach was chosen to kick-start a fresh angle on performance management. The challenges facing the company were:

- *It was too focused on historic financials for tracking and managing performance.*

- *There was a lack of transparency between strategy (value drivers) and management information for local decision-making.*

- *It was internally focused and external investor relations were poor.*

- *The performance management process and measures were inconsistent.*

- *Performance dialogues were poor.*

- *Planning and reporting processes were unnecessarily bureaucratic.*

*The answer was simplification. The dashboard project was split into two phases. Phase 1 was based on pilot exercises; it took advantage of the company's recent investment in portal technology, but was essentially **technology-lite**. This phase was not fully integrated with the rest of the ERP infrastructure and was semi-automated. Phase 2 was a full rollout based on an integrated technology architecture. The company adopted a coordinated, cross-business unit approach with program management. The building blocks of Phase 1 were as follows:*

- *Performance Management: the objective was to develop line-of-sight through the performance measures in the organization. These measures would be prioritized around their contribution to value creation. The emphasis was to be on changing behavior to improve performance. A big issue was the trade-off between long-term investment and short-term profitability.*

- *Dashboards: the company had experimented with various visualization tools, most recently portals. The objective was to make the most of existing systems, providing a degree of automation and integrating data sources without the need for expensive systems integration. The emphasis was on creating flexibility by providing users early in the development with attractive visually presented data.*

Three examples taken from the project pilots demonstrate what can be achieved:

Example 1: Transparency – linking strategy to operations

- *Strategic issue: one of the strategic priorities at the oil field site was to grow production levels. This was achieved by bringing the highest-potential new wells on stream as soon as possible.*

- *Approach: the dashboard focused attention on highest-potential wells. The visualization highlighted problem projects and allowed a reallocation of resources before projects got out of control.*

- *Benefit: for every extra day of production from a key well, the site gained significant revenue.*

Example 2: Monitoring HR capacity against performance management targets

- *Strategic issue: To deliver against corporate's performance goals, it was essential to develop the "right" capabilities.*

- *Outcome: the dashboard focused attention on composite measures, giving a user-friendly snapshot of "well-being," teamwork, and leadership. The drill-downs highlighted training and resource gaps. A link was provided to Web-based training, related to key skills.*

- *Benefit: management gained an up-to-date understanding of people issues.*

Example 3: Leading indicators – moving focus from "why something happened" to "what should we be doing"

- *Strategic issue: optimizing production levels was critical to achieving financial targets. Preventing key wells from "falling over" was essential to achieving overall production targets.*

- *Outcome: the dashboard focused on identifying risks of failure. This promoted a forward-looking perspective.*

- *Benefit: maintenance became preventative, rather than reactive. More accurate forecasting led to faster turnaround for unplanned shutdowns. "Workover times were significantly reduced as a result."*

The Phase 1 solution was subsequently extended to the rest of the organization. Technology change was the key driver in Phase 2, with the goal being a more robust, scalable platform. Overall, the company achieved its goal of a significant improvement in performance. The dashboard program was credited with achieving multi-million dollar savings. Other benefits:

- *Clear definitions and operational focus on value drivers and performance metrics*

- *Redefined roles and responsibilities across the organization, integrating strategic and operational activities*

- *Integrated dashboard solutions providing transparent focus on BU (business unit) operating performance*

- *Improved performance conversations focused on the action for the future – not reconciliation of the past*

As this case study illustrates, a successful dashboard implementation has four characteristics:

1. *Buy-in at the operations level*: the practical benefits are most easily seen where operational decisions are made.
2. *The "journey"*: strong, open communication and shared debates are critical in finding the right solutions.
3. *Speed*: pilot projects deliver benefits within a few months.
4. *Strong business case*: low cost – the project makes the most of existing data systems. The dollar benefits are significant.

Research[2] carried out across a variety of companies on their approach to performance management has revealed a number of commonly experienced pitfalls and their impact (see Table 5.1).

INTEGRATED RISK MANAGEMENT

As we said earlier, good performance management connects strategies with operations. But CFOs need a process which alerts them to key business risks. SEM – a fully integrated approach to performance management – addresses these risks. However, business risk management involves little science, but a great deal of intuition. Formal techniques are becoming established, but this new discipline remains complex. No single

Table 5.1

Pitfall	Impact
1. Business issues	
Project not predicated on agreed business issues	Project becomes about how to push through to completion and resources are not focused on delivering business benefits
Large scale IT-led project signed off, without clear agreement on what the business benefits are	Scope creep, as project later seeks to address customer demands; hoped-for benefits not realized
2. Content	
Focus on existing data versus 'right' data	Project is very complex, all data is cleansed indiscriminately, no change in decision-making process
Try to include everything – managing vast volumes of data	No transparency – can't see 'the forest for the trees' Key issues don't reach the right people at the right time
Everyone's "piece of the pie" is so special to them that design is inconsistent – no balance	No standardization; internal benchmarking of key figures is impossible
One size fits all – no recognition of different local issues (e.g. emerging/growth BU versus mature BU)	Reporting looks at business from central perspective, not local perspective, therefore no common language established to discuss targets and trade-offs
3. Business process	
Apply a controlling perspective (reconciliation and consolidation) to a decision support area	Lack of focus in reported information – no change in conversations between portfolio level and operating unit level
Define a measurement-and-reporting portal that does not fit with performance contract or achievement of strategic objectives	Decision-making dashboard is not used to manage the business, therefore offers limited business benefit
4. Behaviors	
Change the technology without understanding the need to change processes and behaviors	IT works, but does not change review or decision-making process
Reporting focuses on reporting the past in great detail	Conversation does not change to "where we need to go" – does not consider short-term/long-term trade-offs
IT-led project	Lack of emotional commitment to end results from operations people, therefore limited business benefits

approach suits everyone. However, the risk management process[3] that many companies use unfolds in five interrelated phases:

1. *Strategic targeting*: this first step involves the definition of strategies and enterprise targets. The KPIs and strategic success factors are linked to the major risks involved. How much risk is reasonable for your company? What infrastructure and resources must be in place to prevent unreasonable losses?

2. *Risk identification*: do you fully understand all risks? Are they being managed appropriately? Most companies carefully analyze certain areas, such as credit risk. But other areas – often those related to more subjective factors, such as loss of reputation – are not considered in depth. It is important to identify potential risks at the business unit level and store data in an enterprise-wide risk catalogue. Simulate *worst-case* and *what-if* scenarios.

3. *Risk quantification and evaluation*: focus on risks relevant to each business unit and quantify the effect on targets and measures. Evaluate the influence of risk on target values – shareholder value impact, contribution margin accounting. Sophisticated techniques for risk quantification and evaluating *value at risk,* as well as dynamic financial analysis for simulating balance sheet impacts, may be helpful in the right circumstances – but they are only as good as the quality of data and assumptions behind them.

4. *Risk implementation*: this phase involves everything from selecting, training, and developing staff to using new or existing financial instruments. It also involves the documentation of policies, procedures and practices; and the introduction of systems and reporting; hedging and risk financing.

5. *Risk control and monitoring*: internal and external changes come thick and fast. This phase focuses on providing information relevant for decision-making – a kind of early warning system. The questions asked by CFOs in this phase include: how is the company's overall risk position changing? When and how should we alter our strategy?

The better you are at risk management, the greater your ability to make risk an opportunity, rather than a threat. A risk management framework should be used both as a communication tool and a risk mitigation tool. Create an awareness of critical risks in your organization. Clearly articulate your risk management policies, what risks you are prepared to take, and your plans for risk mitigation.

To create a culture that empowers everyone to manage business risk you need integrated processes and systems. What's the impact of technology? Risk assessment necessitates a hybrid architecture – a mixture of textual communication with quantitative indicators. This requires both knowledge warehouses – the textual input – and data warehouses. The balanced scorecard also provides a useful vehicle for turning strategic action programs into specific qualitative/quantitative measures. An integrated SEM-style process architecture adapted to include risk is presented in Figure 5.3.

Recently, there has been a growing demand by CFOs for integrated strategic planning and risk management. In Germany, for example, the Board is obliged by regulation to establish a risk-management framework. The law was made more specific and formal by the German

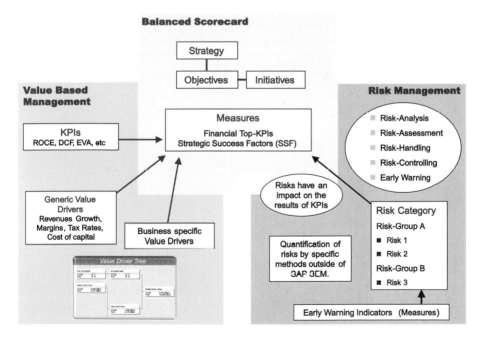

Figure 5.3 *The Balanced Scorecard as Framework for VBM and Risk Management*

standard accounting principles for the preparation of risk reports adopted in 2001. Risk is defined as "the negative impact that events or actions may have on the enterprise." The focus is on risks that have a direct influence on enterprise targets. Companies must report their risks to ensure strong credit ratings.

CASE STUDY
Using a Scorecard to Manage Risk

A German insurance company introduced a balanced scorecard two years ago. Its implementation was judged very favorably. However, one area where the scorecard project did not score well was the evaluation of risks. Although risks and opportunities were discussed in great detail in the strategy workshop, this information did not figure in the actual scorecard.

Parallel with the implementation of the balanced scorecard by the finance department, the internal auditing department introduced a new risk management system in response to new national legislation for reporting risks. Checklists were developed and filled out by the respective risk areas. Risk indicators were added to the checklists. The information was then compiled into a risk report by the auditors to comply with the new German legislation for risk reporting.

A joint project review revealed a problem: very similar information had been processed in the two separate projects. The risk management system and the balanced scorecard had used the same indicators in certain cases. Many of the risks described in the risk management system were also found in the balanced scorecard. However, these two headquarter departments were disconnected on this issue. One was focused on low-level financial performance metrics, the other on risk. There was no integrated view.

Top management wanted one view of performance and risk. It wanted to quantify the impact of individual risk on financial and non-financial performance measures (e.g. impact on sales channels or customer segments). Early warning indicators were to be developed – for example, monitoring the risk of achieving forecast versus actual, versus plan.

The company decided to launch a joint pilot project merging both risk processes. Clarity had to be reached as to how different types of information (checklists on the one hand; objectives, measurement factors, and initiatives on the other) could be brought under one hat. The decision was made to merge the two projects as a pilot in the life insurance business unit. The objective-oriented risk view was added to the risk management system.

All risks were assigned to corresponding objectives. Besides estimating absolute loss potential, they also estimated the factors influencing scorecard objectives. With this approach, the scope of the risk areas analyzed was increased considerably. Specific problem areas could be scrutinized more thoroughly thanks to a differentiated analysis of objectives. By merging the risk assessment process and the balanced scorecard, these two headquarter departments were able to harmonize their activities.

Once companies have implemented the core of their performance management system – the balanced scorecard – and once they *really* use KPIs as the primary source of information to manage the business – they are ready to reconsider the role of planning and budgeting.

BLOW UP THE BUDGET!

"The budget is the bane of corporate America. It should never have existed. Making a budget is an exercise in minimization, i.e. showing how little you can do." Jack Welch, the former CEO of General Electric, isn't the only one who has a problem with budgeting. Bob Lutz, a former vice-chairman of Chrysler, called the budget a "tool of repression." To Jan Wallander, a budget revolutionary and the former CEO of Svenska Handelsbanken, it is an "unnecessary evil."

Here are the results from a survey[4] of CFOs:

- Only 12% believed that budgets added a lot of value to their organization.

- Some 79% said abandoning budgeting was a top-five priority (44% said top three).

- And 65% saw themselves responsible for leading the move towards this abandonment.

In another survey, just 10% of CFOs thought their budgeting process was completely efficient, while 90% said it was cumbersome. But many corporations haven't even taken the first step toward escaping the budget's constraints – acknowledging its limitations.

Why are budgets almost universally condemned?

Budgets can slow the pace of change Responding quickly to changing environments is difficult if you restrict yourself to fixed annual strategies and budgeting cycles – and if you rely on rules, procedures, and budgetary controls that constrain your freedom to act locally.

Budgets can keep you from finding and keeping talented people Hierarchical structures that are governed by rigid plans and inflexible financial budgets offer your ambitious managers limited opportunities for challenge, risk, and reward. Rigid plans and budgets do not encourage entrepreneurial leadership and risk taking.

Budgets may inhibit innovation Bloated bureaucracies and rigid budgetary controls often obstruct insight and innovation. They stifle creativity by failing to provide the management with a climate in which creative people thrive. When fixed budgets are the only target against which their performance is measured, managers are unprepared to aim high. Easy-to-achieve targets and overly cautious strategies are the result. Sooner or later, your company will begin to underachieve.

Budgets do not challenge the cost base One of your best opportunities for cost reduction is to adopt a flat management structure, mainly a networking model, in which your business processes interact at high speed, enabling you to respond quickly to customer requests. But in the traditional budgeting model, resources and costs are hard-wired into the fabric of your business structure. Only by eradicating the old-fashioned budgeting mentality can you encourage your managers to challenge fixed costs and seek continuous cost reductions.

Budgets can get in the way of customer relationships When your salespeople are focused solely on achieving fixed targets for revenue, product volume, or gross margin, they have little incentive to care about whether you are meeting customers' needs or whether your customers are satisfied and profitable.

Budgets can be a barrier to achieving sustainable, competitive corporate results   One of the aims of the budgeting process is to produce earnings forecasts and set shareholders' expectations. Blind allegiance to financial targets and the budgets underlying them can cause long-term problems. Managers who set aggressive targets may be required to take drastic actions to meet shareholders' high expectations – such as downsizing, restructuring, and cutting essential long-term investments in R&D.

How do CFOs overcome the barriers to change that budgeting creates? Some simply cut down the amount of detail involved and target business measures which develop *top-down*. The *bottom-up* detail is deemed unnecessary. Others focus on compressing the amount of time taken to develop budgets – from many months to just a few weeks. Best-practice companies have abandoned budgets altogether. Instead, they target their business economics on shareholder value-driven scorecards – KPIs. To track performance, they rely on rolling forecasts. For these companies, annual budgeting has become a thing of the past.

Best practices in budgeting have been combined to create the beyond budgeting model. This model has been designed by the CAM-I organization to overcome traditional barriers and create a flexible, adaptable organization that gives your local managers the self-confidence and freedom to think differently. It lets them make decisions rapidly and collaborate on innovative projects in multifunctional teams, both within your company and beyond its borders.

Twelve principles provide a robust framework for implementing the beyond budgeting model. Principles 1 through 6 are concerned with the performance management climate at your company. They involve both organization design and the delegation of power and responsibility to people who are close to your customers.

Performance Management Climate

1. *Self-governance*: replace rules and procedures with clear values and boundaries to provide frontline managers with the freedom they need to make fast, effective decisions.

2. *Performance responsibility*: recruit and develop the right people with the mindset to serve customers and take responsibility for achieving results.

3. *Empowerment*: delegate authority and responsibility to your managers at the front line. Keep decision-making power close to your customers.

4. *Structure*: base your new organization on a network of inter-dependent units with fast communication up, down, and across the business. Create as many small, entrepreneurial units as possible.

5. *Coordination*: design processes that work together naturally to deliver customer value. Use process- and project-based relationships to respond to customer demands in real-time. When you make each unit responsible for its own results, market-like forces driven by your network of supplier–customer agreements replace centralized controls.

6. *Leadership*: challenge and stretch your managers to make significant performance improvements and to break free from incremental thinking. Coach and support your managers, rather than command-ing and controlling them.

Principles 7 through 12 focus on performance management. A key feature of the model is that goals, measures, and rewards are decoupled – that is, they are not tied together in a performance contract.

Performance Management Processes

7. *Goal setting*: adopt relative, rather than absolute, targets and dis-connect them from measures and rewards. This will free your local managers to set their sights on ambitious goals. Base your relative targets on a range of KPIs and external benchmarks to encourage your managers to pursue strategic as well as financial goals.

8. *Strategy planning*: free your managers to think differently and to produce new ways of delivering customer value – and to create new businesses altogether. Build your new initiatives from strategic goals rather than from departmental concerns.

9. *Early warning systems*: give your managers early warning of changes that affect their businesses, particularly if the changes spell trouble. Use rolling forecasts to keep an eye on the future. Anticipatory systems can help you manage short-term capacity. If you integrate customer-order information with your supply chain, you need not fix capacity far in advance, which enables you to turn some of your fixed costs into variable ones.

10. *Resource utilization*: delegate investment and resource decisions to people who are close to the action. Uncouple such decisions from the annual budgeting cycle to ensure that they are made only when needed – and to give your managers the freedom to take appropriate action at the right times. Maintain continuous downward pressure on costs through efficient resource consumption. Where appropriate, use an internal market approach in which internal supplier units sell their services to customer units within your company.

11. *Measurement and control*: put in place multifaceted controls that provide actual results, leading indicators, and rolling forecasts – and support them with fast, open information systems. Disseminate measures to all management levels simultaneously.

12. *Motivation and rewards*: base performance evaluations on relative measures to drive performance improvement. Emphasize performance by teams, groups, or companies, rather than individuals. This approach encourages sharing and ensures that your whole enterprise pulls in the same direction.

During the early stages of blowing up the budget, system misfires can occur because employees haven't adjusted to the new approach. Provide your employees with a coaching framework (Intranet) that supports their approach to the new methods. It is especially important to prepare everyone well ahead of time for upcoming changes in financial and performance management. People ask what's cutting edge about blowing up the budgets, and the reply usually relates to getting KPIs right or doing rolling forecasts. But what's really cutting edge is getting an organization to stop reporting detailed yet rearward-looking budget metrics. It requires strong leadership. Swedish bank Svenska Handelsbanken did it 30 years ago and it's never looked back.

CASE STUDY
Throwing Off the Budget

When Jan Wallander was appointed CEO of Handelsbanken in 1970, the bank was underperforming. Rather than introduce a series of small measures and wait for results, he decided on a radical solution. Customer dissatisfaction was the most common reason for switching banks, so Wallander decided to transform his institution into one where the customer relationship prevailed, and non-customer service costs were minimized.

One of his first acts was getting rid of the costly budget, based on this reasoning: either the budget will prove approximately right and it will be trite, or it will be disastrously wrong and therefore dangerous.

Wallander decentralized Handelsbanken and empowered its employees, 90% of whom have customer contact, to focus on pleasing their customers instead of their bosses. Headquarters set targets for the branches using key trends and internal/external benchmarking, and a handful of regional supervisors decided when and where local offices would be opened or closed. All other responsibility for managing the business was turned over to the branches.

The branches aim to provide products that are best for their own customers – even if they are not the most immediately profitable. The bank has a central product development office, but each branch is free to accept or reject any of its offerings. This reflects Handelsbanken's stated belief that the branches are not the bank's distribution system – they are the bank. After the bank exceeds its target for return on equity, one-third of the remaining funds are allocated to the employee pension plan each year, encouraging employee retention.

While there are no budget criteria to meet per se, Handelsbanken does recognize outstanding achievement. Practices developed at high-performing branches, which are identified by internal benchmarking, are quickly communicated throughout the organization, and outstanding individual efforts are rewarded.

How has Handelsbanken fared after 30 years of these "radical" practices? It has grown to 8,000 employees and 530 branches, which earn 80% of the bank's profit. And although there are branches throughout Sweden and other Nordic countries (with expansion to the UK in the offing), the company still has only 10 regional managers.

These practices give Handelsbanken one of the lowest cost-to-income ratios of the 30 largest universal banks in Europe. This ratio is 39%, compared to most US and European banks, which have ratios in the 55–65% range. For 28 years in a row they have achieved a higher return than the average for other Nordic banks, while also maintaining the highest levels of customer satisfaction. Handelsbanken's key metrics are the same as they were 30 years ago:

- *Return on equity*
- *Customer-led profitability (not product-led profitability)*
- *Cost-to-income ratio*

Historical analysis is low on the agenda. Customer satisfaction remains an important KPI, and is independently verified through the Stockholm School of Economics.

Since the day the bank prepared its last budget, it has sent a clear message to its employees: the past is the past. While we can learn from it and it sometimes reflects the future, it can never improve anything.

OPERATIONAL PLANNING AND SIMULATION

Tools and techniques are now available to the CFO for business planning and simulation. These enable you to carry out comprehensive simulations and scenario analyses without investing excessive time and effort. By relating one forward-looking KPI to another it is possible, for example, to model and simulate complex, non-linear relationships between markets, competitors, and your own enterprise.

These cause-and-effect relationships between KPIs can be modeled together to assess value impact. For example, evaluating the impact of advertising on future sales growth. Or evaluating the impact of today's capital investment on future supply chain cost reduction. Or evaluating current R&D expenditure levels on future cash flows emanating from new products. Figure 5.4 provides an overview of how cause-and-effect relationship models can be developed between different functional objectives and their corresponding measures.

Cause-and-effect modeling can fill a gap between assessment of the future value of strategic initiatives and lower-level operating plans. These models are best focused on those parts of the organization where there are major trade-offs between longer-term capital investment and shorter-term operating profits. These are the decision points in the organization where significant shareholder value can be either created or destroyed. Later in this book, in Chapter 8 on intangibles, we refer to these decision points as *value centers*.

Company and business unit plans can be converted into strategic and operational models for multi-level planning purposes. The functionality of today's planning systems enables finance staff to model business activities for each planning unit – ranging from sales volume planning through material requirements, to cost, capacity, and headcount plan-

Perspective	Cause-Effect Relationship	Objectives	Measures	Targets	Initiatives
Financial 	Profitability Sales Growth	Profitable Business Growth	Operating Profit Sales Growth	20% Growth 12% Growth	
Customers 	Product Quality Shopping Experience	Quality Products from a Competent Partner	Complaint Rate Customer Loyalty ■ Number of Active Customers ■ Average Number of Products	50% Reduction Every Year 60% 2.4 units	Quality Mgt Program Customer Loyalty Program
Internal Processes 	First-Class Production Delivery Management	Improving Production Quality	% of Goods from "A" Plants Stock Items Versus Plan	70% in the Third Year 85%	Production Development Plan
Learning & Growth 	Planning/ Building Skills	Training and Education of Employees	Availability of Strategically Desired Abilities in %	Year 1 50% Year 3 75% Year 5 90%	Strategic Training Plan

Figure 5.4   *Simulating Cause-and-Effect Relationships*

ning. Integrated tools are now available to link these more detailed plans to overall profit and loss, balance sheet, and cash-flow forecasts.

Organizations wanting to move to a 24-month rolling forecast must begin by building sales forecasts that focus on strategic goals and supply requirements. The aim is to produce a workable game plan – this isn't a logistics exercise to determine earnings – but a definition of what the corporation is going to be doing for the next 24 months. Specifically, CFOs need to do four things:

1. Develop rolling business forecasts that are continuously informed by sales forecasts and key events.

2. Install continuous, forward-looking exception reporting that provides recommendations to management based on achievable goals and action plans.

3. Stop building sales forecasts primarily on the basis of near-term supply requirements.

4. Separate target-setting processes from operational forecasts.

Creating rolling forecasts is not about managing numbers or hitting an endpoint like a budget target. It's about promoting collaboration among business units and facilitating business-issue management. Integration is the key to success in moving toward a "beyond budget" environment based on rolling forecasts, scorecards, and KPIs supported with cause-and-effect relationship models. This means integration between planning and forecasting systems, performance reporting, and most importantly, business financial accounts. Reconciling the *management view* with the *financial view* is a major headache for many finance departments of large, diverse, multinationals.

BUSINESS CONSOLIDATION AND INTEGRATION

Companies like Siemens AG also have to unify external and internal reporting. They require a central corporate data pool, with worldwide online access for all companies in the group to enable them to publish monthly financial statements and provide reports for US GAAP. By using SAP Consolidation software, their publishing process is faster and more accurate than ever before.

Any company that wants access to worldwide capital markets must harmonize its financial reporting with international standards. Legacy systems are often inadequate for this purpose, especially since increasing business complexity and constant changes in corporate structure – for example acquisitions – make data structures incredibly complex. Large corporations like Siemens, which has approximately 1,200 companies in its worldwide organization, store their data in a corporate data pool and have approximately 3,200 users working on their consolidation system.

All processing steps – from validation and standardization of entries to currency translation – run in parallel and support several hundred users simultaneously. Reconciliations can be made faster by using the company intranet to communicate and process inter-company differences. Traditional inter-company matching processes are compared in Figure 5.5 with those that can be performed electronically.

This simultaneous support is a major prerequisite for a fast close (fast close is covered in more detail in Chapter 9 on integration). Security is ensured through a controlled organization facility, so that everyone involved in the process can access information and use it for their

Traditional Match   **E-Match**

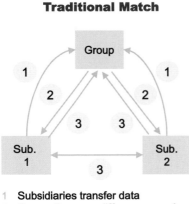

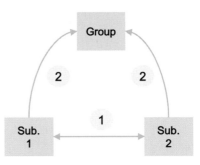

1 Subsidiaries transfer data
2 Group discovers differences and contacts subsidiary 1 and 2
3 Subsidiaries check the differences again and contact the partner
4 Subsidiaries mail the correct numbers

1 Subsidiary 1 discovers differences and contacts subsidiary 2
2 Subsidiaries release the correct data

Figure 5.5   *Faster Reconciliation for Consolidated Results*

various reporting purposes, such as compiling management information by customer segment.

Multinational corporations often choose a centralized data storage system because companies in the group are already using an intranet, making it relatively easy to implement a uniform solution for the group as a whole. Since data is no longer entered and processed manually, error rates drop steeply. Staff engaged in the consolidation process are relieved of many routine tasks and can concentrate on evaluating data. Problems are pinpointed earlier, and the data for both internal and external reporting is now more consistent and supports more frequent, more accurate forecasts. Companies like Siemens are moving towards a Web-oriented, user-friendly interface for accessing key corporate data.

Many companies strive for a common consolidation basis for both accounting and planning. This avoids duplication and has the benefit of one data source for both the legally required company consolidations (for example, by US GAAP, IAS, and local GAAPs) – as well as for management consolidations based on user-defined organizational units.

CASE STUDY
Integrating Global Consolidation, Planning and Reporting

The Coca-Cola Company is the world's largest beverage company, marketing four of the world's top five soft-drink brands to consumers in nearly 200 countries worldwide, who drink more than 1 billion servings of its products each day. Running this global business is not only a daunting operational task, it also involves a mountain of financial information that must be collected, consolidated, and understood to drive financial reporting, planning, and decision-making. The company wanted a single environment for making financial data readily accessible to executive management worldwide.

In the past, Coca-Cola used a legacy system for its consolidation function. The system was not user-friendly, it generated high costs, and it was difficult to maintain. It was also impossible to see consolidated results quickly while the consolidation process was taking place. There was no standard planning tool at the company. Financial planners relied on individual Excel spreadsheets that required manual re-entry from general ledger data. The information was difficult to consolidate and keep up to date. The company depended on paper reports and lacked interactive reporting capabilities.

Coca-Cola chose the SAP SEM consolidation and planning solutions to tightly integrate with its core ERP system, implemented across the company for more than 6,500 end-users in over 20 countries. It also chose SEM for its ease-of-use, Web-enabled access, and drill-down reporting. This enabled executives to gain better access to global financial information for continuous planning and decision support. The implementation was launched in January 2000 and went live in February 2001. The company followed an accelerated method-ology, moving quickly through the five stages of project preparation, blueprint, realization, final preparation, go-live, and support.

Today, financial information is submitted for processing via Coca-Cola's intranet. Consolidation processing is performed at both the legal entity and business unit (profit-center group) level. This information is used to generate consolidated financial statements and internal management reports. The information is also used to create external reports for statutory requirements and as the foundation for further drill-down business analysis.

Financial actuals are extracted automatically on a daily basis. These actual results are then used to assist in monthly forecasting. This enables the company to generate financial reports for financial planners as well as division and regional financial managers at the profit-center level. The information is also used to generate monthly forecasts on sales, cost of sales, operating expenses, and profitability. The forecast data is then summarized and consolidated. This lets the company generate consolidated forecast results and compare con-solidated actuals to forecasts.

Data warehousing enables Coca-Cola's management to further slice-and-dice and analyze this financial information to support decision-making. The solutions are deeply intertwined. The consolidation and planning solutions feed one another data and share the same data, at differing levels of detail. The business intelligence system works with both to refine information into more value-added form for query, reporting, and analysis.

According to Coca-Cola "Management reporting is the endgame here. 'The SEM solution is the foundation for management reporting and our quarterly and annual reports. This is very, very important to Coca-Cola. It ensures that our managers have access to consolidated results and planning information based on the same, accurate data, and that this information is derived from standard, consistent business processes for rolling up financial items and calculating gross profit."

Using SAP Strategic Enterprise Management, Coca-Cola can now integrate actual data into its planning process for their annual budget and monthly rolling estimates. This is the foundation to be able to use dynamic business-strategy models and analysis and simulation tools to identify the impact of possible actions on the P&L, balance sheet, and overall corporate strategy. The company implemented the data warehousing solution as the infrastructure and reporting engine for the overall SEM implementation.

This creates a common repository of information – visible across all Coca-Cola locations worldwide – and a consistent tool to enable value-added analysis in support of decision-making. The company also plans to expand the use of data warehousing as a reporting tool throughout the company. This will enable its financial planners and analysts to add even more value. Previously, they relied on people "eyeballing" rows and columns and pages of data.

These new solutions provide consistent, high-quality information globally. This enables Coca-Cola to compare, in an exception-based way, locations, brands, and accounts. This also enables the company to compare one part of the world with another, one brand with another, to answer crucial questions about its businesses, and to continually improve its competitive position.

When choosing integrated financial and management-reporting systems, CFOs often cite *multi-dimensionality* as the overriding selection criterion. It should be possible to dissect your company's shareholder value into its components and compare scenarios. For example, by *slicing 'n dicing* by customer, by distribution channel, by geography, by investment center. Some application packages can *slice 'n dice* across up to 40 dimensions! Figure 5.6 shows how multi-dimensional cubes can be built up from an operational level to a strategic level, providing rich dimensionality and high levels of manageability.

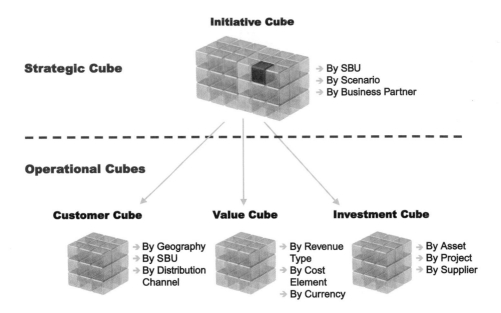

Figure 5.6 *Multi-Dimensionality: Partitioning Information for Reporting and Analytics*

The modular concept based on cubes makes multi-dimensionality more manageable from an information management viewpoint. The best integrated information systems – those which support shareholder value measurement – tend to have the following features:

- *Accessibility*: all relevant information must be easily available at the point of decision-making. Provide a common source of information, allowing people across the organization to make decisions on a consistent basis.

- *Flexibility*: organizational structures and processes will change over time. Focus on adapting the system to reflect resulting changes in information requirements.

- *User friendliness*: while providing sophisticated functionality for advanced users, the system must also be easy to use for non-financial and non-IT literate decision-makers. In addition, it must be easy to configure and manage.

- *Speed of response*: the system should be dynamic and highly auto-mated to support real-time decision-making and ensure that changing business conditions trigger appropriate, timely responses.

- *Robustness and scalability*: the system must be able to integrate large volumes of data from diverse sources. It must also be able to handle simultaneous queries from a large number of users dispersed across the enterprise.

- *Consistency and data integrity*: all users must have confidence in the information the systems provide.

IMPLEMENTING INTEGRATED SEM

During research for this book many CFOs were found to have a common problem. They have invested in their ERP. They have invested in their data warehouse. But they still use spreadsheet software for scorecards and budgeting. Furthermore, strategic initiatives aren't in the systems at all – their progress is just communicated by e-mail. As a result, the scorecards are all different - these tools work for the individuals who use them, but they can't be used across the organization. They require a lot of manual effort for data feeds. CFOs don't feel they can rely on them to run the business because they are based on memorandum entries and don't tie up with the accounts.

These problems are compounded when long-term planning and short-term budgeting processes are taken into account. For long-term planning, the complaint is usually:*"We have to reinvent the wheel each time. We have to collect information on where we are on our strategic initiatives manually; then we have to evaluate them in financial terms. This all takes too long and is prone to error. Also, it's inflexible; we can't change our minds easily. It can take the Board of Directors six weeks to negotiate a budget with the senior business unit executive. Even then, the budget is often rejected as inadequate and we all have to go through a number of wasteful reiterations before we settle on a compromise."*

An investigation among the Fortune 500 of financial models based on spreadsheets revealed the following:

- More than 95% were found to contain major errors
- More than 59% were judged to have poor model design

- More than 78% had no formal control procedures

- But more than 81% of users believe that their model would provide them with a competitive advantage!

We know the problems. But what are the solutions? These are best addressed at two levels: the *process* level and the *data* level.

At the *process* level, the need is to reengineer and integrate the strategic planning, budgeting, scorecarding, and performance-reporting processes. The missing process link between strategic initiatives and budgeted activities is illustrated in Figure 5.7. Reengineering these processes provides opportunities for cost reduction, improvements in workflow efficiency and timing, increased accuracy, and better collaboration. However, process reengineering alone cannot provide the full benefits. Investment in new technology – dedicated technology support for the process integration and workflow management itself – presents the biggest prize! For example: in the planning process, the budget account-

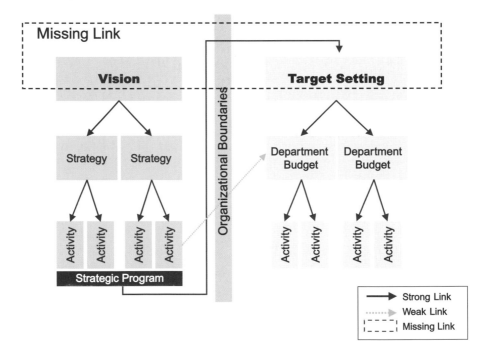

Figure 5.7 *The Missing Link – Strategic Initiatives with Budgeted Activities*

ant has to manage the coordination of input from a variety of cost center managers in a relatively short time frame. The advanced workflow technology provides immediate feedback on the budget preparation, management, and monitoring life cycle.

Let's turn now to the *data* level. In the spreadsheet approach, there are a number of different versions of the truth! There are different versions held in different spreadsheets; data is stored in a variety of different repositories – this makes consistent reporting across different analysis dimensions almost impossible. The suggested solution is set out in Figure 5.8.

In this proposed architecture, the source systems feed the data warehouse; the data warehouse feeds the dedicated data repositories or online analytical processing (OLAP) cubes; and these feed the presentation mechanism, be it a dashboard or portal. Best practice suggests starting with the scorecard using a technology-lite approach, moving subsequently to this more robust, scalable architecture when the pilot implementations have been validated and the processes sufficiently well established from a user viewpoint. Your integrated SEM architecture should enable you to:

- Structure your strategy (strategy map/balanced scorecard) and communicate your goals throughout the entire organization and to stakeholders

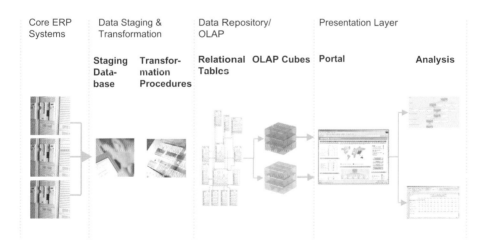

Figure 5.8 *The Integrated Performance Solution Architecture*

- Value your strategy through scenario planning and activity-based planning and link strategy with operative targets and resource allocation

- Support integrated planning, budgeting and forecasting processes, and consolidate actuals

- Collect unstructured information from external and internal sources

- Monitor the performance of strategic key success factors using external and internal benchmarks – either online or in a *management cockpit*-style room

- Communicate your strategy and performance to major stakeholders and gather feedback

A critical prerequisite for the support of the strategic management process is an appropriate information base. The required information can be classified into structured and unstructured information. Structured information is typically numerical information that is available in a fixed data record structure (for example, data from the ERP system, or stock price time series from an external business database).

In addition to structured information, many steps in the SEM process require external information that is usually available in unstructured form. This could be textual information on market events, competitors, their products, their patents, industry sector development, economic developments in target markets, press reports concerning the enterprise or its products and capital market expectations. Software is available which provides functionality for the automated and semiautomated collection of structured and unstructured business information from external and internal sources.

Where should the CFO start in implementing the vision for SEM? Consider the case study of a major international bank.

CASE STUDY
Implementing SEM in Three Plateaus

The main goals of this international bank were to become a world leader in cross-border wholesale banking and become the European bank of choice for clients seeking global financing solutions. In 2001, the bank integrated its global investment and corporate banking activities in the Wholesale Clients strategic business unit (SBU).

This organizational change is part of the new managing for value (MfV) framework that would ensure that every management decision made within every part of the bank would be focused on maximizing returns for its shareholders (to be measured by TRS: total return to shareholders).

To reach the ultimate goal (maximizing TRS), a bottom-up goal-setting process took place, in which business units defined financial and strategic targets. These targets were delegated to the business managers and laid down in multi-year performance contracts. In order to control this process, a set of KPI's per business unit were defined. This meant a change in the way performance was measured and also a change in culture, promoting a greater focus on the creation of shareholder value. Short communication lines and the effective use of modern information technology were critical for the success of the MfV framework.

For every business unit, performance reports had to be defined to monitor short- and long-term performance throughout the Wholesale Clients SBU. These fixed format reports were based on the performance contracts and contained financial, strategic, and non-financial KPIs. Furthermore, these reports reflected progress against predefined milestones and changes to specific business assumptions. Additionally, these reports contained evaluations of the predefined strategic initiatives. The management information system played a critical role in the MfV program: it needed to be robust, affordable, and reliable to generate accurate performance reports. It also needed to be flexible enough to satisfy future information needs and organizational changes.

To this end, the bank decided to start with the implementation of SEM, together with a business information warehouse. The implementation approach was twofold:

1. *A short-term SEM solution to satisfy the most immediate monthly reporting and budgeting needs.*

2. *A vision for a mid-term SEM solution to provide full business intelligence to all business units involved in the MfV program.*

The outputs and benefits of the full business intelligence vision were:

- *An information system, which formed an integral part of management control and strategy setting*

- *Performance (contract) management*

- *More efficient data processing*

- *One information source at different levels*

- *A flexible tool that supports ongoing implementation of MfV*

- *A uniform standard set of IT tools*

- *A common global data model*

Every business unit manager was to receive the information relevant to monitoring and improving business unit performance. Each manager would have 24/7 worldwide access, both globally and locally, to selected screens tailored to his/her needs and interfaces.

The implementation of the business intelligence system was more than just setting up a system and customizing its settings properly. Four key areas needed to be addressed during the implementation:

1. Management and control: *what is the impact of organizational changes and management requirements on implementation and vice versa?*

2. Internal processes: *what is the 'fit' between internal processes and systems – and what changes may occur as a result of the implementation?*

3. Systems: *which systems are affected or replaced during the implementation? How does the implemented solution fit within the total IT infrastructure?*

4. Personnel and culture: *what is the impact of the implementation on the desired cultural environment and how can we ensure that the implemented solution will be accepted?*

In a dynamic environment, a phased approach, from plateau to plateau, leads to a situation in which systems, people, processes, and management and control are kept in balance. In each phase, all four areas need to be addressed with specific deliverables. Two quite separate work streams were defined: one for performance contracts, focusing on the KPI and performance contract reporting; another for budgeting and forecasting. Both these work streams were to be implemented in a coordinated phased approach referred to as "plateau planning." These three implementation plateaus were:

- Plateau 1 "Business Blueprint" *The first plateau in the implementation was the business blueprint. A detailed mapping was made of the bank's functional requirements against the functionalities of the prepackaged SEM software. The implementation plan was subsequently written in detail.*

- Plateau 2 "SEM Lite"   *On this plateau, the KPI reporting and performance contract front-end was implemented and functionality for consolidating the contracts made available. Furthermore, a planning process was defined, a prototype built and piloted.*

- Plateau 3 "Full SEM Dialogue"   *The focus of plateau 3 was on the implementation of full process dialogues, (both for the KPIs and the planning process) and on the full rollout of the planning prototype to the other business units.*

This staged implementation provided the bank with a stable reporting and budgeting environment on which subsequent enhancements could be built. Such enhancements would include: implementation of a Web front-end; automated data feeds via an ETL (extract, transport and load) tool; value driver trees; implementation of more levels of detail at the individual SBU level.

Like the bank in this case study, most organizations build their SEM architecture based on their data warehouses and link them to their enterprise transaction processing systems. Most integrated SEM software packages offer the following applications:

- *Business planning and simulation*: providing functionality to support integrated strategic and operational business planning using multi-dimensional data structures. These functions include: creation of dynamic and linear business models; modeling and simulation of various scenarios; and evaluation of these scenarios based on risk assessment. Business planning features also include analyzing resource allocation; cross-functional enterprise planning and rolling forecasts; and aligning these activities with strategic KPI targets.

- *Business consolidation*: providing functionality for financial consolidation and value-based accounting. These functions include: automated value-based adjustment postings, automated assignments and allocations (for example, of assets to reporting units), currency translation, inter-company profit eliminations, consolidation of investments according to different internal procedures, and monitoring of local and international statutory accounting requirements.

- *Balanced scorecard*: providing functionality for the definition, analysis, visualization, and interpretation of KPIs. These procedures make use of innovative visualization techniques designed to increase management effectiveness. The system provides a comprehensive infrastructure to support better performance management and communication processes both internally and with business partners. This application also helps you create customized interpretation models based on *value driver trees* and *management cockpit* scenarios.

- *Stakeholder relationship management*: providing functionality to support the stakeholder communication process. It ensures that stakeholders are informed regularly and systematically about business strategy and its effects on shareholder value – either through *push* services (e.g. automated e-mails) or through *pull* services (e.g. a Web-based enterprise stakeholder portal). In addition, this application collects formal feedback from stakeholders and distributes it to top management.

SEM systems architectures are designed to allow access to the full range of functional tools via the Internet or company intranet. The relationship between SEM, specialty financial applications, and ERP is shown in Figure 5.9.

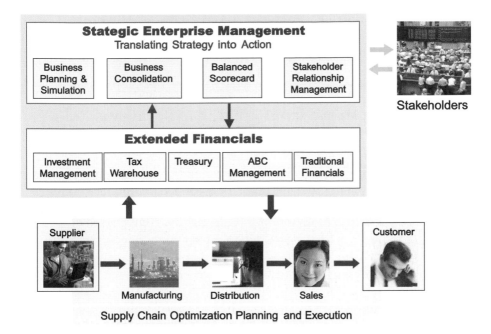

Figure 5.9   *Linking ERP with Strategic Enterprise Management*

The CFO and the CEO should be the most strategically informed people in the corporation. They should have access to any and all critical information needed to successfully manage the enterprise – and *keep their fingers on the pulse*. This information must be consistent with that used by their colleagues, including the head of strategy, the corporate financial controller, business analysts (*internal* and *external*), and most importantly, the executive teams running the business units. At its best, SEM today offers all this and more.

CFO CHECKLIST

MAKE A FRESH BUSINESS CASE FOR DECISION SUPPORT
Formulate a vision, then identify where you are today – what do you need to do to close the gap? Work out how much your existing decision-making and management information processes and systems cost you today. Focus your future investment on SEM initiatives, which create tangible value added.

DEVELOP YOUR PERFORMANCE MANAGEMENT PROPOSITION
Focus on a *living conversation* throughout the company, supported by real-time, event driven information. Engage your divisional CFOs in the process and ensure scorecards are formulated for each significant management layer in the structure.

IMPROVE YOUR ABILITY TO PREDICT THE FUTURE
Translate your growth-creating strategies into KPIs. Focus on the *cause-and-effect* of KPIs on individual strategies.

INTEGRATE RISK MANAGEMENT
Take your risk and opportunity assessment and link it to your scorecard KPIs. Integrate risk into your management reporting process.

BLOW UP THE BUDGET!
Reengineer your budgeting process to focus on what's important. Reduce the time taken and unnecessary detail. Formulate performance contracts with your business units which combine performance-based compensation, strategic initiative reporting, rolling business forecasts, and resource allocation.

BROADEN YOUR CONSOLIDATION BANDWIDTH
Develop your accounts consolidation process into a multidimensional, *slice 'n dice*, reporting mechanism, which provides line-of-sight between the corporate center and the

business units, and across global product market views. Select *one* consolidation tool for both your financial accounting and your management information requirements.

ENHANCE STAKEHOLDER RELATIONSHIP MANAGEMENT
Define your stakeholder management communication needs. Link the external world of investors with the internal world of management through your performance management process.

INTEGRATE YOUR SEM COMPONENTS
Build your new decision support platform on your ERP and data warehouse infrastructure. Integrate your scorecard, planning, consolidating, and stakeholder processes with data from one source and with externally and internally driven transactions.

CHAPTER 6

Analytics: Converting Data into Action

FOCUSING OUR LINE OF SIGHT ON THE END-CONSUMER

Gary Fayard, CFO
The Coca-Cola Company

Coca-Cola has a market capitalization of $110 bn – only $23 bn of this is in physical assets. The majority of our remaining asset value – our intangible assets – is tied up in the Coca-Cola brand and the company's relationships with its bottlers and distributors. The company's business model is well proven over the last century – it has always concentrated on building the brand and encouraging bottlers to invest in physical plant. End-customer relationships are typically managed by Coca-Cola's distributors and retailers. The company has a great long-term track record in creating shareholder value and exceptionally high returns on investment. To quote directly from its annual report, Coca-Cola's strategy is to:

- *Accelerate carbonated soft drink growth, led by the Coca-Cola brand.*

- *Selectively broaden our family of beverage brands to drive profitable growth.*

- *Grow system profitability and capability together with our bottling partners.*

- *Serve customers with creativity and consistency to generate growth across all channels.*

- *Direct investments to highest-potential areas across markets.*

- *Drive efficiency and cost-effectiveness everywhere.*

Gary Fayard, the CFO, explains Coca-Cola's strategy further: "Managing intangible assets is a very big issue for us. We did go through a stage when we owned a lot of assets, but we do not want to have the skills or capabilities to be a truly excellent bottler. We are essentially a marketing company; our primary purpose is to grow brands. We strive to maintain our corporate reputation as the world's leading branded beverage supplier. How do we achieve this? Through marketing efficiency and effectiveness. It's all about growing the value of our brands. Coca-Cola is EVA driven – cash drives shareholder value. And luckily, our cash flow profile matches our earnings profile.

We need transparency of sales data and daily volumes. We have common accounting systems that track financial performance, but we need a full view of value chain economics – from one end of the supply chain to the other. We have different marketing media and we are constantly looking at the relative economics of mass marketing versus segmented marketing. We relentlessly evaluate the profitability of our extended system – at what point in the value chain we add value to customers and how we deal commercially with our bottlers and the retail trade. We do have a common strategic plan – we collaborate closely with our bottlers, but we are constantly having to role sort – sorting out who does what and deciding how to share our respective financial obligations. And for this negotiating process, we need financial, analytical information."

The company's business model is not only based on brand innovation and development; it manufactures concentrate syrup and then sells it to its franchised bottling operators, who then distribute it to wholesalers and retailers. The bottlers can only buy their product from the Coca-Cola Company. The commercial relationship between them is predicated on substantial marketing investment by Coca-Cola in the brand – world-class advertising and promotion. The bottlers are encouraged to be profitable.

In return, Coca-Cola depends upon its partners down the value chain to provide them with critical end-consumer data to continuously evaluate, fine-tune, and focus its marketing investments. As Gary points out: "You could say we are 'asset-lite'! Our current capital investments are largely tied up in our Fountain and Minute Maid businesses – where we control the integrated value chain. For the majority of the Coca-Cola business, we have what we call an extended enterprise – a unique set of commercial relationships with our business partners. As you can imagine, managing these relationships with these external parties creates a constructive tension: balancing the right amount of market invest-ment with the right level of commitment from our partners to ensure the right level of returns for all parties. Our biggest challenge? Better line-of-sight through to the customer via the bottler. Not only do we share marketing cost with our bottlers, but we need to analyze the profit margins by customer segment – both trade and consumer segments. Only where it makes economic sense do we own the integrated supply chain – for example, the Fountains business in the USA. Where we have manufacturing assets (for manufacturing concentrate), these are established, wherever possible, in low-cost, low-tax countries."

Coca-Cola's bottlers have approximately five times the turnover of The Coca-Cola Company. So getting detailed information on sales turnover of the extended value chain can be a problem. This problem has been partially solved by creating a bottler accounting and information system, which supplies much of the data required – on routes, delivery schedules, and consumption. But this system assumes a direct delivery business. In certain parts of the world, the bottlers sell to wholesalers – Coca-Cola knows what product goes to the whole-saler, but doesn't know what goes to the retailer or end-consumer.

Gary goes on to say: "We are interested in having better analytics to support better targeted decisions on brand marketing and advertising effectiveness – more detail, more accuracy. For example, greater granularity of consumer behavior is critical to understanding lifestyle trends, targeting campaigns, and timing our TV advertising at precisely the right time of the day. This precision of promotional timing, reaching consumers at the moment when they are most likely to drink our product, we refer to as 'event-based analytics.' We have invested in our Inform marketing database. This is our main source of market intelligence and the basis for systemizing our analytics. We also invest *in something we call DME – our direct marketing expenditure evaluation tool.*

Most of our analysis, though, is done on Excel spreadsheets and we, in finance, would like to move towards a more structured investment in processes and systems for these analytics. The bottlers do use our prescribed accounting systems to feed us their raw data. We carry out end-consumer sampling on a periodic event basis. We develop lead indicators, which tell us what volume growth and sales to expect. There is huge potential in Inform. However, it doesn't give us the whole picture on marketing efficiency: We may do the national marketing, but our bottlers handle local marketing and we may reimburse them for half their marketing costs. But we don't get feedback on how effective this marketing has been on the local level – we don't own that data.

We are improving our trends analysis and correlating advertising cost to sales growth. We review marketing expenditure against the 'pressure points' – reviewing the impact of marketing at the time of the day it hits the consumer and the consumer's reaction. The timing of the consumer reaction and the relevant cash expenditure are often misaligned. We strive to eliminate this misalignment through a corrective analytical technique we call 'pressure points'. At that moment in consumer behavior – the pressure point – the goal is to align investment with return."

Coca-Cola uses detailed analytics on brand awareness, brand preference, and purchase intent – segmenting, for example, between monthly, weekly, and daily drinkers of its products. This drill-down to different customer groups is so precise that it can reach all the way down to specific occasions – the time of day that certain consumers drink products.

Gary's response to this marketing challenge from a finance function viewpoint is as follows: "I expect my finance people to be both deep in Finance, but broad in the Business. I do need good accountants to keep the books – this is a given. But what I really need is finance people who understand the whole business, the entire value chain. They need to understand the value propositions for the bottler, the wholesaler, the retailer, and the consumer as well: evaluating the pricing assumptions, reviewing channel profitability, and analyzing the economics of a promotional package when it hits the streets. For example, the economics of selling a beverage in Japan can depend on making choices between selling it off the shelf in the supermarket or through a vending machine. Also, we have opportunities to cross-sell between brands and channels. Maximizing the sales opportunity from our advertising investment.

Reviewing all the options. That's where we need to start our analytics program – evaluating all the options, out-of-the-box thinking and accelerating the learning curve. Sharing this expertise across our finance function worldwide and with our marketing colleagues is a problem. We look to globally share our information on brands, knowledge, consumer insights, and to build on our global reach and scale. However, we have a predominantly Excel-driven spreadsheet culture in finance. Spreadsheets are helpful, but inefficient. We do have SAP as our ERP backbone for accounting. What we need now is outstanding decision-support tools, built around our structured database with standardized definitions. We need an analytical environment which will fuel our growth, not just cut our costs."

Every company has oceans of data and acres of knowledge. However, only those businesses able to transform their disparate data streams into timely, relevant, and coherent information will ultimately achieve real competitive edge. Today, companies want finance to be proactive – advising managers on the financial impact of decisions, helping them to simulate alternatives, and pushing operations to support strategic goals. As CFO, one of your prime goals must be to improve strategic performance by cascading information down through every level of your organization.

This urgency places demands on the software supporting business processes that didn't exist just five years ago. Technology has moved on, too – providing new ways of gathering, storing, and deploying financial data. Henry Morris, vice president of International Data Corporation[1], has aptly summarized the role of business analytics:

- Business analytics provides *process support* – helping an organization plan and optimize its business operations, as well as discover and develop new opportunities. This means looking at business operations within individual areas (such as your payment or sales processes) and understanding how they perform in a wider context (for example, impact on profitability or working capital). Process support also means setting targets (such as reducing day sales outstanding), simulating alternatives, and controlling the results.

At the same time,

- Business analytics is *functionally separate* from process execution and operational systems. For example, while an *accounting application* in an operational system must record every business transaction and reconcile all invoices, a *financial analytics application* is far more flexible: it can aggregate and manipulate information to simulate alternative value flows.

In addition,

- Business analytics provides *time-oriented data from multiple sources.* This involves gathering data from different systems – namely, enterprise resource planning (ERP), customer relationship management (CRM), supply chain management (SCM), and legacy systems. The business analytics application then uses this data to identify trends and make predictions – such as customer lifetime value if current buying patterns continue or the customer retention rate if customer churn remains stable.

BROADER BOTTOM-LINE DEMANDS

Today's leading organizations build management dialogue into their cultures and look for software tools that support this dialogue. Success depends on translating business strategy into clear-cut actions and then communicating goals to every employee and stakeholder. Concerns about profitability and growth are no longer confined to a handful of top managers. Today, improving bottom-line results is part of everyone's job description. All business units must now factor cost and profitability into their decision-making – whether designing new products or closing a deal. Collaborating early and often is the name of the game.

Making everyone accountable for bottom-line results has transformed cost planning. Engineers, for example, used to focus solely on product design and hand over all financial responsibility to cost accountants once a new product was completed. Today's engineers are expected to plan new products based on cost targets. Cost accountants are involved early in the product-design process, making suggestions when major changes are still possible. What's more, they remain involved at every stage of the product life cycle, calculating break-even points, costs, and revenues. The result? Cost savings of up to 70% during the design phase alone!

Similarly, a sales clerk once used an inventory-management system to determine whether a product was *available-to-promise*, then checked an automated system to see if it was *capable-to-promise*. Today, that same clerk uses activity-based management (ABM) to decide if an order is *profitable-to-promise* before accepting it. The issue is not whether the clerk *can* meet a customer's requirements but whether, based on profitability, those requirements *should* be met.

The trend is toward giving each employee more control over costs, supported by cost accountants who play an advisory role. This shift to a self-controlling approach has changed the way that organizations execute their business strategies. At one time, strategy was developed at the top and implemented through a centralized command-and-control culture. Today, most organizations operate via decentralized business units and teams that are much closer to the customer.

As we will see in Chapter 8, companies have also witnessed a change in the source of value: competitive advantage now lies in intangible assets rather than physical ones. As a result, tracking investments in inventory, property, plant, and equipment is just one part of your job. You must also measure the value of your organization's human capital, innovation, customer base, and business partners.

Such measurements require more than financial yardsticks. A supplier's rating, for example, must take into account factors such as price, shipment costs, fulfillment track record, and quality scores. And that's not all! Your purchasing manager needs the latest supplier ratings when negotiating contracts.

Besides delivering data to frontline employees, financial decision-makers must help them improve operations. Finance and operations must work as a team. This might mean presenting a list of customers with high day sales outstanding (DSOs) to the accounts receivable to speed the payment process, identify bottlenecks, and make it easier for customers to pay. Linking financial data and operations can help reduce working capital and trim transaction costs.

What does all this change mean for business analytics? First and foremost, it highlights the lack of flexibility that traditional application packages suffer from. As shown in Figure 6.1, most packages offer adequate routine production reporting, but provide only limited analysis capabilities and no support at all for predictive modeling.

Various scenarios exist for integrating the technologies needed to overcome traditional systems limitations. Two common approaches are outlined here, along with their benefits and drawbacks:

- *Scenario 1*: vendor-led suites:

  Pro: Follows pattern established for transactional applications; analytic applications are just business process extensions.

  Con: "Suite-of-suites" unlikely to come from one source; many different core competencies and specialized expertise are needed.

- *Scenario 2*: open framework plus best-of-breed:

  Pro: Follows "build, buy, and integrate" approach; application integration technology is better understood and accepted.

  Con: Unknown source of "open" framework; no existing organization seems capable of establishing metadata standards.

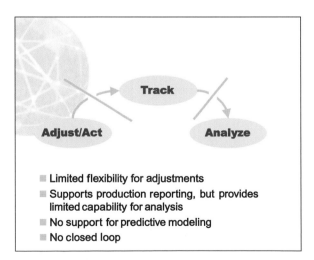

Figure 6.1   *Limits of Traditional Application Packages*

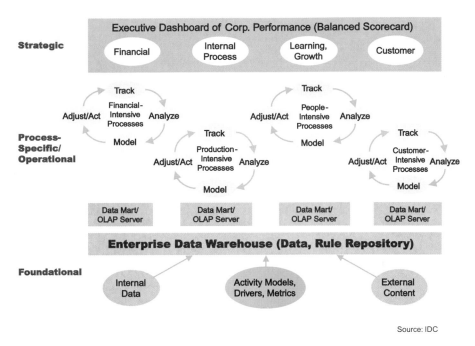

Source: IDC

Figure 6.2 *Analytics Overview – Framework and Applications*

Figure 6.2 provides an overview of analytic suites – the framework and applications – at strategic, process, and data levels.

INTEGRATED ANALYTICS: TRANSFORMING DATA INTO DECISIONS

The average executive spends *82 frustrating minutes a day* searching for information! Multiply this by thousands of employees and the loss is staggering. As CFO, you can help end this waste of time and talent by putting your company on the path to integrated data solutions.

Integrated analytics or "iAnalytics," is a flexible new approach to data aggregation management, distribution, and analysis. It allows the balancing and blending of information in real time – providing true decision support in the fullest sense of the term. iAnalytics captures far-flung intelligence in ways that are agile, actionable, and accessible. Put more simply, it transforms data into information, information into knowledge, and knowledge into wisdom – and action!

Two technologies support the exciting new finance role described here. First, *data warehouses* let you gather information to drive profitability and growth. Second, *Web-based reporting and enterprise portals* help you deliver financial insights to front line employees. Analytical applications generally use a data warehouse, often called an OLAP (online analytical processing) system, which runs separately from the process execution system or OLTP (online transaction processing) system.

Initially, data warehouses were used to gather data for reporting. Now they also provide data consolidation and planning applications. The data warehouse can also dynamically support activity-based costing and management. The data warehouse serves as the technical foundation for business analytics. Since data warehouses rely on multiple source systems, they can pull data from functional silos and present a 360-degree view of customer services or a supply chain that spans many partners.

The benefits of separating data warehousing and process execution systems are twofold. First, business analysts can process high volumes of data without affecting operational systems. In addition, the systems themselves can be built differently. In a *process execution* system, the emphasis is on storing documents such as a goods issue or an invoice and accessing them again quickly. Typically, such data is archived as soon as it is no longer needed. In a *process support* system, data is aggregated in ways that permit multi-dimensional analysis. The data remains in the system for longer and is easier to access for ad hoc queries and simulations.

The Internet, e-Commerce, and online sales have all grown hand in hand with new trends in information deployment. Today, anyone with a browser can read and refresh an intranet report, making it easier to reach more staff more quickly. Such Web reports are not aimed at ERP professionals, but at occasional users who need to know, for example, which plants are producing too much scrap or which sales offices are failing to hit their targets. Generally, Web reports are designed to *alert* users to exceptions rather than to bombard them with information.

Today, enterprise portals provide a single point of sign-on and control for Web reporting. Enterprise portals get the right information to the right user at the right time. Portals make it easy to combine bits of data that managers need – whether details of the opportunity pipeline for a sales manager or feedback on customers with unpaid bills for an accounts receivable clerk. A manager's portal, for example, may link information from finance and HR for use in updates on current projects and costs, while also profiling the skills, career paths, and salaries of employees (see Chapter 7, Portals).

While enterprise portals promise to transform the information landscape, making them a reality won't be easy. Even the largest companies face many challenges on data collection and delivery front. Today, they are struggling to manage and upgrade outmoded legacy systems and to improve data quality and consistency. Overcoming the functional "silo" mentality, which creates *islands of information* that make sharing knowledge difficult, is an ongoing challenge. Communicating with external partners, suppliers, and customers is also critical, but many companies have a long way to go in this area.

What are the iAnalytic opportunities for the finance function? To span functional boundaries. To focus the organization on decisions that create value. And to take advantage of new tools to support those decisions. But perhaps, most importantly, iAnalytics helps to leverage the already very heavy investment in ERP and data warehousing. Typically, data warehouses have consumed vast resources with little benefit. Analytics are the applications that take advantage of data and information in the data warehouse – and bring them to life. Such analytics can *customize* data – and in some cases, *personalize* it. For example, through a portal, customers for financial services products – such as insurance policies or retirement plans – can access their own personal data and use online analytics to evaluate options and configure product solutions tailored to their needs. This transforms the data warehouse from a passive repository to a dynamic revenue-generating tool.

INCREASING CUSTOMER VALUE THROUGH ANALYTICS

A company's customer base is often its biggest asset. As its guardian, the CFO is often charged with finding customer-centric solutions. Since achieving customer profitability usually requires substantial investment, it is crucial to know where customers are in the life cycle – which ones deliver positive value, for example, and how close others are to the break-even point. Yet even today, customer value is often not measured regularly – or value measures are based on past history or outmoded business models.

Analyzing customer relationships from a lifetime perspective is critical for business success. This depends on achieving a complex set of goals:

- Building your asset base by acquiring profitable new customers

- Strengthening relationships with your largest, most reliable customers

- Transforming minor customers into more profitable ones

- Increasing your share of sales revenue (and hence your share of wallet)

- Exploiting cross-selling or up-selling opportunities

CASE STUDY
Leveraging CRM Analytics

A large national health insurance company comprising of close to 20 regional associations currently insures more than 25 million people. The CRM challenges it faces today are similar to those of many other enterprises: how to monitor customer fluctuations (joiners and leavers). How to enrich its marketing information. And, finally, how to retain its most attractive customers.

When the company began rethinking its approach to customer relationship building, it reviewed its progress to date. It had already implemented an SAP CRM program and had designed an in-house business analytics system. However, despite these activities, the company faced growing competition and was losing customers – especially those with higher incomes, who preferred to join private health insurance companies. As a result, its risk structure was changing.

In developing a more sophisticated customer management program, it was further hampered by outmoded technology: its 25-year-old computer system was reliable but unable to meet the data demands of a complex CRM program. What's more, its strong regionally focused structure threatened to overwhelm its centralized customer database, creating isolated islands of information.

From a customer service standpoint, the company's broad goal was to create a "diagnostic view" of healthcare service utilization. Specifically, it wanted the power to:

- *Monitor gross profit by customer groups/segments*

- *Control fluctuation by tracking customer employer changes*

- *Improve customer retention rates*

- *Launch campaigns for selected customer segments*

- *Build local networks between subsidiaries*

- *Improve change processes and structures*

To revitalize its customer base, the company must use integrated analytics and business planning to target customer segments and launch focused marketing campaigns. It must commit to consistent KPIs, conduct detailed fluctuation analyses, and use integrated information to better manage risk. By clustering customers and using demographic data, it can significantly boost its bottom line. The solution: integration!

A well-defined customer value framework[2] can and should be used to measure the health of your customer base and improve performance. This said, in almost all cases, CFOs lack the framework or tools to attain this customer-centric vision. The major issues facing the CFO today in implementing customer value programs are as follows:

- *Do our customer relationships promote loyal, long-term profitable growth?*

   The cost of losing customers is rising. Fleeting customer loyalty has always been a problem, but today's consumers are more fickle than ever. They have more choice, more information, and are more willing to chase a "better deal." Little wonder that churn rates are surging!

   In many B2C environments, a customer must be retained and stimulated before becoming profitable. This break-even model has become a business driver: banks offer cash incentives, phone companies offer free mobile phones, and retailers sell certain products at a loss to attract customers. Companies must monitor the cost of losing valued customers both *before and after* they reach the break even point. This alone justifies the cost of customer value programs.

- *Do we really understand who our customers are and how much they contribute?*

  For example, phone companies often find it hard to consolidate all their contracts with large commercial customers. Many banks also have difficulty consolidating a customer's file if that customer has several accounts and uses multiple financial products. In addition, companies are realizing the fragility of their businesses: often, a surprisingly small segment of their customer base accounts for a high percentage of revenues or profits. In many mobile telecommunications companies, 40% of all profits come from 7% of customers. One large Japanese bank was astounded to learn that 1% of its customers accounted for almost 99% of its profits!

- *How do we deploy our resources to acquire and retain the right customers?*

  Acquisition and retention costs are skyrocketing. In response, most companies are searching for new strategies to build customer and shareholder value. The key is tailored marketing: defining all value-driven activities at an individual customer level so that products can be personalized.

- *Can new customer value solutions be integrated with current/future systems architecture?*

  Data warehouses and other technologies help identify customers, consolidate buying patterns and transaction data, and segment customers. However, these tools do not provide the more advanced techniques needed to measure and monitor customer value. Today's new intelligence-based applications are flexible and feature-rich. Early adopters of these new customer value-building tools will reap huge benefits.

- *Is our investment in CRM systems generating real customer value and profits?*

  CRM systems integrate processes across departments and lines of business. As depicted in Figure 6.3, these systems often consist of call centers, sales and marketing, and customer service vehicles designed to boost efficiency and lower costs. But such tools may not improve customer retention and value. In general, current CRM systems do not address long-term customer value issues (CVM: customer value

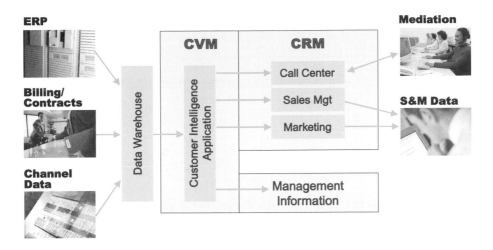

Figure 6.3   *Systems Architecture including Customer Value Management*

management). They also offer little or no intelligence on customer profiles, break-even modeling, and potential lifetime profitability.

- *How can we monitor changes in customer value on a long-term basis?*

It is important to monitor and track changes in customer value over time to determine which customers are increasing or decreasing in value. Analyzing historical customer value data can help pinpoint the reasons for customer changes, making it easier to make decisions about future interaction and investment.

- *Why do we need customer value tools – isn't a customer profitability system enough?*

Customer value is more than just a financial measurement. That's why calculating it requires ongoing (i.e. monthly) tracking of many non-financial measures. Some organizations use activity-based management (ABM) to measure the cost and profitability of customers, products, and services. However, customer profitability is calculated mainly for customer segments or groups, not individual customers. And most profitability models are only updated quarterly or annually.

Customer value drivers are reshaping pricing, services, and processes. Equally important, customer value can be used as leverage with external stakeholders, including shareholder alliance partners and the investment community. Today, a well-planned customer value strategy encompasses:

- Unified customer intelligence
- Customer profiling and valuation mechanisms
- Customer tracking by household, family group, buying patterns, etc
- Break-even analysis for investment and retention programs
- Enhanced sales and marketing capabilities based on personalized contact
- Pricing based on customer lifetime value

CASE STUDY
Maximizing Customer Value through Analytics

A medium-sized European mobile operator had 35% of its market and more than 3 million subscribers. Customer acquisition costs in the lucrative but competitive commercial market were spiralling out of control. The board of directors decided that growing its customer base was essential to sustain market share and financial health. To do this, its customer intelligence would have to improve significantly. So would its customer-facing processes.

The company worked with specialists skilled in designing customer value systems. It rapidly built a system to create meaningful customer profiles while tracking costs and revenues on a lifetime basis. Next, management decided to focus its marketing on more direct customer interaction, with an investment plan based on customer value and break-even. Using customer usage profiles, direct marketing campaigns were conducted. The results were spectacular: cross-selling success rates surged by 200%. Over time, the company expects to radically improve customer satisfaction. It also plans to reduce churn by investing strategically in high-value customers.

Today, the company has totally restructured its customer care department based on customer value: priority customers are automatically directed to specially trained customer care representatives. All CRM systems now contain customer value metrics to allow integration of all customer-facing processes.

The next step: leveraging customer value to assist in designing and pricing new products. Using customer intelligence about family groups, households, and associations – pricing will be tailored based on current profitability, propensity to adopt new products, or loyalty incentives. As this company moves heavily into the Internet world with third-generation networks, portals will be personalized to each customer and products priced based on individual customer lifetime value measures.

As this case study forecasts, using the Internet to reach customers – especially via portals, will be personalized through micro-marketing campaigns. Clearly, the Internet is the best mechanism developed for self-service environments. As a result, it offers a robust route for one-to-one marketing, cutting service costs, and increasing dialogue with consumers.

Yet even now, using the Internet for micro-marketing is a distant dream for most companies. However, they are improving; for example, most Telcos still mass market via costly product campaigns: European companies alone spend approximately $7 bn a year on mass marketing! Most operators lack the ability to track campaign results or to distinguish between marketing impact and natural customer behavior.

All this is rapidly changing, however – and not a moment too soon! New, more advanced customer value programs are reshaping strategy on many fronts. Today they are empowering companies to:

- *Proactively identify subscribers at a high point in the profitability cycle.* When an attractive customer segment is targeted, it is now possible to calculate the investment cost for reaching each subscriber – this data can then be used to budget more accurately for a marketing campaign.

- *Allow the customer value system to track campaign impact on each subscriber.* New systems can slice 'n dice any and all metrics associated with a campaign – for example its effect on profitability and usage.

Without doubt, these new approaches will affect call center programs. Customer value tools may be used to route customers. The CVM – customer value management – system can deliver real-time data on customer profitability, usage, payments, and product usage. As a result, customer representatives will have a rich array of fresh data at their fingertips.

Customer profiles will also be more detailed and more accurate. They will capture more detailed customer attributes: which products/services they have purchased, how they use them, payment patterns, and any links they have to individuals, organizations, households, family groups, and associations. Not to mention geo-demographic and socio-demographic data.

As steps like these are taken, once elusive possibilities emerge:

- New products can be created more intelligently, based on the requirements of customer segments or even individual customers.

- Marketing can be targeted to individual customers, messages tailored, and 'best-fit' product proposed.

- Reinvestment can be targeted to individual customers.

- Organization design and staff training can focus on customer segments.

- Websites can be personalized based on the unique characteristics of an individual customer, and products or services priced to reflect lifetime value.

Customer value measures are fast becoming a focal point for management. As Figure 6.4 shows, 6% of customers can contribute 40% of the revenue. Customer segmentation by value and characteristic can hugely influence a company's strategy. Customer value analytics are likely to reshape how products are priced, how and what services are offered – and radically redefine CRM programs and strategies.

BRINGING ANALYTICS TO SUPPLY CHAIN MANAGEMENT

Supply chain analytics are aimed at supporting operations, improving delivery, and offering differentiated services – all while keeping costs down. A tall order! To support existing ERP and best-of-breed supply chain systems, there are four key analytics elements[3] that must be in place:

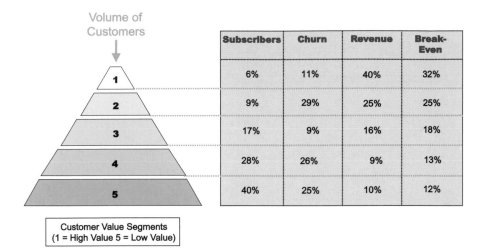

	Subscribers	Churn	Revenue	Break-Even
1	6%	11%	40%	32%
2	9%	29%	25%	25%
3	17%	9%	16%	18%
4	28%	26%	9%	13%
5	40%	25%	10%	12%

Volume of Customers

Customer Value Segments
(1 = High Value 5 = Low Value)

Figure 6.4 *Monitoring Company Performance by Customer Value*

1. *Concept*: get the initial design right, whether for a new product, a new business, or a result of restructuring. Inefficient/inappropriate design can cause unnecessary costs to be designed into a supply chain system. Good design recognizes "envelopes" of possibilities and explicitly trades off key performance and risk factors.

2. *Consistency*: give priority to service-driven supply policies, consistent with design, performance, and demand. This will ensure smooth operation, high-quality service, and working and fixed capital efficiency.

3. *Coverage/Cross-functionality*: align operating plans and policies across the extended enterprise. Proactively manage risk and respond to market events quickly when big gains or losses are at stake.

4. *Cost drivers*: understand cost to better determine value drivers. One example: analyzing the cost of complexity and its net value added when measuring both working and fixed asset usage.

Integrating iAnalytics into supply chain programs isn't easy. It requires strong commitment and follow-through. Structural flaws must be eliminated at the design stage and operating plans adjusted for demand uncertainty and supply side risk. Bottlenecks must be anticipated and preventive measures installed from the start. Cross-functional solutions must support trade-off decisions. And all these steps must be facilitated by responsive, robust, and fully integrated tactical planning. The benefits can be huge. They include increased revenue, often up to 5%, which goes straight to the bottom line; reduced capital expenditure and increased asset utilization of 15% or more; working capital reductions up to 30% and lower sourcing costs.

To improve supply chain results, a business analytics program must operate on four levels. First, it must cover every facet of the extended supply chain, including partners and outsourcers. Second, it must offer operational depth and agility. Third, it must be event-driven – it must assess, in real time, the full impact of any event or change. And finally, it must be flexible and forward-looking – offering fact-based scenarios so you can quickly see all your options and take action.

Sustained improvement depends on fine-tuning – upgrading the systems, analytical, and people skills you need to do all this routinely. But the really big issues are: How strong will demand be, and how much capacity at what stage in the process do I need – and when? Throwing lots of capacity at a problem may not be the answer, since the cost of making the wrong decision will be high. For example, in addition to volume variances, both mix yield and supply reliability can affect timing requirements across the chain – making it unclear exactly where and when additional capacity is needed.

As Figure 6.5 shows, the earlier you build supply chain requirements into your product design process, the lower the overall life cycle cost will be. The best approach is to generate scenarios based on different combinations of forecast data, supply-side variables, batch size, and lead time during the design stage when these factors can still influence cost. Scenario results let you understand the required operational "envelope" – along with associated costs and risks along the chain.

Initial insights can be gathered and applied in a matter of weeks. Get started by choosing a pilot with a strong potential for success – using a single product, for example. Your pilot should address a "hot" stakeholder issue. The lessons learned will help you shape and roll out a more ambitious program across your supply chain.

As always, effective planning depends on setting policies attuned to your business's underlying dynamics. This helps ensure both reliable, predictable supply, and highest (net) value outcomes – reflecting the right combination of fixed and working capital investment, operating cost, and revenue risk. For example, as shown in Figure 6.6, businesses are

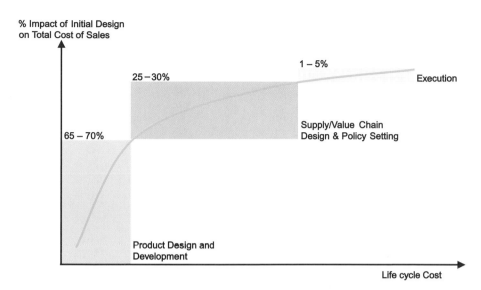

% Impact of Initial Design
on Total Cost of Sales

1 – 5%

25 – 30%

Execution

Supply/Value Chain
Design & Policy Setting

65 – 70%

Product Design and
Development

Life cycle Cost

Figure 6.5 *Impact of Initial Design on Total Cost*

responding to demand-and-supply uncertainty by setting policies based on a four-way trade-off.

Tactical planning aims at short-term benefits. However, supply chains also need to be managed at the aggregate, "what if I could break this constraint," level. The preferred approach is to generate scenarios providing:

- A snapshot of "as is" status along with the associated risks, sensitivities, financials, and decision points

- Forecasts on potential bottlenecks and options for removing them

- Estimates of how quickly the supply chain can react to market/internal changes

The results? The power to manage the chain by exception, using prerun scenarios as part of the sales and operations process – immediately broadcasting "synchronized" operating plans and policy changes. This has been done at the product or product group level within 10–12 weeks.

Operations' task is to manage "here and now" supply chain demands. Business analytics looks at what drives cost and value. The ability to evaluate operating configurations, including operation/conversion cost, and capital requirements can be a significant source of value. In many

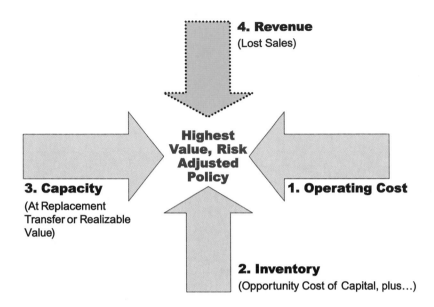

Figure 6.6 *The Four Way Trade-Off*

supply/value chains, product variety and rigid control architectures comprise 50% of total conversion costs.

CASE STUDY
Integrating New Product and Supply Chain Analytics

AstraZeneca is one of the world's leading pharmaceutical companies. It provides a wide range of innovative healthcare products. In the highly competitive global pharmaceutical market, a successful product launch is critical. Any mismatch between product costs and market demand can mean huge revenue losses.

A major new drug AstraZeneca was developing exceeded all expectations, sparking much higher than anticipated product demand. The challenge was how to reliably meet this demand while controlling manufacturing and working capital costs. The problem: balancing capacity investments against inventory in a cost-effective way.

As Andrew Smith, Head of IS Demand (Operations), comments: "Supply chain analytics was chosen to model AstraZeneca's new product supply chain. With limited data requirements, this new tool was soon delivering results. We were able to identify and evaluate constraints, visualizing when they would come into effect. Rather than optimizing within our existing framework, we were able to explore the space and ask questions we never had the frame of reference to ask before."

Using supply chain analytics, AstraZeneca developed a model of the new product looking forward 10 years. The model covered the total global supply chain, including suppliers, manufacturing, distribution, and customers. AstraZeneca developed a model that identified ways to relax constraints without increasing risks.

Says Smith: "We tested different design possibilities to determine which design promised the best results. In two days, we charted 60 discrete scenarios against design options. Increasing uncertainty and shrinking timeframes are driving the need for greater agility in supply chain design. Analytics is the only tool we have found that can significantly improve performance in complex global supply chains."

Supply chain analytics gave AstraZeneca the data it needed to:

- *Ensure possible demand scenarios could be supported*

- *Reduce expected inventory investments*

- *Improve asset utilization and planning*

- *Reduce sourcing and material costs*

- *Mitigate major risks*

The results? Lower working capital requirements, reduced costs, and enhanced value. The company was asking questions it never asked before. As Andrew Smith noted, "We understand our supply chain better now and have more confidence in how it behaves."

Supply chain analytics lets you model structure, service, supply and demand options. It helps boost overall performance by adjusting design, policy, and operating levers. This flexible tool also lets you identify savings in supply chain design, identify constraints, and assess the financial impact of breaking through them.

ANALYTICS: TRANSFORMING THE FINANCE FUNCTION

Mention financial analytics and most people's minds turn to financial reporting. Some think of spreadsheets and some, of enterprise portals. Still others visualize data warehouses. But financial analytics is about far more than financial reporting. It is about using data to influence bottom-line results.

Take customer profitability, for example. Most organizations report on contribution margins for each customer or customer groups. Financial analytics goes beyond contribution margin reporting to show what drives those margins. How? By providing a 360-degree view of all customer-related activities and costs. It uses data from customer touch-points to find out which customers respond to which marketing, sales and service activities. It uses the information on order fulfillment gathered through SCM (supply chain management) to determine which customers are over-burdening your logistics processes. And finally, it monitors payment behavior to find out which customers make your accounts receivable staff work extra hours.

Financial analytics "explains the numbers" and how they affect your bottom line. Today, many marketing and service activities are still treated as period expenses. By integrating financial analytics and customer data, you can nurture your most profitable customer relationships or renegotiate service agreements with marginal customers.

In other words, financial analytics provides real decision support – not a list of numbers, but the ability to get behind the numbers and simulate alternative approaches. It also lets you manage costs dynamically. By the time a product goes into production, for example, 95% of its costs are fixed. Concurrent costing helps you assess product costs much earlier, when you can still redesign components or processes to reduce costs. This requires simulating a number of options – such as choosing new suppliers, remapping transport cycles, or sharing product components.

Financial analytics involves mapping the allocations between functional areas as well as products, customers, and service channels. It also provides the transparency that old allocation tools lacked. You can use it to start small – introduce shared service pricing for IT services or HR – or apply activity-based management (ABM) methodologies across the board.

Financial analytics starts where controlling once left off by letting you use ABM to increase efficiency. After using ABM, you will quickly see the depth and breadth of financial analytics tools it puts at your command. The potential for integrating cost analytics with performance management – or scorecard – analytics is presented in Figure 6.7. Whether you are pricing external goods or internal services, you will see in graphic detail the costs that all parties are incurring and why.

But financial analytics is more than controlling on a new platform. It goes beyond profit-and-loss statements to include data from accounts receivable and accounts payable systems. Indeed, it uses the business information warehouse to bring together relevant data from all the ERP applications – and external data providers as well.

This opens the way to new, more profitable solutions, such as how best to manage working capital. Financial analytics lets you accelerate time-

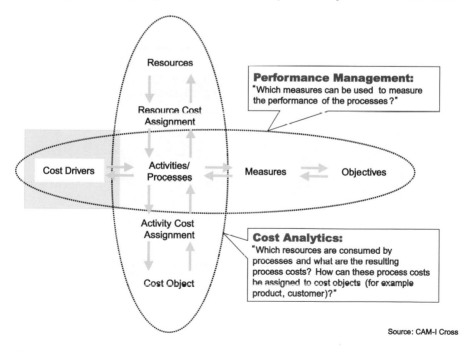

Source: CAM-I Cross

Figure 6.7 *Linking Financial Analytics with Performance Management Analytics*

to-cash by applying ABM methodologies to your payment processes. And of course, modeling payment processes isn't just about reducing working capital. Invoicing costs also mean administration costs.

Financial analytics tools help your credit managers analyze payment behavior, letting them adjust payment conditions based on day sales outstanding for each customer. Tools for liquidity and cash-flow analytics let you manage short- and medium-term payment streams with several financing alternatives. The integration of financial supply chain management with corporate finance management and associated analytics is illustrated diagramatically in Figure 6.8.

Besides being tightly integrated with transactional systems, financial analytics is linked to strategic enterprise management (see Chapter 5). This gives you access to tools like the balanced scorecard and management cockpit. As you translate strategy into action, you can map performance measures to the processes modeled in financial analytics. The result? A tighter focus on both strategy and your bottom line.

Getting there from here will take time. Consider the results of a recent survey[4] by the Aberdeen Group on spreadsheet analytics. Excel rules! Despite a host of high-powered new solutions, 88% of those surveyed still use spreadsheets. Today, in fact, they may be doing "double-duty." With the ability to support Excel-based views and input formats, advanced financial analytic solutions appear to be supplementing – rather than supplanting – spreadsheets as a stand-alone tool. Consider these findings from the Aberdeen Group showing how survey respondents ranked, in preference order, their top-five spreadsheet uses:

1. Consolidation/financial reporting

2. Financial performance metrics

3. Cash-flow optimization

4. OLAP-driven planning, budgeting

5. Enterprise risk management

How respondents defined the top-three benefits of spreadsheets:

1. Facilitates better decisions

2. Introduces greater granularity in data

3. Sharpens perspectives on profitability

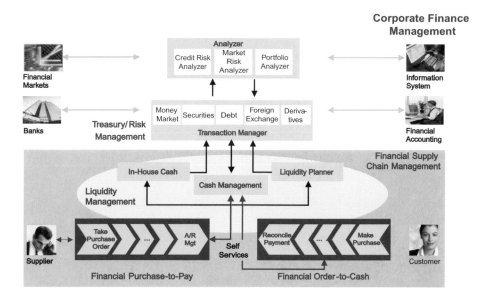

Figure 6.8 *Integration Financial Supply Chain Management – Corporate Finance Management*

How respondents defined the top-three disadvantages of spreadsheets:

1. Little or no integration with transactional and other systems

2. Increases maintenance and cost of other systems

3. Unable to update software business models

As these survey results suggest, adoption of new integrated analytic applications has been slow. Why the sluggish response? According to survey respondents, they are reluctant to adopt new business analytics tools because:

- *Integration benefits have been understated*: managers don't understand the benefits of integration between financial analytic software and their enterprises' transactional systems.

- *The spreadsheet format is well-liked*: most end-users continue to cling to the comfortable, familiar spreadsheet format – even if it used in conjunction with more sophisticated financial analytic solutions.

- *Established suppliers still reign*: many buyers are rejecting newer, more innovative suppliers, who provide integration, and continuing to opt for the safety offered by better-known suppliers whose products are in danger of becoming obsolete.

CASE STUDY
Global Margin Reporting Reaches a New Level

Along with a complex supply chain, a major oil company found itself managing a cumbersome, heterogeneous systems landscape. Usage was plagued by problems with data reliability and quality, risk management, and data/coding inconsistencies. Another thorny area: ensuring transparency of the value added generated between legal entities, profit centers, customer/products, geographies, fiscal and physical flows. The solution: group costing – a global model for monitoring revenues generated internally and from third parties (customers and joint-venture partners).

Global margin reporting depended on efficiently managing costing practices for individual supply chains. The regional versus global sales picture differed dramatically, with added value generated from the UK, US and Asia-Pacific, individually and collectively. The result? Growing complexity! Data flow and process design, predictive tools, and the what-if toolkit (the key to this case study) all needed to be more fully integrated.

The oil company had an ambitious vision for improving its global margin reporting. It wanted reporting to provide margins at the variable cost level by customer and by product. It wanted quick reporting "snapshots" of market changes. It wanted to standardize financial reporting terms and policies so that its global margin framework was consistent from business to business. And finally, it wanted the ability to slice 'n dice information locally, regionally, and globally.

The company spent considerable time designing the specifications for its proposed global margin reporting improvements. As a first step, it chose in-house, prepackaged functionality. In addition, it opted for:

- *Information on sales data (volumes and revenues)*

- *Margin based on current month raw material costs*

- *Margin reporting when sales invoices are generated*

The oil company also chose to use variable margin calculation (VMC) – margin results are based on calculating "netback" at supply points minus full variable supply cost up to the last supply point. All netback components are related to an actual sales transaction. VMC is used to calculate the margin and is based on "monthly" average costs ("monthly" relates to the month the sale occurs). The VMC engine uses the following sources of information:

- *Bill of material for each product at each plant*

- *Routing information through the supply chain (plant to plant, plant to storage location, storage location to storage location)*

- *Inbound transaction costs (driven down to the product level)*

With its new margin reporting system in place, the company's calculation engine can now estimate production processing and transportation cost throughout its integrated supply chain. The result? Its new global margin model framework is now a reality.

As the case study shows, improving gross margin reporting across a complex supply chain is a demanding, but rewarding process. Many of the CFOs we work with face similar challenges as supply chain complexity increases, both internally and among collaborating companies. The CFOs we talk with are asking some tough questions:

- How do we estimate the value added between single entities and groups?

- How do we break down cost and profitability data by product and customer?

- How do we estimate transfer prices in a heterogeneous systems landscape?

- How do we deal with exceptions (joint ventures, tax and legal requirements)?

- How do we improve data quality while speeding up the group costing process so we can avoid the usual "end-of-the-month" panic?

As Figure 6.9 illustrates, new business analytics applications are making it far easier to manage and control the group costing process. Integrated analytics vendors now offer group costing applications which provide new flexibility and features without forcing you to jettison what you already have. These analytical applications build on a heterogeneous, reconcilable ERP infrastructure. They offer built-in currency conversion to group currency plus conversion to standard units of measure.

To achieve the full benefits of group costing applications, be sure to build in:

- Extensive syntax and plausibility checks on different levels

- Alert-based error detection linked to correction processes

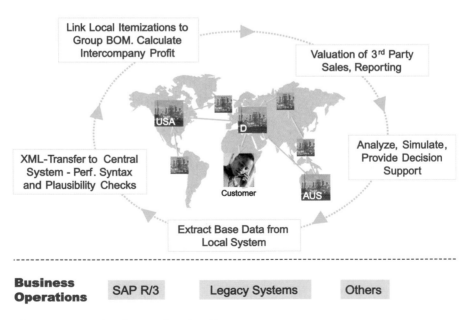

Figure 6.9   *The Group Costing Process*

- User-friendly navigation and interface capabilities

- A manual intervention mechanism at the group level (with audit trail)

- Fault tolerance through alternative valuation rules (previous period/ product group level/% share)

As your group costing solution evolves, it should provide drill-down insight to the lowest level. It should let you easily view item level and customer data with all linked characteristics. To ensure group-wide implementation, resist the temptation to go for a big bang. Instead, opt for a smooth run-up with incremental improvement.

ENRICHING PRODUCT LIFE CYCLE MANAGEMENT (PLM)

PLM analytics provides a holistic view of the economics of product life cycle – from new product planning through design to market launch (via production, service, and warranty) to final decisions on product withdrawal.

PLM is usually defined as covering:

- *Life cycle data management*: provides integrated product and process engineering capabilities, bills of material, routing and resource data, recipes, computer-aided design (CAD) models, and technical documentation. Product change management functions safeguard consistency of product information.

- *Life cycle collaboration*: internal and external partners can be linked virtually and in real time to give them shared access to project plans, documents, service bulletins, and other information.

- *Program and project management*: spans the entire product development process. Covers planning, managing, and controlling all product portfolios. Monitors project schedules, costs, operations, and processes.

- *Quality management*: provides integrated capabilities for comprehensive quality management. In addition to the classic forms of quality assurance, audits and other types of e-Quality management are also supported.

- *Asset life cycle management*: covers all performance requirements, including product-related maintenance services, management of machinery and equipment, and availability of plants and physical assets.

- *Environmental issues*: tracks health and safety data. Applies legal requirements to environment concerns, health and safety management.

CASE STUDY
It is the Development Process that Differentiates

In an interview[5] with Michael D. Capellas, Chairman and CEO of Compaq Computer Corporation prior to the merger with Hewlett-Packard, he discusses his company's PLM strategy.

"Poor product design will haunt you throughout the entire life cycle. But good product development processes will help you not only save your manufacturing costs downstream but also give you the ability to adapt products to ensure long product life. With the Internet, you have a fundamental shift toward com-moditized distribution and manufacturing.

For example, if we look at the manufacturing of laptop computers today, it is the development process that differentiates. Every laptop is produced in a similar factory in Taiwan. The key is to reuse standard components across different products to lower costs and develop new products much faster. You start with the same, solid base for multiple products, and then you mass customize for multiple markets.

What is more important for business success, time-to-market or product quality? In the old world, there used to be a trade-off between speed and quality. Today, you have to have both. I would also argue that a high-quality product can be taken faster to market because you do not have repetitive development tasks or extensive reworking. This not only helps you decrease time-to-market, but also provides an important boost to ramp. If you are redesigning products on the fly, with little regard for quality, you may be first to introduce the product. But you are never really the first in time-to-market because time-to-market means achieving the ramp volume you anticipated.

So what is Compaq's overall strategy for product life cycle management? A comprehensive strategy is critical. This strategy includes market research that shows exactly what your customer needs. It shows that you have developed the products not only from a design point of view, but also from a manufacturing point of view. It increasingly means that you are developing products that meet customers' product needs for service and support.

It also says that you understand that more and more customers require that you have a transition plan when you bring products to market – a plan that clearly protects the customer's investment so that when a product comes to the end of its life cycle, a customer does not have to spend an exorbitant amount of money to put the next generation in place. All this is part of an increased focus on return on investment.

We no longer implement large projects where the entire business is stopped for rollout. We are increasingly sensitive to the fact that implementing a new product should be a transitional process, not a start-and-stop one. We are also focusing on understanding the implications of how one product fits with another.

For example, if we introduce a new handheld product, we want to know how it works with a wireless infrastructure. This overall process flow is why portfolio companies are creating better products, as opposed to niche players. The Internet has extended the internal collaboration between engineering, manufacturing, and service to one of external collaboration. This is increasingly important as manufacturing is outsourced. Another major need is the tight and intelligent coupling between in-house development teams and the manufacturing teams that might be outside your company's four walls."

The ability to develop products quickly and cost-effectively has become a crucial factor for success. Companies must also offer products and services as complete solutions to boost customer loyalty and tap into new sources of revenue. Only seamless processes made possible by product life cycle management can meet these challenges head on.

Most cost-reduction opportunities occur early in the product life cycle, during the innovation window of concept design. Your opportunity to cut total life cycle costs diminishes over time. The positioning of the innovation window for life cycle cost determination is shown in Figure 6.10.

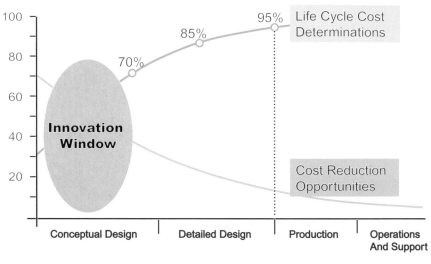

Source: DARPA Rapid Design Exploration + Optimization Project

Figure 6.10 *Life cycle Cost Determination*

With PLM analytics, your company can profit from:

- *Lower costs*: through the close integration within ERP of the PLM application with customer relationship management, supply chain management, enterprise resource planning, CAD, and supplier management

- *Reduced time-to-market*: through the exchange of up-to-date product information; faster, better decision-making; and greater control over product development and production ramp-up

- *Increased revenues*: thanks to the ability to develop innovative products more quickly and to spot new market opportunities more effectively

- *Improved product quality*: thanks to integrated quality management reaching into all phases of the product life cycle

- *Increased customer satisfaction*: through customizing products and extending customer service to include maintenance and technical support

Managing the innovation pipeline is a key issue for every company. The PLM analytics tool supports new product design and launch. Support for concurrent costing lets you calculate product costs early in development, when design changes are still possible, but data for costing is incomplete or non-existent. You can access costing data from any product data management system and set specific cost targets.

CASE STUDY
Product Life Cycle Costing

Nokia, the world leader in mobile phones, is known for its speed-to-market, leading-edge technology, and fertile innovation pipeline. Nokia is constantly fine-tuning its approach to product life cycle management by aligning product innovation and supply chain processes.

Nokia's overwhelming success in mobile communications has been attributed in large part to its emphasis on investment in R&D. Recently, its spending in this area was increased to EUR 3 bn or 9.6% of total net sales. Its highly skilled and motivated staff are another key asset. What makes Nokia special is its ability to synchronize the different functional players in bringing product to market. Nokia is developing an integrated costing approach taking advantage of the latest in financial analytics. For example:

- Material project leaders *are responsible for global sourcing for mobile phones. They have a background in the company's ABM methodology and use it in negotiating purchase agreements with suppliers. Negotiations with part-ners (internal and external) involve material pricing and related activities, which add on 30– 40% to material costs.*

  Negotiations focus on supplier performance as well as material price. The material project leader will challenge partners based on comparative supplier data reflecting total cost, material cost, activity cost. The same principle is used for the benchmarking of internal suppliers (comparing cost per phone in each plant).

- Logistics project leaders *manage the total demand-fulfillment process. They, too, have a background in ABM methodology. They are looking at Six Sigma initiatives. They measure on-time deliveries, manufacturing failure rates, costs per phone. There is an internal benchmarking system that compares 18 manufacturing plant results based on total costs per phone (including process costs). It also looks at inbound and outbound logistics costs. In some cases, it is cheaper to manufacture in Finland than in China once the extra delivery costs are factored into the production model.*

One aspect of the fulfillment process not modeled in the costing system that Nokia uses is the extra costs for customer-specific configuration. They need to separate orders with customer-specific requirements from standard orders and include the extra processes for customer-specific configuration.

- *Program project leaders are charged with overseeing R&D use the same costing techniques and systems as materials and logistics staff. R&D is a key issue at Nokia: 20,000 of the 56,000 staff worldwide work in R&D. For a new phone, they will estimate the product cost using concurrent costing and the activities required for the entire fulfillment process before production begins. This includes make-or-buy decisions for each component, quality cost, manufacturing processes, and logistics.*

Today, Nokia is pushing the innovation envelope still further by expanding their use of ABM – as an integral part of their decision support infrastructure – in addressing these issues: optimizing the product portfolio; matching current resources against future requirements; budgeting for new product development. For Nokia, integration of costing with its balanced scorecard is also a key issue. So is fully exploiting the benefits of Web-based reporting. Nokia has much to do to improve in these areas. Innovation and costing go hand in hand. Both are constantly changing. So even an industry leader can't afford to rest on its laurels!

IMPROVING HUMAN RESOURCE (HR) ANALYTICS

New HR analytics products[6] have a management by objectives (MBO) capability. This lets you streamline internal processes. MBO also frees personnel development and compensation management experts from administrative tasks by allowing them to use balanced scorecard data in evaluating employees and in goal-setting agreements. HR systems can also automatically transfer appraisal data to personnel development and compensation management applications.

All these advances mean that HR departments, too, face completely new tasks. It is no longer enough to support strategy by recruiting high-quality employees and containing personnel costs. Today, like everyone else, HR departments must ask themselves what part they can play in adding value and reaching enterprise goals. With a shift in direction and focus, an HR department can develop into an important link in the value chain – and position itself as consultant and partner for management and employees alike. The human capital analytics capability provides a vertical link between your goals for training and your workforce-management processes.

So why are HR analytics so important? Today's management systems were designed to meet the needs of stable enterprises that were changing incrementally. But you can't manage transformation strategy with systems designed for tactics. Consider these all too common performance obstacles:

- *The vision barrier*: only 5% of the workforce understand the strategy; 9 out of 10 companies fail to execute strategy.

- *The management barrier*: 85% of executive teams spend less than one hour per month discussing strategy.

- *The resource barrier*: 60% of organizations don't link budgets to strategy.

- *The people barrier*: only 25% of managers have incentives linked to strategy.

How do business analytics improve HR effectiveness and what do pre-packaged HR analytics offer? The answers may surprise you:

- *Workforce analysis* (planning, simulation and forecasting): allows you to analyze your current workforce with strategic planning tools, such as headcount planning and cost simulation.

- *Reporting and benchmarking*: reporting tools to track KPIs and bench-marking services to optimize enterprise-wide processes.

- *Strategic alignment*: keeps activities synchronized with corporate strategy by using workforce performance indicators.
- *Balanced scorecard techniques*: let you define targets, milestones, and KPIs.

CASE STUDY
Transforming HR into a Service Center

The key HR issue confronting this airline was cost pressure. Personnel costs and travel expenses were rising at an alarming rate. The solution proved to be creating an HR shared services organization. During the redesign, a set of problems very common to shared services surfaced. First, there was the issue of determining the prices and costs of the HR services and how to automate internal expense request and approval processes. A key financial challenge proved to be integrating procurement with HR recruitment, together with Web-based expense claims management. For HR service pricing, it was necessary to integrate HR costing applications with HR scorecard applications containing service volume and quality metrics.

The technical challenges: the company had already installed its ERP for financials and was implementing the activity-based costing module. They were to supplement this with modeling and simulation capabilities for pricing purposes and with drill-down capability to provide transparency on cost. This information was to be shared with their business partners – the new customers for the in-house HR service center.

To meet its financial and technical objectives, the company is developing its HR and financial analytics in stages, prioritizing its developments for quick wins. Not surprisingly, the first new services to be offered through this shared services center include payment processes and compensation. The next target will be personnel recruiting and assessment. Following on from that, it intends to address medical services, since frequent check-ups are vitally important for pilots, flight attendants, and staff in the airline industry. Once all these services have been implemented by the center, the company plans to design a user-friendly Web-based portal to encourage employee self-service.

The new integrated analytic software allows you to link the HR function with other functions in the organization – not just for transactional processing as in the past – but now for real value-added management tasks. Linking the HR function to the finance function. Linking HR functions with strategic functions.

GETTING STARTED: ANALYTICS CRITICAL SUCCESS FACTORS

Consider the following 10 critical success factors, outlined by W.H. Inmon in a recent article,[7] in designing and implementing a holistic and responsive analytics environment:

1. *Be aware that there is an important infrastructure behind analytics.* Beware the façade with no substance behind it. The value of analytics appears obvious, but the internal demands on your resources are deceptive: a large infrastructure is needed. Unfortunately, people buy "sizzle" without recognizing they need "a griddle and a fire."

   Many analytics software suppliers sell their products as if there were no infrastructure required, or as if the infrastructure suddenly and magically appears when needed. Not so! Therefore, the first critical success factor in building the analytics environment is recognition that an infrastructure in support of analytics is required – and that it is harder and more costly to build than it is to obtain the analytic application itself.

2. *The analytics infrastructure has a standard framework and features.* The world of analytics has some very predictable needs. These include: uniformity of meaning and definition, especially when it comes to important subject areas such as customer, product, and transaction. Completeness of data is also key. Limited data greatly limits the type of analysis that can be done. Ease of access is vital. If data is hard to access then analytical efficiency will be hampered. Flexibility is also key: limited analytic processing capabilities reduce data usage.

   In short, data that resides in the data warehouse provides an ideal basis for analytics. But the data warehouse does not exist in a vacuum. It is at the center of a larger architecture – the corporate information factory. The corporate information factory supports many types of informational processing, such as real-time processing, statistical processing found in exploration processing and data mining, departmental processing, and so forth.

3. *Business analytics must evolve.* Analytics needs to be developed in an iterative manner. The inevitable result? Requirements are not discovered until the user understands what the possibilities are. Once users see what can be done, they unleash a new set of requirements. By staging development, results are put in front of the user on a reasonably regular basis.

4. *Don't expect to get all the requirements in the first iteration.* Gather and analyze user community requirements as a starting point. It is a mistake to build analytics in isolation from end-users. If analytics are built in isolation, then the final results may prove irrelevant to user needs.

5. *Link analytics to other corporate data.* An analytics environment that stands alone has a limited life span and limited usefulness. Nevertheless, it is a real temptation to view analytics as a stand-alone application. Remember, however, that a superficial attempt at integration always yields disappointing results and leads to faulty decision-making. Thorough integration of data is required, for example at data structure, data code, and reference table, calculation, and semantics levels. This integration is necessary for compatibility, consistency, and uniformity.

6. *Business analytics depends on historical, as well as current data.* Historical corporate data is very important for providing insight and perspective, especially in the area of customer service. History about customers is important because consumers the world over are creatures of habit. The habits they form early in life are the key to their lifetime buying patterns. Understand a customer's history and you are in a position to predict the future. And once a corporation can anticipate the tastes and dislikes of a customer, then it can be proactive, not reactive.

   All this depends on historical data being readily available for analytic applications. Here, volume is a huge issue. As a rule, inactively used data far exceeds actively used data. Because of the cost of storage, be prepared to store inactive data in an inexpensive location. Usually, historical data has little or no documentation. Metadata describing the historical data needs to be stored for future analysis.

7. *Transaction performance must be factored into the analytics environment before the system is built.* Systems performance is always a key issue. In the online environment, performance means two to three seconds response time. In the data-mining world, responses may take longer. Performance expectations need to be spelled out at the start of the analytics exercise so that there will be no surprises at the final delivery of the system. The performance expectations of the organization are usually outlined in what is called a service level agreement (SLA). SLAs often include system availability parameters as well as performance parameters. It is noteworthy that the SLA for analytics will be different from the SLAs for other processing initiatives. Merely adopting the SLA found in the online environment will not suffice because the analytics workload is fundamentally different.

8. *Analytics can be purchased, developed internally, or both.* It is tempting to say that analytics software developed by an external vendor can be purchased off the shelf. There is much to recommend this approach. First, there is no development time. Second, the software is maintained by the vendor. Finally, the talent for developing such software is not usually available internally.

   But there are some problems with purchasing one-size-fits-all analytics solutions. The first problem: what competitive advantage is there in buying software that everyone else in the industry has access to? Another disadvantage: if a third-party vendor builds and maintains the software, how responsive to changes will the vendor be? One alternative is to purchase some portions of your analytics software and develop other parts internally. Internal development may be as simple as having information put on a spreadsheet.

9. *Analytics are intuitive and may defy standardized systems design.* Try as the systems developer may, a certain (and important!) part of analytics is informal. This is the area in which creative minds that use the analytics system branch out and extend its functionality. To a limited degree, spreadsheets capture this aspect of analytic processing. And those spreadsheets are found in the desks of a few individuals. This could be where you find real competitive advantage.

There are several problems with trying to incorporate informal analytics with formal analytics. For example, the statement of the problem being addressed by the informal part of the system is fluid. By the time the informal aspect is formalized, it has changed. Information that is useful today may not be useful tomorrow.

10. *Analytics must address both current and future requirements.* In order to be successful, analytics *must* not be locked into a rigid set of requirements. When analytics software becomes static, the solutions it provides quickly lose their immediacy and value. The technical and design foundation of analytics must accommodate change – and rapid change at that.

An overview of the analytics landscape from an applications viewpoint is shown in Figure 6.11. Analytics for operational functions are linked through financial processes to strategic analytics.

It is in analytics that the payoff of information processing becomes apparent, unlike the data warehouse environment, where cost justification is difficult to achieve. The analytics environment has two levels – a micro level and a macro level. Both levels have important value to decision-making.

So, analytics are flexible, actionable, real-time, accessible and integrated. They transform *data* into *information* into *knowledge* into *action*. Recent experience of implementations show by following these five steps you can help ensure success:

Step 1: Start with a business case   The challenge: to define the specific value proposition and the business benefits, based upon best practices and research. Focus on value-creating analytics across the value chain. The benefits should link the analytics investment to corporate value drivers and ROI.

Step 2: Plan your information strategy   Define with users (internal and external) their information requirements. Outline your target technical architecture. Formulate a clear process for mapping information needs to technical solutions. Identify common usage patterns and align them with the proposed solutions.

Step 3: Agree on governance and structure   Seek best practices for defining and implementing internal governance structures to guide

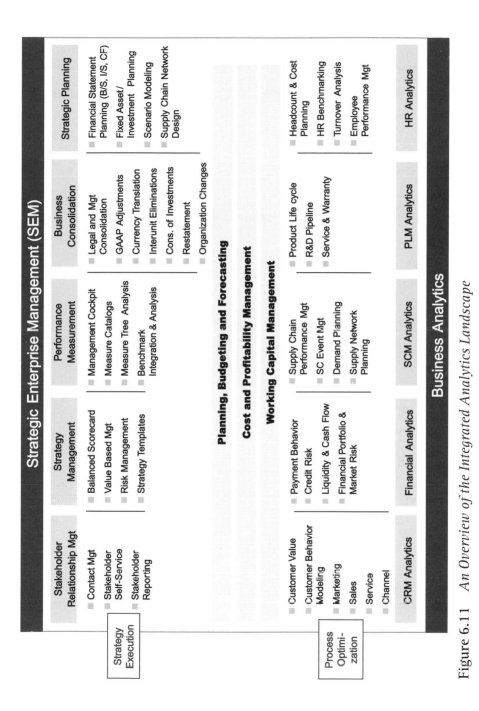

Figure 6.11 *An Overview of the Integrated Analytics Landscape*

239

business user and technology communities. Governance issues include: accountability and collaboration, and information governance – data stewardship, information consistency, security, and communication.

Step 4: Draft the architectural blueprints for conceptual and logical design
This blueprint serves as a framework and set of best practices to aid the definition of an integrated data model, set of information management processes, integration services, and analytical application architecture. This will support vendor and technology decisions.

Step 5: Take action!   Appoint a highly skilled and motivated project team. Deliver in small, high-impact, end-to-end solutions. Follow up quickly with timely training and skills development. Follow a solid methodology for sound project execution. Pay particular attention to the integration requirements of your ERP, CRM, and related applications.

These steps sound very formal. They are! Don't forget, many of these steps become iterative. For those parts of the analytics suite which are hard-wired into the organization and which support business processes on which others depend, structure and development discipline is essential. However, do leave scope for the individual to experiment and innovate. These one-off initiatives could be the secret to your future competitive advantage!

CFO CHECKLIST

GO HORIZONTAL WITH ANALYTICS ACROSS THE VALUE CHAIN
Span functional boundaries to build a better understanding of your value chain economics. Develop an analytics vision, focused on value creation. Evaluate the profitability of the extended enterprise system.

CHOOSE YOUR iANALYTICS STRATEGY
Decide between vendor-led, integrated application suites and best-of-breed, open systems frameworks. Bring your data warehouse investment alive! Use integrated analytics for preemptive decision-making. Separate business execution processes from business support processes.

LEVERAGE YOUR CRM INVESTMENT
Understand who your customers are and how they add value. Achieve line-of-sight across your entire value chain to optimize your marketing investment through a better understanding of end-consumer economics.

BE SURE YOUR SUPPLY CHAIN DESIGN IS RIGHT
Model structure, service, supply, and demand options using supply chain analytics. Boost overall performance by identifying supply chain constraints, savings in design opportunities, and working capital efficiencies.

REDEFINE THE ROLE OF FINANCE
Move from a spreadsheet mentality to a more dynamic, more robust and scalable decision support infrastructure. Use new technologies to integrate isolated, stand-alone financial tools and techniques. Leverage your prior investment in activity-based management, group costing, and customer lifetime value.

APPLY ANALYTICS TO THE INNOVATION PIPELINE AND
PRODUCT LIFE CYCLE
Consider the economics of each stage of your life cycle – from
new product planning to design to launch. Use concurrent costing
for integrated product and process engineering. Share
collaborative information internally and with external partners.
Relentlessly monitor financial performance over the asset life
cycle.

TRANSFORM HR INTO A SERVICE CENTER
Get the full benefits from HR. Select prepackaged analytics for
workforce planning, simulation, and forecasting; integrate HR and
finance with enterprise-wide performance management. Cut cost
and improve communications through the employee self-service
portal by adding analytical functionality on demand.

FOLLOW THE FIVE-STEP IMPLEMENTATION APPROACH
Build an infrastructure behind analytics – with data, process, and
technology. Develop analytical applications with users through an
iterative approach. Standardize and structure only where essential
for collaboration. Remember, truly successful cross-functional
analytics depend largely on intuition, creativity, and informality!

CHAPTER 7

Collaboration via the CFO Portal

BUILDING A PLATFORM FOR GLOBAL COOPERATION
Jochen Krautter, CFO
Henkel

Henkel is one of the world's leading manufacturers of cosmetics, toiletries, and homecare products. On the industrial side, the company makes adhesives and surface treatment products. Headquartered in Germany, it employs 60,000 people worldwide and has annual sales in excess of $10 bn. Jochen Krautter rose to his current position from a business rather than a financial grounding. Jochen has been a member of the executive board since 1992, with responsibility for the surface technologies business, information systems and the Latin America region. In 2000 he was appointed CFO of the Henkel Group.

His is a somewhat unusual background for a CFO. In particular, his former responsibility for Henkel's IT program gives him a unique insight into the convergence of information integration and finance. According to Jochen, his finance role has changed significantly: "As CFO, my main value drivers certainly must be business transactions. What has changed today is that I must now assume global responsibility, not only for general finance guidelines, but also for execution. Ever since we launched our shareholder value program, I have also been very involved in capital market management."

Beyond these changes, Jochen has also found himself heavily involved in redefining the finance function to embrace the new information integration possibilities that technology has created. In the past, Henkel had a relatively simple but nevertheless ambitious IT vision: the company set out to manage its businesses worldwide seamlessly in real time. The business requirement for IT was viewed from three levels: the transaction level, the communication level (networking), and the information level.

What is new today? With the emergence of the Internet, Henkel now has enormous opportunities for networking with external market partners, suppliers, and customers. Internet technology and portals provide the ability to run systems and processes in a totally integrated way. As a result, Henkel and Jochen, as CFO, are working toward a new vision for an informal enterprise: managing all key processes worldwide with seamless interfaces both internally and externally.

What does this mean in practical terms for running Henkel's diverse, world-wide operations? It means collaborative planning with suppliers; global management and delivery of inventories; and closer linkages with the supply chains of Henkel's far-flung customers. In addition to linking to supply chain partners up- and downstream through Web technology Henkel's ERP systems are consolidated in all regions.

As Jochen points out: "You have to know your customers extremely well in order to make all flows of information converge and achieve worldwide key account management. Ultimately, the goal is to have comprehensive data providing all information about every customer, wherever he or she enters our worldwide corporate network. This is a very painstaking process, but we are very committed to making it happen. As early as the mid nineties, we launched an 'International Data Harmonization' project."

Jochen goes on to say: "Business drives IT. IT must enable. We want to control our businesses globally, but to have this control, I need global and standardized information, and that means synchronized processes. And I must be able to control business events seamlessly and in real time. Whatever portal and systems solutions we develop need to be harmonized in 70 countries and must take into account country-specific legal and regulatory requirements. This is the big picture: worldwide standardization and harmonization of information and processes."

Henkel's portals and extranet solutions create exciting new opportunities for customer management and relationship building. These new tools support real-time collaborative planning and enable Henkel to continuously monitor customer service and product delivery. As a result, the company's employees at every level can keep customers fully informed about scheduling and order changes, about the availability of new products, and other important product information. Henkel's new systems and portal capabilities also provide its customers with other valuable benefits. As a result Henkel is able to maximise the use of its VMI (vendor managed inventory) capabilities with more customers which enables it to monitor the on-the-shelf inventories of its trading partners, incorporating an alert system which signals threshold values. This results in enormous productivity gains.

Internally, Henkel's finance function has also been transformed. Along with the impact of collaborative planning and supply chain integration, other finance responsibilities are benefiting from newly created portal and systems initiatives. As Jochen notes: "Within the Henkel Group, we do worldwide internal cash pooling. We collect our financial assets on a daily basis via a cash pool system with Citibank and Deutsche Bank. We exchange financial data with all our major trading customers.

We recently launched a portal project at Henkel, specifically for our order-to-cash processes; our goal is to provide a collaborative platform for community working. In addition to sharing knowledge across the organization, this portal initiative facilitates central services for answering questions, speeding up processes, and cutting costs. Ultimately, our plan is to integrate our multiple systems and processes into one seamless user interface – providing ease of access worldwide. Our business is necessarily complex, but our goal is to make things simpler for the user, whether that user is a finance executive within our company, a trading partner, or a customer. In a nutshell, we consider our worldwide ERP consolidation program enhanced by web technologies, using portals and extranet solutions, to be the best vehicle for the harmonization of information and the standardization of processes in order to maximise efficiency for Henkel and it's business partners."

In today's world, no one is an island. Every individual, every department, and every company is part of a larger value chain[1] that includes colleagues, customers, trading partners – even competitors. And today, more than ever, information is power: having the right information at the right time is paramount. All employees, from the CEO to the help desk analyst, need information to be effective. Certainly, the Internet has created explosive growth in the depth and breadth of information available. In fact, the sheer scale of this corporate data has emerged as one of the Internet's weaknesses as well as its strengths. Having virtually unlimited information is one thing, but sharing and integrating it to support faster, smarter decision-making, is something else entirely.

To thrive and compete, businesses desperately need to improve application services, integrate diverse sources of information, and empower users to access only what they need, when they need it, wherever they need it. Companies also need proactive data systems that guide users to information instead of forcing them to conduct extensive searches or data manipulation. To accomplish this challenge only provide the information relevant to each user, based on their business role or function in the organization.

Now, for the first time in the history of IT, there is a tool that puts the user in the data driver's seat: *the portal*. Portals offer a single point of entry for every user across all systems, providing the resources to integrate and deliver data quickly and easily. And within a portal, these resources can be harnessed using a role-based approach that hides unnecessary complexity from the user. Something an intranet could never deliver. The information can now be structured by tasks and responsibilities instead of system boundaries. Thus the portal has enormous potential for cutting across business units and functions, for supporting data management and transactions, and for sharing knowledge. What's more the process chain no longer stops when it reaches corporate boundaries: external communities can be integrated into an enterprise portal just as easily as internal ones.

DOUBLING PRODUCTIVITY

Who leads portal development? Some say the CFO. Isn't this IT's job? How can portals help my finance group and me in my role as CFO? Which portal strategy will give us the best results? How do we leverage portal technology to transform our business?

We hear these kinds of questions from clients again and again. They underscore the need for some practical guidelines for portal design and use – and that's exactly what we intend to deliver in this chapter. But first, let's build the "business case" for portals. In our view, the case is a rock solid one. The question isn't whether or not portals are necessary or if they offer a return on investment (ROI) – it's how quickly they can be established – and how big the ROI will be. Let's take a look at the major strategic benefits that portals offer:

- Closer collaboration among staff, business partners, and customers
- More efficient intelligence gathering and distribution
- Rapid data integration, making it more useful and timely
- Cost reduction and increased efficiency
- Better, faster decision-making
- Connectivity with shareholders and financial markets

The list of benefits goes on and on! In short, portals are exactly what the name implies: gateways to untold riches in the realms of information, customer data and relationship building, operating efficiency, and enhanced productivity. For example, portals can:

- *Boost business efficiency*: they let you gather and integrate information from diverse sources and systems so that it can be accessed by single or multiple users via a Web browser or mobile devices. Users can receive updates, research solutions, track projects, and respond to business events instantly.

- *Enhance the quality of your business relationships*: portals let you strengthen relationships and use advanced processes through real-time collaboration across functions and businesses. They transcend traditional enterprise boundaries by enabling users to work seamlessly across the value chain.

- *Maximize the value of your business*: portals leverage your physical and intangible assets to improve both short-term results and long-term ROI.

Portals empower users to transform data into knowledge and knowledge into decisions – and action.

A study[2] of the impact of portals on selected business processes showed a doubling in productivity. The study compared more traditional ERP systems with role-based portals for three separate applications involving the employee, the sales representative, and the general manager. The results for experienced users are shown in Figure 7.1. For inexperienced staff the differences proved to be even higher. The portal reduced processing time from 40 to 60%. In addition to doubling productivity, the enterprise portal also helped users to better understand their role within their companies. This dramatic increase in productivity was the result of the following portal capabilities:

- *Single point of access*: there was only one point of access – via a Web browser – for all applications, content, and services.

- *Single sign-on*: users only had to log onto the portal once to access all other systems.

- *Personalized and role-based user interface*: the portal provided personalized access to all relevant activities, applications, information, and business processes. Since they were assigned special roles with specific menu entries, end-users didn't have to navigate through the system to

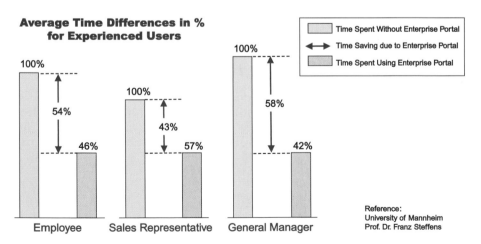

Figure 7.1 *Enterprise Portal: Doubling Productivity*

perform their tasks. All business functions related to their work were accessible from a user-specific menu structure.

- *Integration*: the portal coordinated internal and external data sources, research information, and applications, as well as their underlying systems.

- *Drag and Relate*: thanks to this feature, the portal integrated business software and Web-based resources. A task could be easily transferred from one application to another for further processing.

- *iViews*: iViews are simple and intuitive Web applications or documents that provide users with an instant overview and access to important information.

Intranet capabilities and information-based aggregation are still relevant in gathering and organizing data, but portals have made it possible to advance interactions with colleagues, customers and partners in important ways. For example, a portal enables a business to organize and provide data efficiently.

For example, a company might decide to offer online bill presentment and payment as well as dispute management on their web site. They will face the following direct and indirect benefits:

- Direct benefits – savings of up to 70% for bills sent via the internet instead of paper, improved cash flow as a result of reduced Days Sales Outstanding (DSO), dramatically reduced costs per dispute case because all dispute cases come in and can be traced through one channel (and not by a combination of e-mail, telephone, fax etc.)

- Indirect benefits - such as improvements for the customers. Customers can arrange payment, checkup and settlement of bills and, since all of these steps can be done electronically on the biller's website, the customer has better control of the timing of payments and management of outbound cash flow.

CHOOSING THE RIGHT PORTAL

Today, everyone is a knowledge worker. For the first time in the history of IT, there is a technology suite base that uses common, message-based infrastructure for integration – of portals, Web applications, exchanges, and IT infrastructure. Portals put users into the driver's seat when performing their daily tasks, whether they are CFOs or call center representatives. Improved access to application services and integration are the keys to fully opening the door to the diverse information users need within an extended enterprise. Via the portal, these users can be notified proactively, alerted to relevant events, and guided through a proactive resolution path.

When we analyze the typical work patterns of different users today, we can separate information sources into four categories: applications and legacy databases, business intelligence, unstructured documents, and Web content and services. These *four pillars*[3] of the enterprise portal are illustrated in Figure 7.2.

Pillar 1: Transactional systems and legacy database access   Enterprise applications encompass both critical information and the logic required for meeting transactional needs. Legacy databases contain information

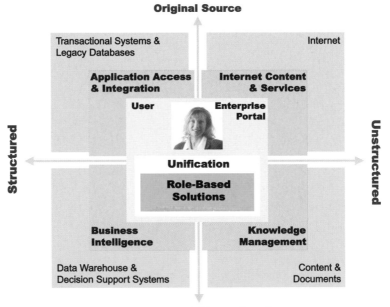

Figure 7.2   *The Four Pillars of the Enterprise Portal*

which is manipulated through a variety of codes, screens, and reports – all too arcane to be replicated. Yet, these systems represent an enterprise's informational backbone – all the data required for day-to-day operations. Most organizations amass hundreds or thousands of these data sources through normal growth or acquisition. In most cases, the data lacks consistency and the systems are so diverse that the average user is familiar, at most, with only two or three applications.

Pillar 2: Business intelligence   Most business events require a broader perspective than can be achieved through a single transaction record. This perspective encompasses internal patterns or industry trends, which help alert users to situations well before they prove problematic or even harmful. Enterprises use a variety of metrics to measure performance and gauge where change has been effective. But, most important, they want to integrate information observed through the rear-view mirror with current situational data in order to drive the enterprise forward safely and accurately. This requires a business intelligence platform that can aggregate information and simulate the impact of current events and data on the future.

Pillar 3: Knowledge management   In every company, massive amounts of unstructured information exist in a variety of documents. Employees, partners, and industry sources generate this information constantly. Some of this data must be aggregated, classified, and disseminated to relevant parties. Users want on-demand access to that information through a variety of seamless search capabilities that approximate natural language searches. Within the enterprise portal, all data is accessed through a single interface, making knowledge sharing and active collaboration a reality.

Pillar 4: Web content and services management   Much of the information a company needs comes from external sources. Employees are accustomed to gathering what they need from a variety of sites. They have their own trusted locations, such as my.yahoo.com, where they can access data and services. The same features that websites have developed to attract and retain users (such as "stickiness"), are now being applied to portals to enhance their ease of use in viewing information and making decisions. Just as knowledge management systems offer a hierarchy of unstructured documents, so Yahoo! for example, provides a similar hierarchy of Web content. The enterprise portal connects directly to the full range of Web services. This means that as the content and structure of Yahoo! change, so will the information offered via the enterprise portal.

Seamless navigation across multiple applications can only be achieved by creating a unified world of data. To integrate these four information sources and to better pinpoint key data and insights, an abstraction layer is used. This layer correlates and analyzes the data and logic received from these sources. This layer also "knows" users, their profiles, their authority, and their requirements to fulfill a function or a request. It can present data and logic in effective ways whenever a user requests information or when a business needs to deliver data to users based on ongoing business events. *Focus on total cost of ownership (TCO).* When evaluating different portal vendors one of the major decision criteria should be TCO. The following case study clearly makes the point.

CASE STUDY
Total Cost of Ownership: Making the Portal Business Case

Portal solutions are about more than just technology. They are about content. The company profiled here had carefully compared different technology vendors. Some offered excellent technical features for manipulating, retrieving, and visualizing information. Others excelled in providing connectivity with a variety of information sources over the Internet. Still others provided strong integration with existing ERP applications. However, for this company, the overriding consideration was content. The CFO and CIO together chose a portal that provided out-of-the-box, ready-to-run standard premium content. Nothing had to be built from scratch, making the total cost of ownership and installation very reasonable.

The business case focused on two work environments: on the one hand the workplace of a manager in administration and on the other of a plant manager. They were looking for the following benefits: saving money by replacing paper-based reporting and providing their managers with real-time data access to enable them to base decisions on high quality, detailed and up-to-date information. Data access would be possible via an easy-to-use and intuitive interface so that they did not have to train their users longer than one day. They wanted to ensure that all managers are better informed, always aware of their KPI's, the situation on their cost center, budgets and project status in their own area of responsibility. Additionally, tools for monitoring and initiating of administrative processes would be made available.

The ROI calculation showed a positive net cash flow in year 1, even after taking into account costs incurred from the pilot's rollout and detailed user involvement. Benefits were found to be greatest in the areas of financial and cost accounting, as well as through process integration. The pilot and test phase lasted three months and was rapidly followed by a full production system with integration to ERP and other transaction-processing systems.

In summary, the portal connected employees to systems through a uniform, global access point. Employees perceived heterogeneous system landscapes as homogenous. There was less disruption and less training time required following replacement of legacy systems with new ones. Certain relevant legacy systems were retained and made accessible to a broader group of users than ever before.

Portals abound, but their capabilities vary greatly. Competitive businesses demand more from a portal than Web-enabled access to applications. Next-generation enterprise portals offer far more: they can unify information, applications, and services from heterogeneous systems to promote efficient collaboration, better decision-making, and faster responses to critical business events.

Tasks that traditionally require navigating through multiple systems are now accomplished with a few clicks of the mouse. The outcome is quicker, the results more accurate, and the entire process remarkably efficient. By combining powerful enterprise solutions with data warehousing, reporting and analysis, and prebuilt business content, portals deliver immediate, out-of-the-box value. Beyond this, they let you leverage your investments in data warehouses and enterprise applications.

The importance of prepackaged business content and its delivery via portal applications is illustrated in Figure 7.3. This figure shows the relationship between technology platform and business content – referred to as iViews - and the role-based approach to portal design.

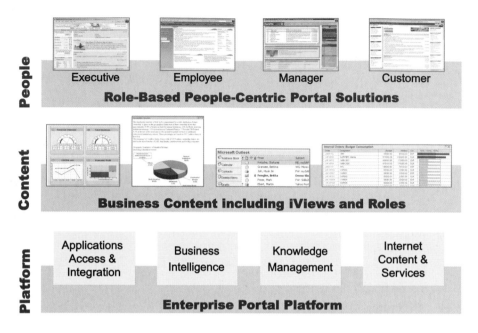

Figure 7.3   *Business Content Delivered for the Portal Platform*

INTEGRATION OUTWEIGHS BEST-OF-BREED TECHNOLOGY

Portal content must streamline access to the business processes that users inside and outside your company need most – whether this involves applications, data, documents, or the Internet. Delivery of this content, tailored to the specific roles and responsibilities of users, results in better efficiency, decisions, and customer service.

In the age of e-Business, companies are turning to enterprise portals to create order out of the chaos of information overload. They want to give users across the value chain a single point of access to the information they need to do their jobs. Access is nice, but let's face it, users' responsibilities are diverse and demanding. What they *really* need are tools to streamline and accelerate the many tasks required of them, regardless of what applications, information, and services are needed to complete those tasks.

In addition to a powerful portal platform, companies need sophisticated portal applications – and content. Delivery of standardized data saves companies time and money in developing portal content and quickly empowers users to take advantage of rich, new data at the touch of a mouse. The basic building blocks of portal content are mini-portal applications or Web services, which retrieve and push answers to individual questions to users from any and all information sources.

Some portal vendors offer thousands of mini-portal applications as standard delivered content. This type of input can simplify tasks, such as creating an expense report – or it can alert users to critical events, such as an overdue payment. Packages of mini-portal applications exist for horizontal functions, such as employee self-service, manager self-service, and collaboration – as well as for vertical functions, such as financials, HR, and e-Commerce. Since every organization is unique, off-the-shelf packages must be modified to create custom portal applications or extend applications as business needs evolve.

THE PERSONALIZED DESKTOP

As a portal enables user-centric presentation of services and applications through the role concept, people will be provided with a working environment suiting their function in the enterprise[4]. But the role concept alone is not sufficient, not all employees performing the same function need the same information. For example, each sales manager should oversee only his or her respective area of responsibility – such as a specific region or customer group. Therefore it is crucial to filter information so that users only see what is relevant to them. Within a portal this is achieved through personalization.

Since the user's role and area of responsibility are known centrally, the enterprise can provide employees with a personalized portal that suits the user's basic requirements. Beyond this, end-users can further adapt their portal to their personal needs or preferences. All this results in a tailor-made desktop through which people can now manage even highly complex tasks in heterogeneous system landscapes. This opens the door to new opportunities for decentralization of processes, employee empowerment, and self-service scenarios.

For example portals can fundamentally change quite ordinary administrative tasks and turn them into value-added collaborative processes. Take the following case study as an example.

CASE STUDY
A Technology Services Provider Transforms Internal Service
Processes

A leading European technology company wanted to use portals to transform its internal service request process. The problem it wanted to eliminate was simple, but troublesome: it lacked a standardized process for making requests for internal changes. As a result, considerable clerical and management time was spent updating systems, communicating via e-mail and telephone, and managing paperwork. The individual responsible for initiating a change had to contact the relevant clerk in the central department. For example, when an employee was transferred from one department to another, the employee's manager would have to send e-mails to (and call) the person responsible in every department involved. The status of the task was time-consuming to track. The existing process (pre-portal) is illustrated in Figure 7.4.

When a portal was introduced for such requests, the entire process changed dramatically – and definitely for the better! The manager involved needed only

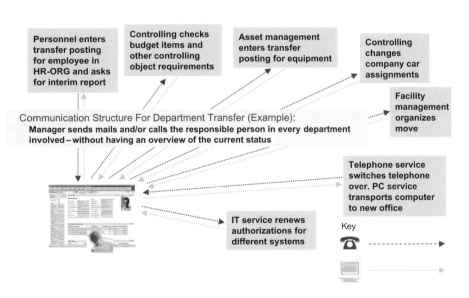

Figure 7.4 *Self-Service: Internal Service Request Scenario (Pre-Portal)*

to send one communication, a form to be filled in online in the portal. This form was then instantly distributed electronically to all the departments involved. The status of the request was always available via the portal. This particular reengineered process passed the department transfer through the HR function for records and maintenance, the finance function for budgetary control, the telephone service department, and, finally, the facilities function for physically relocating the employee.

The benefits? Management time was released, administrative and clerical costs were cut, and action was taken more quickly and decisively. Back-office resources were freed up to focus on value-adding tasks, and communication between the portal and the ERP system was substantially streamlined. Today, the process is decentralized and employees are empowered to initiate a wide range of internal service requests.

The company now enjoys the benefits of globally standard content and standard administrative processes. Portal applications were piloted first in one location covering a relatively small number of users and implementation was quickly rolled out on a global scale. Using this portal strategy, the company cut costs for processing employee changes by 50%.

As this company learned, portals can add value to processes which cross a number of functions. For example, manager self-services within an enterprise portal can streamline administrative tasks, particularly between managers and central departments, such as finance and HR. The net result? Central departments have better control of processes, and receive fewer questions regarding the status of requests. Thus, central resources that used to be tied up in administrative duties are now available to support more strategic tasks, such as projects driven by the CFO.

Take another example - how can portals help you to push compliance to a central travel policy in your organization? Wouldn't it be smart to offer value-added services for travellers? Travellers would use the portal for online booking of hotels, flights or car rental. They could plan complete business trips (maps, guides, information about flight status, weather, visa status, vaccination requirements, etc). Your employees would be highly motivated to use the portal: these central services would save their time and provide them with additional information. You will notice the positive affect on your travel budget - the subsequent bookings would comply with centrally managed travel policies.

WHY SHOULD THE CFO DRIVE PORTALS?

What value can you, as CFO, gain from portals? A better question: what have you been doing to increase the financial information available to your staff and across your company? Most likely, you first worked with a paper general ledger, then with an electronic general ledger. Later, you started using stand alone spreadsheet applications for costing and simulation. Today, your cost accounting applications are integrated into your ERP system. You've made lots of progress, but not enough!

Let's view this from a different perspective. Users. Who is really working with this information in your company? Perhaps it's 30 people in all – most of them financial professionals, such as controllers or bookkeepers. How do you distribute this information to more people? You make paper printouts. But in doing this, you actually *reduce* the amount of information available. Why? The printout is static, not dynamic. It does not let you sort data, drill down to gather integrated information, or set any alert parameters. As Figure 7.5 shows, the greater the number of information users, the greater the value of fully tapping into information deployment technology.

How do you distribute more valuable financial data more widely? Via an enterprise portal. This incredibly flexible vehicle doesn't just allow you to reach more people, it lets you give them richer, more valuable information – and then lets them enrich it still further. Users, for example, can set up alerts geared to their specific needs.

Squeezing maximum value out of your financial data may require some work up-front, but it is definitely worth the effort! Non-financial users, for example, may require different applications and reports than your staff does. This is because occasional users – and that is who we are talking about here – will need information that is different in its focus and structure. Tools for non-financial users will be less powerful but more intuitive and easier to use than those appropriate for, say, a cost accountant. Only few portal vendors offer portal solutions for occasional users out-of-the-box, which will help to increase the ROI of portal projects.

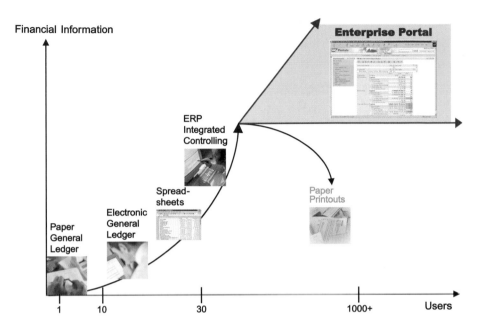

Figure 7.5   *From "More Information" to "Information Deployment"*

Consider the steps that the CFO of a global beverage manufacturer took to automate dissemination of performance-related data to his global finance team. And how, when the new finance portal proved to be a huge success, the company rolled it out to support decision-makers worldwide.

CASE STUDY
CFO Portal for Self-Service Decision Support

A global beverage manufacturer recently underwent a merger, leaving it with finance operations in 15 countries and non-standardized processes and systems. Finance staff found it difficult or impossible to access all the information they needed to operate effectively and deliver value-added services. Furthermore, there was little sense of community within the finance function and little opportunity for sharing knowledge and expertise.

As head of IT and a key player in planning e-Business strategy, the company's CFO was well placed to initiate a solution: an enterprise information portal that equips each finance professional with an intelligent website. The portal was designed to connect the CFO and his team to useful data and tools, based on four priorities:

1. Stepping up decision support capability: *users now have access to mission-critical performance data refreshed on a continuous basis, making it possible to monitor key performance indicators (KPIs) dynamically and to conduct scenario modeling.*

2. Gathering intelligence from external sources: *the portal combines up-to-date corporate information drawn from internal sources with relevant industry news, economic indicators, media comment, and investor alerts. The portal also supplies external benchmarking data on financial management best practices.*

3. Facilitating collaboration among finance staff: *bulletin boards, video-conferencing, and virtual team rooms now bring people together to interpret incoming results and intelligence. The CFO uses the portal to provide regular business updates and to host question-and-answer sessions.*

4. Meeting personalized data and communication needs: *individuals can self-generate content through searches and personalized feeds. Along with e-mail, they also have access to other tools for handling informal tasks, such as tracking portfolios of shares.*

How did the CFO make all this happen quickly and efficiently? By turning to portal specialists for advice on both design and implementation. The key to success? Addressing users' most important needs, rather than trying to build in all relevant information right away. This led to quick wins and avoided a lengthy content-management exercise. Phase 1 of the portal project focused on improving awareness of newly devised KPIs for the merged business, in order to deliver better reporting, budgeting, and forecasting.

The project team moved quickly: in just five weeks, the finance portal was up and running. Acceptance and enthusiasm for this new tool were high. Its winning strategy? Taking a practical approach that limited initial functionality but captured the company's style and ethos. A snapshot of KPI data was used to road-test the solution and confirm navigability. The portal was Web-enabled from the outset, with high-quality visual presentation and an intuitive organizing structure, helping to excite demand among users.

The same team of senior finance people that defined the portal's requirements in Phase 1, also worked on Phase 2. During this follow-on stage, detailed technical architecture was developed. At this point, the team made a critical decision: the portal was linked to an operational data store for real-time capture of both KPIs and information from finance databases.

By this time, finance staff in the group's different companies were finding it easier to work across international boundaries. Their standing with business managers was also improving, thanks to their newfound ability to provide insights into the factors underpinning financial results and targets. The CFO readily gained board approval for Phase 3, a year-long undertaking. During this phase, the portal will be integrated with enterprise-wide systems beyond the finance organization, so that it can be accessed by other functional teams, including marketing and HR.

This success story offers some important lessons. First "sell" the benefits of portal usage upfront by designing a pilot project that has high value and visibility. Second, involve end-users in portal planning and design. And finally, invest strategically in giving users access to high-priority functions that make their work easier and foster collaboration. In the case of the company described above, the drive to put valuable information at the fingertips of more employees is amply repaying the investments of time and money required. The CFO sums it up nicely: "An enterprise information portal is one of today's most powerful tools for enabling the kind of knowledge-based collaboration on which e-Businesses will thrive."

Collaborative processes in finance that lend themselves to inclusion in a portal range from investment management to closing/accounts consolidation. In the next case study we will see an approach via a collaborative platform called the corporate finance portal. How can such a portal solve existing problems in the relationship between a parent company and its subsidiaries? Processes in this relationship include management accounting processes:

1. Annual planning

2. Rolling forecast

3. Cash-flow analysis

4. Management reporting

as well as accounting processes:

1. Consolidation

2. Period-end activities

3. Invoice processing

4. External reporting

The portal addresses problems and challenges that aggravate or complicate daily work. We all know that *forecasting* and *budgeting* consume tremendous resources, occupying finance staff for most of the year. In the pre-portal financial environment, historical data was not easy to access or compare. Simulation tools and other utilities supporting the local specialist did not exist. On top of all this, heterogeneous system landscapes multiplied, inhibiting efficient data gathering and distribution. Moreover, multiple data entry often resulted in inefficiencies and errors. Concurrent access to spreadsheet-based forms created severe consistency problems. Either the form was locked, resulting in a deadlock for all other users, or the last user to save the spreadsheet would overwrite previous changes.

Consolidation processes consume much of the year and even then do not fit differing requirements. The main challenge for all participants is working with consistent databases. Currency translation inconsistencies, differences between internal and legal reporting, and other problems, can all slow down data delivery. Centralized organization puts pressure on subsidiaries with respect to prompt *period-end activities* without providing concise time schedules. Sound chronological ordering is often missing in critical documents. In most cases, this information is inaccessible via the corporate intranet.

The area of *cash-flow analysis* produces frequent duplication and con-fusion. Unequal valuation standards and amortization methods, as well as different local legal regulations for accruals, are critical issues. Often, they make daily loads exceptionally cumbersome.

In the accounting area, *invoice processing* often causes problems because much-needed, standardized processes for dunning and claims doesn't exist. Very often, subsidiaries have no choice about whether to accept services by the parent company or to buy them from an external supplier. After consolidation, the finance staff of a subsidiary may face the problem of reconciling varying reporting periods and definitions within and between its organization and its parent company. Repeatedly, central specialists require *reports* that differ from those needed by local top management.

Improvements in these vital areas touch on only the most urgent obstacles preventing collaboration between a corporate center and sub-sidiaries in a company's financial community. The following case study exhibits some direct benefits from providing a platform for global collaboration in a group's finance community.

CASE STUDY
A Global Manufacturer Develops a Corporate Finance Portal

This multinational wanted to speed up its corporate finance processes. Head-quartered in Germany, the company had more than 1,000 subsidiaries world-wide and coordination was a big issue. This is why the company wanted a portal for worldwide information exchange. The aim was to unify application and information stores into a single, simple "cockpit" for driving the consolidation processes. To quote the group financial controller: "We wanted to establish a state-of-the-art communication forum for finance and accounting to improve performance and quality of financial processes, increase knowledge sharing in the corporate finance function, and strengthen the group's financial community worldwide."

The situation before the portal: access across the intranet to specific infor-mation required by a variety of users for the closing process was difficult; much of the information valuable to the process wasn't easy to find, and some wasn't used at all or was difficult to retrieve. Communication between employees involved in the consolidation process was often slow or unclear. After implementing the corporate finance portal, the decentralized subsidiaries were able to contribute to corporate-wide processes more quickly and efficiently.

The company's portal strategy was twofold. Firstly, a direct exchange was built for sharing relevant unstructured material. This was done by bringing together all the group's content management solutions - for example accounting procedures, timetables, definitions and charts of accounts - into one portal. This supported financial collaboration around the world for planning, closing and consolidation. Besides that, the stored information was reduced from 14 gigabytes to 0.5 gigabytes by eliminating multi-copies and by establishing a process for controlled deletion of outdated information. The second step was to focus the portal development on the integration of structured reporting and process interventions - collaboration of the worldwide finance community through the corporate finance portal.

The ultimate benefits included fundamental improvements in quality and timeliness. Relationships between the corporate center and the subsidiaries improved and now there is a healthy balance between user control content ("pulled" information) and news distributed by the central corporate finance function ("pushed" information).

Figure 7.6 demonstrates the potential reach of the corporate finance portal as a collaborative space for streamlining processes and information flows.

To ensure that the corporate finance portal will be used by subsidiaries, it is mandatory to provide local specialists with *additional services*. Some examples might include offering issue resolution, decentralized creation of mailing lists, or the ability to register for functionally oriented or centrally hosted services, such as a currency simulation tool or a calculator supporting lease-or-buy decisions. Other ways to enrich the value proposition of a corporation finance portal include knowledge sharing or advanced training, for example.

The case studies in this chapter clearly indicate that the CFO will not only benefit from enterprise portal projects indirectly through cost reductions but that there are also a multitude of *direct benefits for CFOs themselves.*[5]

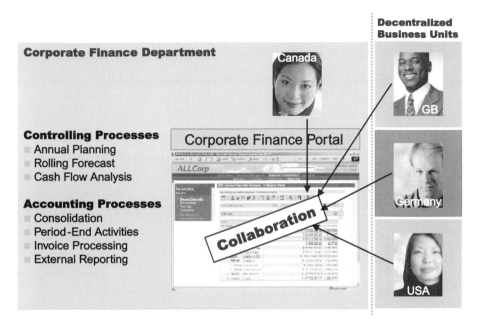

Figure 7.6 *The Corporate Financial Portal – A Collaborative Forum to Streamline Processes and Information Flow.*

These include performance monitoring applications even in heterogeneous system landscapes (after mergers, for example), a platform for global collaboration in processes like group consolidation, and freeing-up of finance professionals by providing decision support and - service applications through a portal (see the TransAlta case study below). Therefore, from our experience of portal implementation projects, the CFO should always make sure to get involved from the very beginning.

A JOURNEY, NOT A DESTINATION

Start small – think big! Experience has shown that powerful portals tend to grow organically. Those that are seen as corporate success stories have been implemented to react quickly to take advantage of hard business opportunities. They have been launched with minimal effort and cost. And, most important, they are not viewed negatively by staff as a cost-reduction tool, but as a positive means of individual and collective empowerment. As all users will learn from using collaborative applications through a portal there will be user-driven process innovation. Therefore portal solutions should not be seen as a one-time deliverable with a fixed design, but as flexible and adaptable solutions to immediate and long-term needs.

Start with initial design concept and planning   Use small, prepackaged portal building blocks known as mini-portal applications or iViews. These can be put on any portal page. In addition there is a navigation structure between portal pages. Even the combination of several portal pages and the navigation between them is reusable. These so-called worksets can then be reused to support different roles, such as enabling a sales manager and a production manager to monitor their own cost centers.

Move on to prototyping   Creating a prototype on paper is a good way to begin. This involves presenting prebuilt mini-portal applications in printed form and encouraging users to arrange them into simulated portal pages. Consider setting up informal prototyping workshops. In this kind of brainstorming environment, potential users can freely discuss what information they really need and what's missing from the portal prototype. They can also gain a "feel" for what a portal can offer them and how it can make their work both easier and more productive.

Involving users in this very concrete way helps them understand the business value and benefits that a portal can provide. Train users during this prototyping phase to experiment with the portal's exciting capabilities. Don't just consult them on the design. Encourage your users to *think portal* and you will be amazed at how much value they can contribute to reengineering your business process content.

After prototyping, move on to role definition   After a prototyping workshop, which focuses mainly on content and applications, you can specify the functional roles that need to be addressed first. Try to reuse as much of the predesigned content – the work sets – as possible. Here are some helpful comments from users attending a recent portals workshop:

> "I want a simple, Web-based tool for getting my job done fast. I only want to see the things that are relevant to my role as a purchasing agent pushed to my desktop."

"I want to have a single point of access to all of the internal and external functions and services related to my job."

"I am looking for a personalized work environment where I can customize the way I see things and add functionality as I need it."

Enterprise portals typically involve role-based user interfaces – these simplify application and information access. Only by creating roles can you deliver different types of content to different groups of users. This approach lets you define roles according to user responsibility and fields of interest. The benefit? Tailored content based on individual needs and community-specific roles. Remember that users can be assigned to more than one role. Also remember to enforce some measure of discipline through a role administrator.

The next step in portal development is personalization Although you reuse roles for many users, each user sees only his or her own area of responsibility. This is possible through personalization. By setting user parameters, for example, managers will only see their own cost centers.

The final step is technology integration As your portal evolves and wins acceptance, you will want to integrate more and more information sources. Start with those systems that can be easily linked to standard, pre-built content. Then expand capabilities to include more information sources and systems based on user demand (consider revisiting the prototyping process). Keep in mind that you can bring information from different sources into one portal page. This enables you to cut information by topics, not by system boundaries. For example, you can combine cost center reports from your ERP system with information from your costing department supplied through your intranet system.

When you define the scope of a portal project, take small steps, but think big. This strategy will maximize the benefits by giving you quick wins. It will also lead to continuous improvement. After you have defined the total scope of your enterprise portal, segment development into easy-to-manage phases. When you prioritize these phases, take a careful look at end-user commitment. Implement according to user priorities; ROI is important, but it should not override user needs, since user motivation is critical for success.

CASE STUDY
Evolution not Revolution: Designing a Global Portal with
Small Building Blocks

*The Freudenberg Group is a manufacturing conglomerate. It produces every-
thing from household products to rubber floorings, circuit boards, and lubri-
cants. A family owned company, it has sales in excess of $4 bn and 30,000
employees scattered among 244 companies in 41 countries. To quote a senior
executive on the company's strategic vision: "Throughout the workplace
environment, we're organizing ourselves more and more in networks and working on a project basis in global teams. So it makes good sense to exchange
existing knowledge and experience within the whole Group, and to tackle new
undertakings together. This should foster our portal."*

*Freudenberg comprises a high number of small, results-driven business units.
Organization hierarchies are relatively flat, but increasingly, these business
units need to collaborate globally. Virtual global development teams have been
formed to expand and retain technical product knowledge, to cope with expanding information flow, and to reduce costs. Portal technologies were the obvious
solution for promoting greater communication and collaboration. Making information available more quickly by designing more efficient work processes was
the name of the game.*

*The objective: to link employees, customers, partners, and suppliers across
Freudenberg's far-flung organization. To quote the company's IT managing
director: "Setting up our portal is a long-term project. That's why it is important
to implement an innovative solution that we can easily incorporate into our
environment and that will still be viable well into the future." He characterized
the implementation as an evolutionary development, taken in small steps, over
short time frames. In short – a living project.*

*The portal planners took their first cautious step toward an inter-company
communication platform. Now that this first step has been completed, they have
grown more ambitious. In the next stage of portal development, they expect to
take a quantum leap which, in a short space of time, will deliver an enterprise
portal that spans the enterprise's global operations. The portal will facilitate
knowledge management, software infrastructure design, communication,*

training, and marketing. Why does Freudenberg expect to be that fast? It is because they use as many pre-built portal applications from their ERP vendor as possible. These standard building blocks avoid unnecessary investments in in-house development.

Security was a high priority and the group security policy for portals covers standards, processes, and procedures through a meta-directory. The finance function, for example, uses the portal for implementing international account-ing standards, acquisitions integration, and reporting. Diverse and detailed applications cover product development, project management, HR, and IT functions. The portal development process starts with users and concept work-shops – these workshops expand business content, fine-tune search functions, and seek out performance improvements.

The benefits? The enterprise portal provides central, role-based access to critical applications, information, and services – decisively accelerating and improving corporate communication and business processes. Freudenberg is on the road to success in 41 countries!

For Freudenberg, building an enterprise portal is a dynamic process – deployment is on a huge scale and the driving force behind the project had to be top management. Senior management executives were actively involved in crafting the portal's plans from the beginning.

Companies like Freudenberg are using portals to assist in integrating heterogeneous systems landscapes – giving them worldwide central access to ERP systems, CRM solutions, HR modules, and their consolida-tion system. And giving them, as well, access to e-mail, the Internet, data-bases, and office applications.

What are the learning points from this and other portal implementa-tions? The following nine-step checklist has been prepared to help you, the CFO, take full advantage of current best practices:

1. *Formulate an enterprise portal strategy.*
   What will an enterprise portal mean for your company?
   What information and knowledge should the portal provide?
   What processes must change in your company?
   What business case must you make?

2. *Choose the "right" portal design.*
   What type of portal are users most likely to take advantage of?
   Think less about IT investment or ROI – and more about end-user acceptance and operating costs. A successful portal amplifies ROI in the long run.
   Focus on integrating your business processes.

3. *Include users from the start.*
   Recruit prominent sponsors.
   Investigate users' communication relationships (interviews).
   Find out what users are "itching to get out of the way".
   Create paper prototypes together with users (concept workshops).

4. *Define the scope of the project.*
   What processes should be mapped first?
   What existing applications must be available through the portal?
   What new data and applications are your highest priorities?
   What goals should you reach for in the first phase of the project?

5. *Set milestones.*
   Present initial results and feedback from concept workshops.
   Select a pilot project that promises early success.
   How long will the pilot project take? Set clear milestones.
   How many project phases do you anticipate?

6. *Create maximum value by mixing content from different sources.*
   What are the different sources of content you need?
   How is this diverse information interrelated?
   Can you formulate a win–win strategy for these content chunks?

7. *Develop a pilot.*
   How large is the pilot user group and which employees are included?
   Concentrate on speed and accuracy.
   Check whether applications are correctly configured in your back-end system.
   Install existing standard content.

8. *Execute the rollout.*
   Build excitement through internal marketing. Consider a portal naming competition, create internal brochures, distribute portal "driver's licenses."

Advertise your success by having satisfied pilot users share their experience and advice.

9. *Learn from using portals*
   Keep your portal projects open for user-driven process innovation. New processes will evolve - they cannot all be pre-designed.

A suggested portal implementation road map is set out in Figure 7.7. Experience from pilot implementations has shown that a structured approach avoids serious mistakes. An accurate and detailed conceptual design up-front leads to clear and precise goals. Implementation teams should combine business, functional, and technical expertise.

Portals are new. Organizations have yet to experience their full potential. Be prepared to learn and adapt your approach. Existing implementations indicate that quick wins can be scored in areas such as customer relationship management, routine financials, and HR self-service.

Today, some forward-thinking companies are moving to the next level of portal usage and design. Their early execution successes are encouraging them to radically overhaul traditional business processes and introduce entirely new processes. The focus: new ways of communicating and collaborating. Imagine the creative power of thousands of users connected in communities, both internal and external! The results are positively mind-boggling! Don't limit your portal goals or constrain your

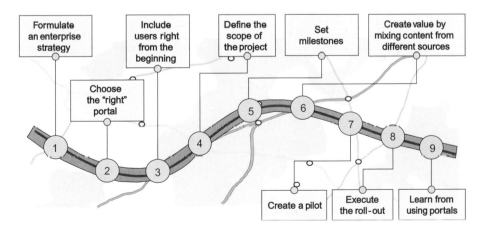

Figure 7.7   *A Portal Implementation Road Map*

portal development. As with the Internet, new processes will evolve – they cannot be predesigned.

GROWING YOUR FINANCE COMMUNITY

Today's employees have to deal with unprecedented volumes of information. Yet they are often expected to make their decisions in double-quick time as well. Against this background, it is essential for data – particularly of a financial nature – to be accessible to a large circle of users within a company in a straightforward, no-nonsense format. An enterprise portal must therefore be designed not only to support the financial professionals in management and financial accounting, but also to draw everyone else's attention to relevant content and information through proactive information distribution.

For example, manager self-services offered through an enterprise portal will contain information and services that team leaders, project leaders, and cost-center managers need to manage their budgets and their staff on a day-to-day basis. Running a cost check will no longer involve selecting various options and compiling a report of even calling the central department. Instead, adequate monitors actively provide visual alerts if certain key figures are a cause for concern or if costs are close to running over budget.

Financial portal solutions make it possible to distribute financial information across a broad base in your organization. Moreover, they enable your staff to work more efficiently than ever before. Rather than wasting precious time searching for information, they get a combination of exactly the information and services they need served up on a plate.

This is all thanks to the new portal-driven techniques such as personalization, which allows you to customize portals to suit individual jobs and tasks. And because the portal integrates information from different areas and focuses on key processes, it delivers better-quality business analyses at much higher speeds than you're used to. Efficiency also gets a boost – simply because all the services and information required to complete a task are available in a single location.

Enterprise portals integrate more than the organization. A complete enterprise solution provides everything users need to get their jobs done more productively. Innovative portal design encompasses:

- *All users*, including employees and external communities

- *Personalized* information – by role and content relevance

- *Convenient access* via point and click, drag and relate, and single sign-on

- *Everything needed*, all required information, applications and services

- *Anytime, anywhere access* through Web browser and mobile devices

- *Maximum flexibility* – in both content design and delivery

- *Secure usage* – robust, reconfigurable security features

Last but not least, portals protect your IT investment, cut costs, and hide the complexity of both your system landscape and your business processes from the user. This integration capability is illustrated in Figure 7.8. And that all adds up to greater profitability – at both employee and company level.

Take the case study of TransAlta, Canada's largest nonregulated electric generation and marketing company. It offers a great example of the benefits of bringing information together around individual roles and then integrating portal applications with underlying ERP and data warehouse technologies.

CASE STUDY
TransAlta: Make Every Decision-Maker a CFO!

The business case for TransAlta was all about process improvement: making business processes faster and more efficient, with less waste and rework. This meant applying new technologies to optimize and sustain process improvements – starting with plant maintenance, employee/manager self-service – and moving toward business intelligence and knowledge management.

TransAlta envisioned its enterprise portal as a single gateway to internal and external real-time information and applications. Its main goals were to provide transparent integration of business applications and information to enable better, quicker business decisions; to facilitate collaboration; and to leverage existing investments in ERP.

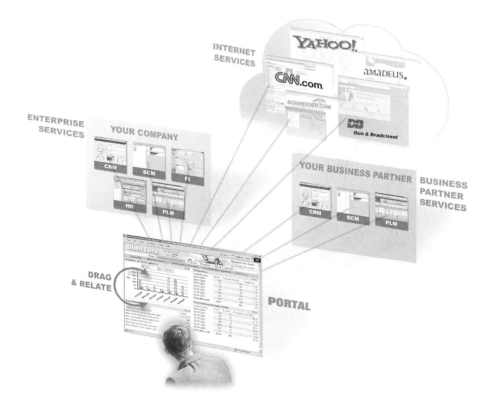

Figure 7.8 *Intelligent Portals Allow Seamless integration*

TransAlta chose a portal solution that provided straightforward integration between the portal and its existing ERP resources. It took standard portal content offered by its ERP supplier and presented it to its internal user community – this was known as the "Manager Self-Service" package. The proposition was sold to users as "easy access to detail". In addition to information provision, the portal included support for administrative tasks, such as recruitment and HR, and finance processes, such as accounts adjustments.

The total target population of portal users was estimated at 2,400 – 500 users in the first phase of development. TransAlta started with a pilot which was up and running very quickly. This success encouraged senior executives to give their support, confirm direction, and validate the business case for the portal.

Subsequent stages included the connections between the ERP and the portal, extracting ERP premium content for use in the portal, and finally, connecting the portal with the data warehouse. The initial plan was scaled down in terms of prepackaged functionality to meet tight project implementation timetables. This richer, more flexible functionality was subsequently incorporated into more advanced releases.

TransAlta chose its portal solution based on a variety of criteria. It was looking for an easy-to-use portal builder, a variety of prepackaged content, connectivity with business intelligence and knowledge management, and "drag and relate" capability. Not only was the solution to improve productivity, reduce costs, and improve process efficiency, but it also provided real-time information. Information was grouped logically by task, making it easy to find and quick to access.

TransAlta's approach also provided tools for better decision support. Information alone was not enough – the solution empowered managers to learn, review their options, and then take action. For example, the plant maintenance solution covered not only the business processes, but also the reporting and analytics. User-friendly access was provided to a library of drawings and related documents; alerts triggered milestone reminders. Managers could share common information from the same sources, particularly on budgets and timetables.

Research for this book has revealed that few executives today actually use their ERP, CRM or supply chain management applications to make decisions – they are used primarily for transaction processing. Increasingly, portals are being used to fill this gap in decision support, helping to tear down functional and geographic boundaries.

When considering your portal strategy, remember to think big! Promote a radical, but winning idea: "*Making every employee a CFO.*" Provide global visibility of relevant business-critical information for every employee – any time, anywhere. Why is this visibility important, particularly for the CFO? Because, prior to portals, more time was spent gathering data and determining "whose numbers were correct" than on meaningful analysis. In the portal there is just *one version of the truth*, accessible for everyone. Build community within your financial organization. Leverage your IT investments. Minimize the cost and complexity of your systems landscape and business processes.

In Figure 7.9, we show how the CFO and the extended finance community can play key roles in realizing an innovative, easily implemented portals strategy.

Finance professionals, and occasional users – inside and outside the organization – can use the existing new capabilities that portals offer for real-time control and accountability. When coupled with business analytics – the subject of the previous chapter – fresh insights into ways of improving financial performance can be shared and secured. Collaboration becomes a reality, not a distant goal!

Figure 7.9   *Expanding the Financial Community*

CFO CHECKLIST

FOCUS ON BUSINESS GOALS, NOT TECHNOLOGY
Make the business case an enterprise-wide issue. Lead from the top – portal projects need high visibility! Reengineer business processes – creating fundamentally new ways of doing things. Shift the burden from central departments to end-users – decentralize without relinquishing central control.

THINK ABOUT THE TOTAL COST OF OWNERSHIP
Choose the right portal – consider the cost of integration to your ERP, exchange and data warehouse. Take advantage of prepackaged content – project development times are shorter, results are more visible quicker, and user motivation increases. Maintenance and training are cost issues too!

GO FOR QUICK WINS AND KEEP THEM COMING!
Involve users at the outset – start with a paper prototype. Take small steps. Phase in the scope and sequence the implementation phases according to user priorities. Committed active users of the portal will ensure maximum pay back.

DEVELOP YOUR CFO PORTAL
Each user sees only their area of responsibility – choose a role-based approach and put personalization at the top of your list. Define who should do what. Then harmonize business processes, accounting practices, and systems worldwide. For example, achieve a faster close and consolidation.

TREAT PORTALS AS LIVING SOLUTIONS
Experiment by mixing content from different sources. Keep the landscape open – a portal project is under constant development. You will want to integrate more and more information sources – cut information by topics, not systems boundaries. Start the technology integration by connecting with those systems that link most easily to your standard prebuilt portal content. Keep the scope open – users will drive process innovation as they learn by using portals.

GO MOBILE WITH YOUR PORTAL
Keep in touch, always have your financials to hand! Collaborate and communicate with your business partners worldwide – both inside and outside the company.

MAKE EVERY EMPLOYEE A CFO!
Use portals for global consistency and visibility – for every employee, anywhere, anytime. Deliver Web-based access to real-time results directly to employees' desktops. Empower employees by integrating portals with business analytics. Provide "one version of the truth" to everybody in the organization and expand your financial community.

CHAPTER 8

Managing Intangibles

CREATING A MEANINGFUL DIALOGUE WITH CUSTOMERS

Phil Bentley, CFO
Centrica

Centrica has redefined its business – its focus is based on customer relationships. Traditionally, we were the UK's largest gas supplier, British Gas. We merged this with the leading motoring services organization, the AA, and have diversified into other segments such as electricity, telecommunications and financial services. We are driven to build scale. Today, we reckon we have 400 million contacts with customers every year – from telephone contacts regarding bills and moving home, to home services visits and roadside recovery. The biggest issue we face: leveraging our customer databases across our businesses into an integrated picture of individual customer "life-time value".

Why do we focus on the customer end of the value chain? Quite simply because that's where we can get the highest returns on our capital employed, by broadening and deepening the product relationship that our brands offer our customer.

We believe we have done well so far with building customer relationships; from our single gas product relationship, we now sell over 2 products per household across the UK. We have more than trebled our shareholder value over the last few years. Our target is to deliver 15–20% total shareholder return annually over the next five years. Shareholder value will be created by investing in the tools to maximize the value of our relationship with customers. We aim to reduce our cost-to-serve and the cost of customer acquisitions whilst growing customer loyalty – this can only be done by offering great service and value-for-money products through our brands, and having the most efficient processes backing us up.

British Gas and the AA are two of the most trusted brands in the UK – we seek fresh insights into consumer choices and we review the effectiveness of our distribution channels to cross-sell within the brand. We're only just beginning to get all our customer data together to know which customers take which products and what other services they might be interested in. For example, we have 12.5 million AA members, but today only one million take our motor insurance products despite our competitive offer – we have great potential if we can target our customers more effectively.

We already have a vast store of customer data; for example demographics, size of household energy consumption, propensity to take other products and propensity to churn. The challenge is to understand better the potential value of each of our customers – in short, to determine which customers create value and which destroy value. We can slice and dice our customer data but currently much of this data is analyzed offline and cannot be used online at the point of customer contact. The "Holy Grail" of Customer Relationship Management (CRM) is to have all this information – from sales, billing and cost-to-serve data – at our fingertips.

We are investing heavily in new customer relationship systems. Currently, this is costing $700 million over the next 3 years – our single most important strategic investment. When complete, this should provide the integrated picture for customer value. This investment is all about integration of processes, data, technology, and crucially, our culture. Training our people and getting them to focus on – indeed be passionate about – our customers is critical.

The market is beginning to recognize the value tied up in customer bases. Our competitors, for example those based in Germany and France, have paid over $400 per customer to acquire UK utility customer bases. But at Centrica, we have the biggest customer base, the best data and the best brands – a winning combination, we believe.

We have a business model though, which is not purely based on customer value; we have invested in physical assets, too, in order to hedge our risks on *energy supply. Energy procurement is a risky business if you get it wrong. The market for gas and electricity can be volatile and is susceptible to peaks in demand and supply. That's why owning assets as a hedge is important to the success of our model.*

We also believe in communicating our performance both internally and externally. We regularly keep track of the KPIs on our scorecard – particularly those lead indicators for brand equity, customer and employee satisfaction. Our investors can find it difficult to value companies in our sector since the intangibles are not always well understood. Increasingly, we are moving away from just historical financial results to communicating our leading value drivers – those of cost-per-acquisition, churn, cost-to-serve and economic profit by customer.

"The times, they're a changing!" Value drivers and value-creating activities have shifted from the tangible to the intangible. Companies like Centrica are focused on getting the right balance of investment and strategy to differentiate them from the competition. Figure 8.1 shows how the balance in market value between physical and intangible assets has shifted. The new value drivers are product and process innovation coupled with customer relationships.

By the late 1990s, in fact, intangible assets represented *more than 80%* of the Fortune 500 market value, up from 40% in the early 1980s. As a result, *only 20%* of a company's market value is reflected through traditional accounting and financial reports. That figure is even lower, often under 10%, for knowledge-based companies such as SAP or Microsoft, or companies with strong brands, such as Coca-Cola. A recent study[1] of the chemical industry, for instance, revealed that the R&D investments of 83 chemical companies over a span of 25 years yielded a 17% after-tax return, while typical capital spending earned just 7%.

This raises a critical issue: managers who rely on standard accounting data to make investment decisions and optimize business efficiency are often acting in the dark. Why? Because the traditional financial tools they are using are relevant to only 10 or 20% of the resources they are responsible for.

Why this disconnect between what traditional accounting systems capture and how financial markets value companies? The answer requires a close look at how today's companies are creating economic value.

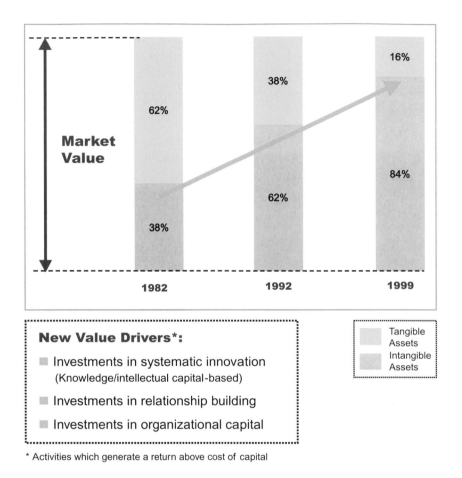

Figure 8.1 *Changing Corporate Value Drivers*

INTANGIBLE ASSETS: THE NEW VALUE DRIVERS

Ever since the 1980s, globalization, new technologies, and industry deregulation have created severe competitive pressures, forcing companies to fundamentally restructure. Many firms responded by investing capital in two phases: in the first phase, they revamped organizational structures to exploit global economies of scale by using best practices via physical assets such as production facilities. Throughout the 1990s, ABB is a prime example of this new business model.

In phase two of the restructuring process, production resources became commoditized and failed to provide sustained competitive advantage; instead, value was created increasingly through new product development and customer-focused service. Companies abandoned vertical integration and began decapitalizing. They outsourced activities, focused on customer relations, and jumped feet first into e-Business ventures. Actually, most companies are still grappling with phase two: they've just started to invest in new organizational structures and related e-Business infrastructures. Nor is *organizational innovation* the only intangibles area that companies are hoping to exploit: product innovation and R&D are also top priorities.

As the shift toward intangible asset building continues, the focus is now on leveraging human capital and building alliances in order to create more productive collaborative business processes. Companies want to build customer value, reap new competitive advantages, and reduce costs at the same time. Cisco is among the most often quoted example of this model.

But accounting and management tools haven't kept pace with changing corporate dynamics. In most companies, activities which create the greatest value for stakeholders are not systematically reported. As a result, companies may under-invest in their real value drivers, and ultimately, even destroy value. Today's CFOs must push accounting and financial systems to the next level so they can report, manage, forecast, and tap into new value-creating activities and processes. The rewards can be enormous!

A survey[2] among more than 800 CEOs and board directors from the UK, France, Germany, Spain, Australia, Japan, and the US revealed that companies that generate 80% of their revenue from new products have typically doubled their market capitalization in a five-year period. High-performing companies, with annual total shareholder returns in excess of 37%, average 61% of their turnover from new products and services. For low performers, only 26% of growth comes from new products and services.

THE PROBLEMS WITH TRADITIONAL ACCOUNTING

Accounting no longer reflects the true value created by a company. This has become obvious for many investment bankers through their statistical analyses. Reported profit does not correlate well with a company's stock performance or total shareholder returns. This is why concepts such as economic value added (EVA), which was first introduced by the consulting firm Stern Stewart, have been so widely accepted in recent years – both by investors wanting to assess the performance of their actual or future investments and by managers hoping to optimize the profits of their internal business units.

EVA treats expenditures for R&D, advertising, brands, and customer relationship building as what they are economically: investments. What had been expenditures according to GAAP reporting are now capitalized through so-called adjustment postings and are part of a company's financial capital base. Corporate returns must now exceed total cost of capital, including investments in intangibles – therefore the name, *economic value added.*

EVA is a step forward in measuring enterprise performance. However, it still fails to capture the full value of today's knowledge-intensive companies in which intangibles are their biggest assets. Even when R&D investments are capitalized, this is done on the basis of costs spent for R&D. Assessing the value created through such investments or based on progress in creating intended value (of a development project, for example) isn't possible using this approach.

In his work on shareholder value management concepts, Alfred Rappaport[3] asserted that calculating economic results by deducting actual return from the cost of capital of a business no longer reflects reality and should not be the basis for executive compensation. Why? Namely, because return expectations of investors, especially for top-performing companies (which typically have high intangible assets), are reflected *already* in the actual share price, and are usually much higher than the cost of capital.

The bottom line? Innovation activities, not capital investment, drive the value and growth of companies today. These innovation activities provide customers with a unique set of value-creating products and services. Measuring economic value added therefore gives you only half a loaf. Companies must also measure the effectiveness (from a customer point of view) of their value-creating processes in product development, supply chain management, and customer relationship management. They have to fully exploit all critical resources (not just financial capital, as EVA does) – including human resources, information, intellectual property, and alliances. They also have to successfully manage all aspects of their value creation recipe.[4] Figure 8.2 shows just how important these intangibles assets, such as innovation, are in creating shareholder value.

**Total Shareholder Return
(10 Year Average)**

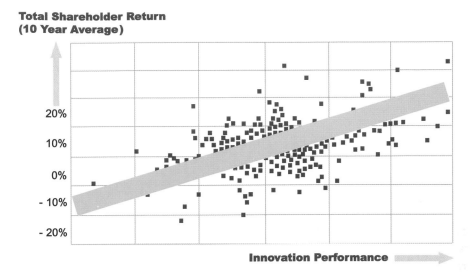

Innovation Performance

Figure 8.2 *How Total Shareholder Return Correlates with Innovation Performance*

Structural capital comprises all the resources that support people in their work: all those intangibles left behind when they go home at night. These include internal processes and structures, databases, customer relationships and so on. Structural capital helps people work smarter, not just harder. This ability represents the real value of an organization. Not financial capital, not human capital, but structural capital: "packaged" internal processes, computer systems, and relationships with business partners. And while human capital cannot be "owned" by a company, structural capital can.

CASE STUDY
Creating Structural Capital and Fueling Innovation

In the 1990's ABB was an example of a company which built up structural capital to fuel global innovation and intellectual capital. Percy Barnevik, ABB's CEO, completed Europe's biggest cross-border deal in 1988, in only six weeks, following his rule: "act fast, even at the risk of making mistakes." Barnevik *immediately structured 1,000 ABB companies into small, distinct businesses; each employing about 200 people and generating about $50 million in revenues. Barnevik's basic objective was to remove "the false sense of security of belonging to a big organization and to develop the motivation and pride to contribute directly to their unit's success." At ABB, there is only one level between the group executive and frontline company managers. "Think global, act local," ABB's philosophy as expressed by Barnevik, is real: its Zurich headquarters offer guidelines and oversee global strategy.*

ABB's transformation converted front line managers into entrepreneurs. Middle managers (the heads of business areas and regional segment head-quarters) now coach and support front line managers. Where other companies use a top-down, staff-managed, financially driven model, ABB created an interactive, bottom-up/top-down process designed to engage managers in an ongoing dialogue about how to build and defend intangible assets.

Key financial targets – long term and short term – are defined at the group level for each business segment. ABB used simulation models to track financial planning and external changes. The most probable scenarios were integrated into strategic planning. Managers then segmented targets at business area level.

ABB's ABACUS financial reporting system serves as an integration tool. This is a data warehouse, where information from decentralized transactions on ABB's operations are stored and sorted. It allows managers to run reports on consolidated financial data in any dimension. ABACUS is also used to assist the strategic planning process at ABB, such as strategic financial planning, world-wide budgeting, and forecasting. Through ABACUS, managers around the world communicate using integrated, consistent data.

With ABACUS in place, ABB focused on value creation from R&D and product innovation, with the ultimate goal of adding value. Value creation through R&D is supported by several measurement vehicles: patents and invention dis-closures, annual sales from new products, and ROI from R&D.

ABB was the first in its industry to organize fully around customer groups instead of products, aiming to boost growth by helping customers succeed in a world of accelerating globalization, deregulation, consolidation, and e-Business. It replaced product-driven business segments with four new ones based on customer industries: utilities, process industries, manufacturing and consumer industries and oil, gas and petrochemicals. In addition a new division, New Ventures Ltd, acted as an incubator.

The main lesson: the importance of organizational capital and culture in boosting productivity. The culture created by Percy Barnevik at ABB proved that large global organizations can fuel individual initiative. The key is the matrix organization, which empowers front line managers while keeping some centralized controls. Knowledge sharing among units inspires people to view the company's mission very personally.

Today ABB is having to scale back dramatically to turn the business around. The changes referred to in this case study may have been too late. The cost base is still too high and the benefits of earlier restructuring programs have been slower than expected. Certain divisions have been prepared for sale and a major break up is on the cards.[5]

A NEW APPROACH TO PERFORMANCE MANAGEMENT

As Figure 8.3 shows, the shift from physical supply chains to intangible assets requires an overhaul of most corporate performance management systems. This overhaul is only possible through a deep understanding of today's value drivers – intangible assets, such as good customer relations, product innovation capabilities, and codified or uncodified knowledge. A key differentiator in today's intangibles-dominated, knowledge-based economy is that input and output, investments and results, are no longer linked: there is no meaningful correlation between input (costs, investments) and output (sales price, revenue, profits).

Put another way, the value of intellectual capital is not necessarily related to the cost of creating it. The costs of producing knowledge products bear less relationship to their value or price on the market than did the cost of producing a ton of steel in the industrial age. The value of a pharmaceutical company's R&D pipeline, for example, can't be derived from its spending. Money invested in software development or to create a movie does not tell anything about future revenues generated by these new products. The value of a knowledge product to a customer – a software program, a movie, a drug, etc. – is not based on the number of software code lines, or on the cost to create a film or develop a new drug

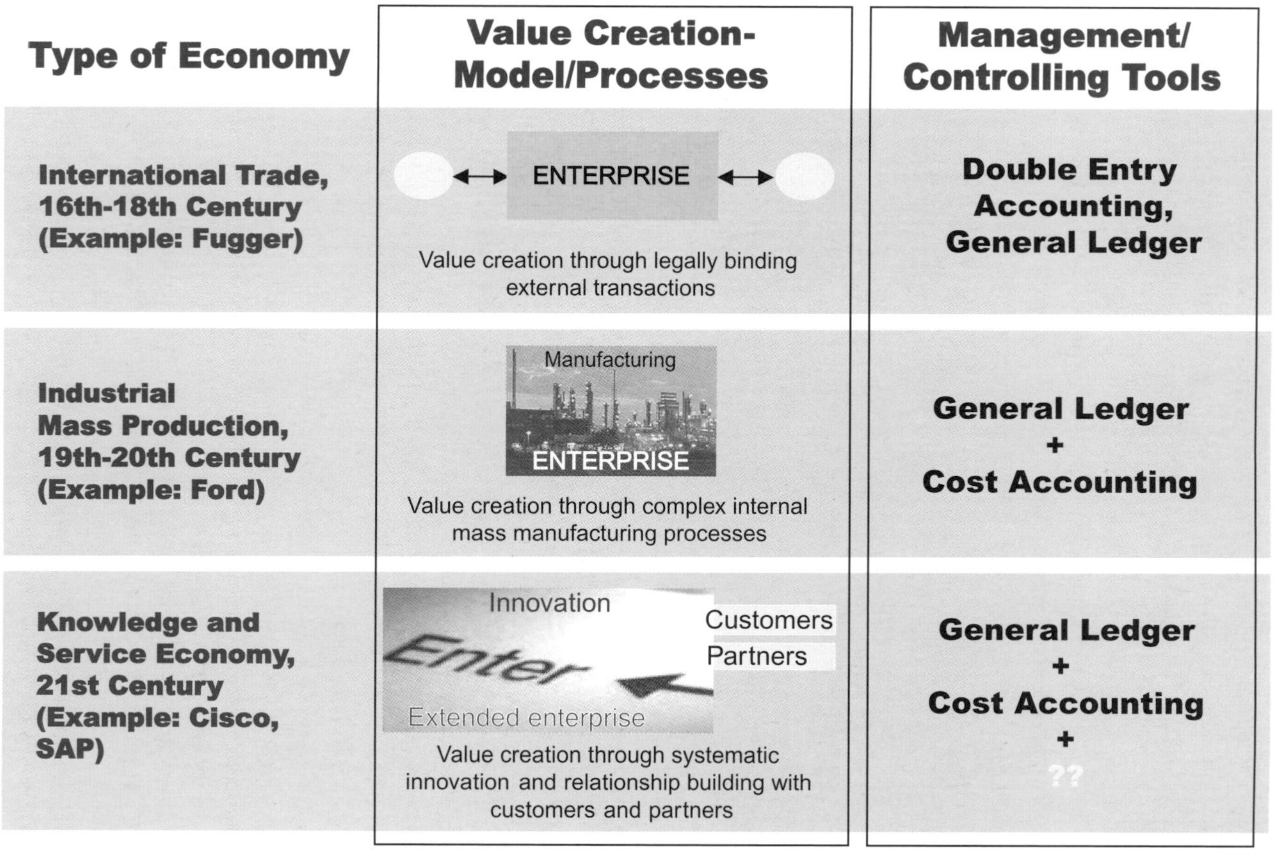

Type of Economy	Value Creation-Model/Processes	Management/Controlling Tools
International Trade, 16th-18th Century (Example: Fugger)	● ↔ ENTERPRISE ↔ ● — Value creation through legally binding external transactions	**Double Entry Accounting, General Ledger**
Industrial Mass Production, 19th-20th Century (Example: Ford)	Manufacturing — ENTERPRISE — Value creation through complex internal mass manufacturing processes	**General Ledger + Cost Accounting**
Knowledge and Service Economy, 21st Century (Example: Cisco, SAP)	Innovation — Customers — Partners — *Enter* — Extended enterprise — Value creation through systematic innovation and relationship building with customers and partners	**General Ledger + Cost Accounting + ??**

Figure 8.3 *The Evolution of Performance Management Systems*

compound. It is based purely on the value its use creates for the consumer – on its perceived quality and market demand.

What's needed is a new performance measurement system that links cost, market value created, and time – one that integrates market perception with cost and resource management – and takes into account the economics of intangibles, both positive and negative. It has to provide, for example, data on the efficiency of the entire life cycle of customer relations and products (see Figure 8.4). And it must offer predictive information that is revised and updated on a rolling basis.

A company must constantly push to improve the effectiveness of its product innovation chain by balancing technical, cost, and market-related issues. This helps a company leverage benefits and control limitations systematically.

Managing value-creation processes in product innovation, customer relationship management, supply chain management – and supporting processes, such as HR, finance, and IT – are critical tasks. But without strategic coordination a company at best, couldn't tap its full potential and at worst, would be impossible to run. As depicted in Figure 8.5, the role of strategy in integrating performance management with operations is shown to be more important than ever. On the left-hand side of this figure, we show the strategic measures – the "content." On the right-hand side, we show the business process interactions. Together, they comprise the new enterprise management system.

The role of strategy is threefold: first, to show *how* the enterprise wants to create value for its stakeholders; second, which assets it plans to use; and third, how it will combine them into a unique value recipe. Strategy's task is to provide a common goal for all corporate activities and enable managers to make fast decisions if trade-offs have to be made between different value-creation areas.

Value related to intangible assets is not created directly, but through business processes that either *create* intangibles, such as in product development or business development, or *exploit* intangible assets, such as customer relations.

Over the past decade, numerous approaches to measuring non-financial value drivers and intangibles have emerged. Among the most useful are:

- The balanced scorecard, proposed by Kaplan and Norton, which provides an excellent framework for reporting on general performance and strategy implementation.

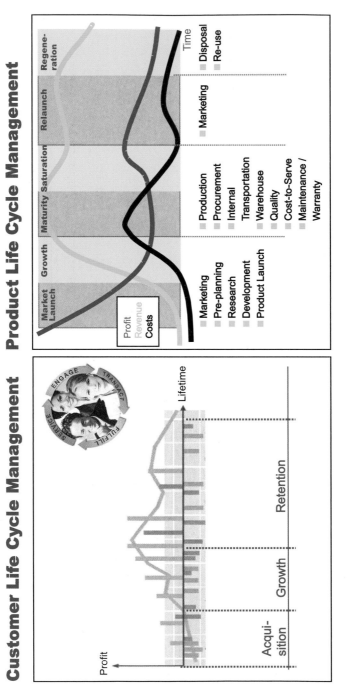

Figure 8.4   *Performance Measurement Over the Entire Life Cycle*

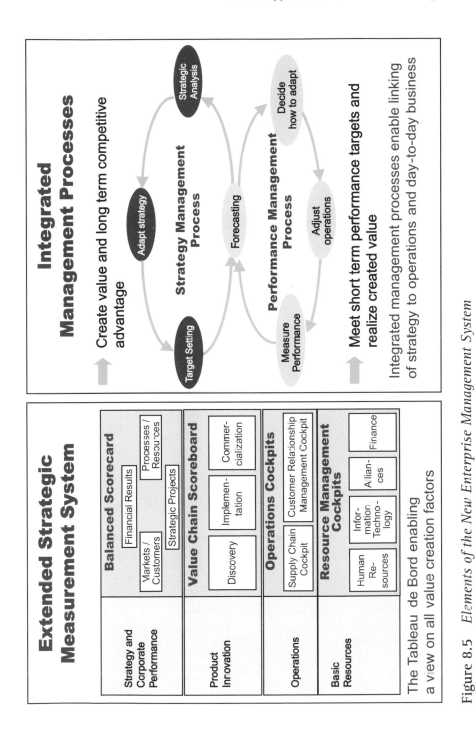

Figure 8.5   *Elements of the New Enterprise Management System*

- The concept of real option valuation provides a valuation scheme for future "real" business options created through new strategies. It also offers decision support tools to manage these options, investment projects, opportunities, and risk.

- The concept of customer lifetime value, which enables a company to value the intangibles created in customer service organizations.

While widely accepted, these approaches fail to offer a comprehensive framework that encompasses *all* important value-creation activities. One new tool that does a better job of assessing intangible assets is the value chain blueprint[6]. Like the balanced scorecard, the value chain blueprint identifies both financial and non-financial value drivers. But in contrast to the balanced scorecard, it focuses on *innovation rather than strategic implementation.*

What does a value chain blueprint look like? It consists of nine sets of measures that provide information – mainly non-financial indicators – about the innovation cycle of successful business enterprises. These nine sets of measures are assigned to three main areas of an innovation value chain: (1) *discovery and learning,* (2) *implementation,* and (3) *commercialization.*

In the discovery area, three sets of measures capture information about *internal renewal* – such as R&D activities, about *acquired capabilities* – such as technology purchase, and about the status of *networking in discovery and learning* – such as R&D alliances or communities of practice.

For the implementation phase, another three sets of measures report about *intellectual property* created – such as patents, trademarks, or licensing agreements, about *technological feasibility* – such as the status of clinical tests for a new drugs or beta tests for software programs – and about *Internet activities* – such as degree of online purchases, Web traffic, etc.

And finally, for the commercialization phase, three sets of measures provide information about *customers* – such as customer churn and value, brand value, or the status of marketing alliances about *commercialization performance* – through revenue figures such as innovation revenues (from recently introduced products), patent royalties and knowledge earnings – and about *growth prospects.*

The value chain blueprint is designed to link resources and outcomes. It differs from most other information systems in that it is scientifically based. Each of the proposed indicators has been shown by economic research to represent a specific value driver and as such, is statistically linked with a company's value.

THE ENTERPRISE CONTROL PANEL

While very useful, even the value chain concept does not go far enough. To support strategic planning, managers need *short-term*, objective data on the status and outlook for all critical activities and processes and *long-term* information on creating strategic value and future competitive advantage. Such a comprehensive performance measurement system is called an organization's *tableau de bord*.[7]

This tool is based on the French concept of an enterprise control panel, which is designed to inform both internal and external constituencies about a company's total performance *and* about the status of its most important value-creating processes. As illustrated in Figure 8.5 (left side), it includes measures related to strategy management and general performance, to product innovation, to market and business development, and to operations and support processes. These measures provide managers with the "big picture" – updating them quickly and easily.

The *tableau de bord* has four components:

- A balanced scorecard focusing on strategy, execution and general performance

- A product and market development component, based on the value chain blueprint concept, which measures effectiveness and efficiency in product innovation and market development processes

- Various "cockpits" for the control of processes in supply chain management and customer relationship management

- An operating view of the most important basic support processes

The result? A performance management system that helps a company coordinate tactical plans and resource allocation across operating processes and functions. The *tableau de bord* does not replace accounting. It precedes and complements accounting-based data. Of course, financial information is still needed, especially since it provides a reality check of the value creation or destruction as products, services, or processes move along the value chain.

Specific scoreboard indicators or measures should satisfy three criteria. First, they should be quantitative. Second, they should be standardized, meaning that they can be compared across business units and across firms for valuation and benchmark purposes. Third, and most important, they should be confirmed by empirical evidence as relevant to users, both internal and external.

Prime management for the *tableau de bord* approach uses the following checklist:

1. Start to monitor the status of intangible assets in your company. By monitoring non-financial indicators of the major value creation processes in your company, over time, you'll gain insight into the relationships among the indicators and of the logic that underlies your intangible resources and financial results.

2. Regularly exchange insights and experiences with managers from other companies. Seeing the problems and solutions used in other industries helps you gain a more precise view of your own business and management systems.

3. Experiment with new ways of collaboration. Invite an external expert as facilitator. Try to develop your own style for management cockpit-like meetings.

4. Insist on using more sophisticated measurements and improving them continuously. Identifying the areas of your company where performance should be measured and reported regularly. Schedule monthly, or at the beginning, even weekly, "research days," where you talk to employees and other managers in your organization about their business processes. Talk with external stakeholders as well, like customers, business partners, industry analysts, and perhaps even competitors about value creation.

5. Start with systems thinking. Attend introductory training in systems thinking in order to understand fundamental principles. Begin designing systems dynamics models on paper yourself on a small scale.

Then try to remodel a business process for your company with your management team.

HARNESSING INNOVATION AND CUSTOMER RELATIONSHIPS

Innovation as the key driver for value creation in the new economy has to happen on the *operational level*, where companies deal on a day-to-day basis with customers and other business partners – for example, through new processes and structures. It must happen on the product-and-market development level, where new technology is discovered, new products are developed and commercialized. And finally, it has to happen on the strategic level, where companies decide whcrc to invest to create value in the future and how they will combine intangible assets to create growth – such as melding a new organization design with an innovative new product, either home-grown or acquired. Even more challenging, *all these innovation activities must be interlinked* as in Figure 8.6.

This requires a focus on *profitability and value generation* to help companies measure the effectiveness of enterprise activities, their efficiency, and business success. Combining the power of intangible asset investment in both innovation and customer management can provide a very successful business model. Take Cisco, for example.[5]

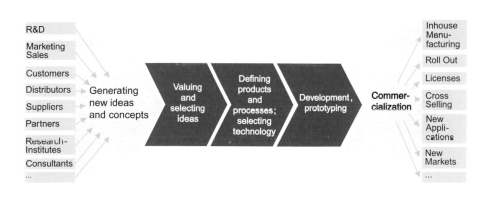

Figure 8.6 *Integrated Measures for Innovation*

CASE STUDY
Cultivating Innovation and Customer Responsiveness

Why is Cisco a global success story? The two-part answer: innovation and the Internet. When networks became the backbone of corporate information technology, Cisco pushed to find innovative networking solutions. Using the router invented by its founders as a springboard, Cisco continued to innovate by building core competencies, increased R&D spending, and targeted acquisitions of small innovators, which it integrated successfully. The result? Worldwide market leadership in Internet networking.

Customer orientation and organizational design are two other keys to success. Cisco concentrated on probing customer needs, developing the right products and services, and organizing employees, suppliers, and other business partners so that customers are served in the best way. Cisco used its intangible assets in R&D, and know-how in designing organizational structures – that is, its business network of suppliers – and its human capital to deliver customer value through new technology.

To make that happen, Cisco created a networked e-Business structure and used information technology to link its employees and its own organization with its customers and suppliers. Today, Cisco manufactures virtually none of its products; instead, it relies on a digitized network of suppliers linked via Cisco directly to its customers and vice versa.

Financially, this has led to decapitalization, reflected in a lean balance sheet – much leaner, in fact, than those of Lucent, Nortel, and Alcatel, which operate in similar markets. Cisco's physical assets and working capital counted in 1999 for only some 3% of its total assets; the same ratio at Alcatel was 15%, 30% at Nortel, and 50% at Lucent.

Cisco's success also comes from its use of information technology and Internet applications to leverage information flows with key constituents, tightening these critical relationships. By improving its own internal network, Cisco is seeing financial benefits of nearly $1.4 bn a year. This has led to high customer, partner, and employee satisfaction, a competitive edge in customer support, order management and delivery – and to improved internal HR and training.

Today, Cisco is the world's largest Internet commerce site, with 90% of its orders transacted via the Web. Says John Chambers, President and CEO: "Cisco's success and our increased productivity gains are due largely to the implementation of Internet applications to run our business. The ability to harness the power of the Internet to create a New World business model is driving survival and competition in today's fast-paced economy."

Cisco needed a strategy to keep up with this pace of innovation and the Cisco management team decided to embark on a strategy of acquisitions. This decision marked a major shift. The company was founded by bright technologists who invented something unique. But in order to remain a market leader and extend its market position, Cisco needed to buy ideas rather than rely on internal innovation. The concept: Cisco could increase the value of acquired technologies and products quickly by combining them with its own intangible assets – its customer base, knowledge about customer needs, and how to serve them. Cisco was able to create far more value because it could concentrate its management power on the most lucrative activities: developing new products and markets – and understanding customer needs.

Technology acquisitions are notoriously difficult to pull off. Cisco solved this problem by developing what it called an Internet operating system (IOS). It let Cisco quickly integrate newly acquired technologies into its existing technology platforms and deliver integrated solutions to its customers. The IOS connected different Cisco technologies, such as routers, hubs, switches, PCs, and workstation file servers.

Cisco developed a structured acquisition process. Acquisition candidates were carefully evaluated for cultural compatibility and other criteria. Once a candidate is approved, the acquisition process has three phases: selling the acquisition to the CEO, followed by a rigorous appraisal, and finally, by the integration and retention process. Once an acquisition is negotiated, Cisco's integration team jumps in and quickly integrates all important functions of the new company, including its information technology infrastructure. The goal: to present the acquired company to customers as part of Cisco within 100 days.

While ABB used its organizational design, culture, and structures to stimulate entrepreneurship and facilitated exchange of knowledge and best practice across countries, Cisco went further and looked to relations with external parties to create additional value.

For ABB, the big step was to become a global player and leverage its tangible and intangible assets on a global scale. In contrast, Cisco's key step was to optimize and manage the company from an outside-in approach, driving everything from the customer side. ABB is now following the same path as Cisco. The key lesson Cisco offers: in an industry characterized by complex products and fast innovation, you need an intangibles-based strategy in which customer service is the cornerstone of growth and value creation.

Cisco has consistently proven that value creation from intangible assets can yield much higher returns and shareholder value than traditional manufacturing and tangible assets. But companies pursuing this route must follow some guidelines:

- Decide how to create economic value by concentrating on core competencies through product or service offerings

- Define a clear strategy for targeting corporate goals and market segments based on anticipating new customer needs

- Outsource non-core activities to business partners, but integrate these tasks tightly into their ecosystem through well-designed collaborative business processes so that the whole structure responds to customers as a single enterprise

- Use advanced information and network technology internally, but also in collaborative business processes with partners and customers, making these relationships more productive

- Define a clear strategy for making employees and teams more productive, as this is vital to generating value from innovation and customer relations

- Maintain a unique relationship with customers, treating them as partners and letting them influence product design. If your company does not sell directly to end customers, then focus on creating a strong corporate brand

- Manage innovation as an outside-in process driven by customer needs. In this process "buy options" have to be taken into consideration as well. If your company pursues an acquisition strategy, it must be able to integrate acquired employees and technologies quickly and efficiently

VALUE CREATION THROUGH VALUE NETWORKS

What is your recipe for value creation? What is a value center? How does it differ from a traditional business unit structure? How do you create value from intangible assets? The fundamentals of value creation are clear: *invest* in business areas, that is in market and product segments and related assets, which yield the highest (financial and non-financial) return from a stakeholder point of view; *manage these investments* by maximizing benefits and overcoming the limitations and negative effects; and *control operations and business processes* as efficiently as possible by generating maximum revenues and profits for the company.

Traditionally, a corporation disaggregates its reporting structure into either profit centers or investment/cost centers for the purposes of management planning and control. The financial chart of accounts tends to follow the same structure. The focus tends to be on reporting sales and costs, usually by either geographic or functional responsibility. Value creation through value networks requires a subtly different approach. The emphasis is not just on sales and cost accountability, it is on the impact of capital investment, and most importantly, on the impact of *intangible* capital investment.

Companies are trying to manage the trade-off between long-term investment and short-term returns. There is nothing new in this at either the corporate or the legal entity level. What is new is how far down into the organization the capital/profit trade-off should be pushed. Shareholder value driven companies with a high proportion of their investment tied up in intangible assets are rewriting their charts of accounts and coming to terms with the resulting changes in organization and responsibility. This new approach is called *value centers*. In Figures 8.7 (a) and (b), we compare the value center approach with the traditional profit center approach.

Surprisingly, most executives don't know how their business units create value. In our research, we found that half the retailers in the United States don't earn their cost of capital. Yet managers at many companies demonstrate an obsession with growth that threatens to destroy value unless they figure out how to improve their returns on capital.

In the pharmaceuticals industry, for example, where the leading companies manage to earn after-tax returns on capital in excess of 30%, growth has a much larger impact on value than does increasing returns. Yet many pharmaceuticals companies don't effectively measure or

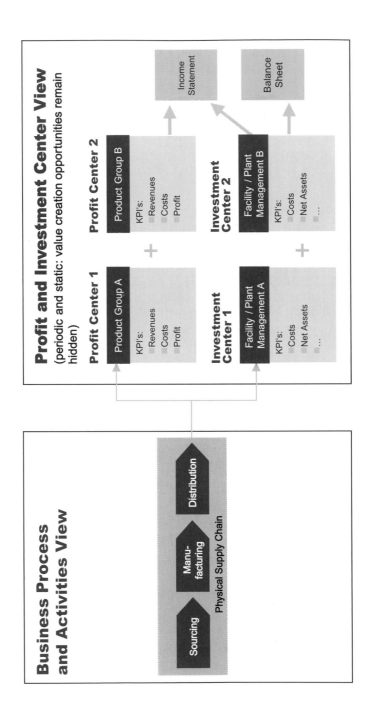

Figure 8.7a *Value Creation through Value Networks – Traditional Model*

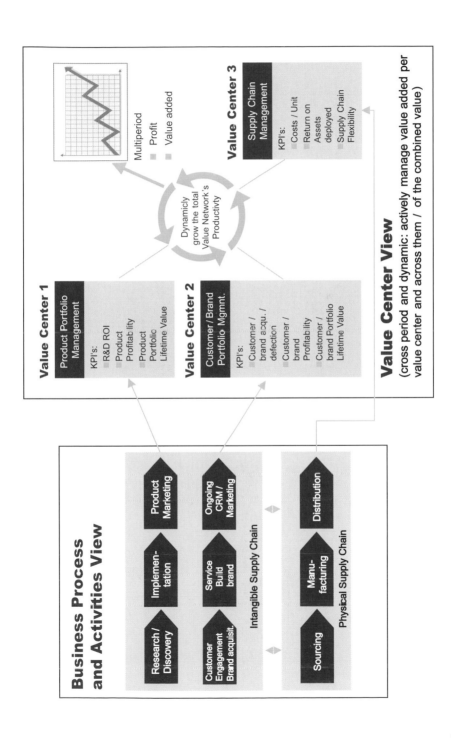

Figure 8.7b *Value Creation through Value Networks – New Model*

manage the value of their research, development, and product launch activities.

In the absence of strong CFO leadership, it is easy for executives to focus on the wrong value-creation measures. At one company, top managers agreed to vote on performance measures. Product innovation was popular with the management team. Analysis of the way the company really created value, however, demonstrated that product innovation was not nearly as important as customer service and process management. Focusing on product innovation was distracting top management from real opportunities to create value.

The story of a leading consumer packaged-goods company offers another cautionary tale. One of this company's most successful business units reported substantial operating-profit growth year after year, consistently meeting or beating targets. As long as the unit appeared to be doing well, senior management didn't question its performance. Only later was it revealed that the unit achieved its profit growth by raising prices. Over several years, steady price increases created an opportunity for competitors to take market share. Declines in market share eventually reached a point where operating-profit growth could not be sustained. The crisis that resulted led financial markets to lose confidence, forcing a major reorganization.

The CEO of BP puts it simply: "Our strategy is our organization." Nokia executives are even more concise: "Strategy = Structure = Implementation." These sayings indicate a change in the way that global firms discern their future. They no longer believe it can be precisely determined in advance through a carefully constructed strategy. Instead, the future emerges from the complex and hard-to-predict interactions of leaders, followers, and structural capital. The idea that "organization follows strategy" no longer works.

CASE STUDY
Balancing the Long Term with the Short Term

A global leader in software development and distribution faced a major dilemma. Short-term profit performance reported in accounting quarters for the benefit of the stock exchange required vigilant management of the sales pipeline. Information from all over the world had to be processed quickly and a view taken on the quality of future sales forecasts. The executive board members spent a considerable amount of time visiting the field, meeting up with strategically important customers and playing their part in final negotiations leading to major sale contract closures. Since most of the revenues were for software license fees, maintenance charges, and consulting support services, the related operating costs were relatively easy to predict and varied according to quarterly fluctuations in sales volumes and prices achievable in the globally competitive marketplace. Sales and marketing were organized on a territory basis and were reported up to a main board of directors through a field organization. Keeping the finger on the sales pulse was the name of the game.

However, software companies have to invest in product development and R&D to survive in the longer term. Major sums of money are committed annually to development projects, some of which succeed, but for which the revenues take many years to come through. Others are commissioned to react with product improvements at short notice in response to unexpected competitive moves. In fact, product development – a major intangible asset – is the real source of long-term value creation. The product development organization was also globally managed, but through product groups rather than geographic territories. The executive board could not easily turn the development tap on and off. The pressure to abandon development initiatives when short-term profits were at stake was immense. The trade-off between the two conflicting agendas was always a difficult and frustrating judgment call.

To quote the CFO, "We needed new financial management processes for providing rolling global forecasts of sales and operating costs; these needed to be integrated with those for reporting the longer-term progress and value of investment projects. We also implemented an integrated balanced scorecard with lead indicators, which became crucial in anticipating structural changes in our costs and organization. These indicators include market share, project milestone reporting, and the customer management life cycle. The scorecard is now integrated in our medium planning and shorter-term budgeting."

The company is now considering investing in a "management cockpit" which fully integrates its scorecard visualization with its data warehouse, ERP, and external intelligence feeds. The global organization structure is also under constant review since accountabilities for investment and commensurate revenue returns change shape with product acquisitions and fast-changing conditions, which vary from one market to another.

Many chief executives recognize the impact that market pressure can have on managers' performance. By decentralizing decision making, they seek to increase autonomy and accountability, boost entrepreneurship, enhance business flexibility, and improve access to opportunities. The most important effect is to put decisions in the hands of the managers who are most familiar with day-to-day business operations.

Corporations can be disaggregated in several different ways: internally, externally, or by combining elements of both. Internal disaggregation, where decision-making authority is given to managers of business units but full ownership of assets rests with the corporation, is the most conservative option.

NEW PROCESSES, NEW SKILLS, NEW SYSTEMS

In today's knowledge age, success depends on having objective information on the process and market status of all enterprise activities <u>and</u> on the fast, efficient knowledge exchange between the managers – a continuous strategic dialogue. In the strategic planning process, methods such as scenario planning should be used (for identifying and managing long-term strategic risks), real option valuation (for managing larger project and investment risks), and system thinking (for identifying growth restrictions).

Budgeting is the central instrument of traditional management systems. All management processes and methods are based on and aligned with it: from strategy planning through resource allocation and cost management to monthly performance measurement and rewards. The budget determines how managers behave and on what activities and objectives they focus. And the main problem today is the inflexibility of the budget-based management system. But a strategic instrument that locks managers into something they thought and found right at the end of the previous fiscal year, cannot be effective in a global knowledge economy with rapidly shifting market conditions and quick and nimble competitors.

Companies are moving instead to continuous rolling forecasting as part of their management processes. The key: a dynamic forecasting process. In contrast to the monthly actual/budget comparison, rolling monthly forecasts of financial performance and other non-financial value drivers related to the different value-creation processes of a company, focus managers on current and future opportunities and risks and not on the past. For the company as a whole, an institutionalized rolling forecasting process delivers more realistic projections. It enables senior management to react in time to negative developments as well as sudden opportunities.

As covered in the earlier chapters on strategic enterprise management and analytics, the implementation of information and software systems that underpin these new management processes looms as one of the most highly visible CFO missions. This includes deploying new analytic applications to support strategy and corporate performance management and operative management processes, as well as the implementation of Web-based portals for managers and eternal stakeholders.

Using a new IT infrastructure powered by open, flexible interfaces is central to success. In this way, operational systems to support new business processes can be plugged into the e-Business accounting system providing 24/7 information for management. Information can be transferred periodically or in real-time, along with data from other sources, to a data warehouse system.

The result is an integrated view across business functions and the entire systems landscape. In addition, the data structures of the data warehouse system are optimized for multidimensional and time-based analysis (called online analytical processing – OLAP). The data warehouse supports analytical software applications for better decision making and captures data for the *tableau de bord*.

COMMUNICATING VALUE INTERNALLY AND EXTERNALLY

Through a manager portal, the CFO can provide management self-services that include instant access to the new analytic tools and data, to a questions and answer catalogue, and/or to an electronic discussion forum, where managers can ask questions or discuss critical issues with colleagues from other functions.

Using such portals, the CFO is able to create a virtual community that links different people within the corporate "ecosystem" in a continuous dialogue about performance management issues. Managers, controllers, and analysts from within the company, but also partners, investors, financial analysts, or other external stakeholders, can all take part in this communication process. The business intelligence center can serve as the back office for this community.

External reporting and communications with stakeholders are more important than ever before. Research has revealed that companies with an active and efficient information policy are treated more favorably by the stock market. Reliable information from management about the potential for the future is important for investors in making informed judgments on shareholder valuation. External communication and internal management processes should be closely interlinked.

Today's statutory financial reports are too narrow: they reflect the financial aspects of executed transactions, but they do not cover adequately information on a company's intangible assets, risk exposure, or unexecuted obligations. Furthermore, 21st century business enterprises are fast changing; they involve a complex network of alliances, joint ventures, partnerships, and other related entities. These are a source of value and growth along with other intangible assets. But these networking activities are also not adequately covered in reporting disclosures. Worse, they are often ignored altogether.

In addition to covering past transactions, reports to investors should include comprehensive disclosures of networking activities, obligations undertaken (executed as well as unexecuted), and risk exposure. The major benefits of a more comprehensive disclosure system will be to improve resource allocation in the economy at large and to enhance the integrity of capital markets. The rooting out of occasional misrepresentations and instances of fraud is a vital, yet secondary objective. Skandia breaks new ground in all these areas.

CASE STUDY
Promoting Communications and Corporate Disclosure

Skandia, the financial services company, has been a pioneer in disclosing KPI-based supplementary reports, a policy started by its director for intellectual capital management, Leif Edvinsson, in 1997. Figure 8.8 shows an extract of the company's supplementary report. The concept has become part of official disclosure rules for companies in Denmark. Since January 2002, Danish

American Skandia	Year 4	Year 3	Year 2	Year 1
FINANCIAL FOCUS				
Return on capital employed (%)	21.9	27.1	28.7	12.2
Operating Result (MSEK)	1,027	579	355	
Value added/employee (SEK 000s)	2,616	2,206	1,904	
CUSTOMER FOCUS				
Number of contracts	189,104	133,641	87,846	
Savings/contract (SEK 000s)	499	396		
Surrender ratio (%)	4.4	4.4		
Points of Sale	45,881	33,287		
HUMAN FOCUS				
Number of employees, full-time	599			
Number of managers	88			
Of whom, women	50			
Training expense/employee (SEK 000s)	2.7			
PROCESS FOCUS				
Number of contracts/employee				
Adm. Exp/gross premiums written (%)				
IT expense/admin.expense (%)				
RENEWAL & DEVELOPMENT FOCUS				
Share of gross premiums written from new launches (%)				
Increase in net premiums written (%)				
Development expense/ adm. exp (%)				
Share of staff under 40 years (%)				

Figure 8.8 *Extract from Skandia's Intellectual Capital Report*

companies disposing of "significant" intellectual capital are obliged to pub lish, in addition to their annual financial reports, an "Intellectual Capital Statement."

Leif Edvinsson, was brought in to help the company transform itself from a narrowly focused life insurance firm into a successful financial services enterprise. He describes the process in great detail here.[8]

"The traditional insurance company does not make money on operations. It makes money on money. Which means, if the rules for capital gains change, then its entire business model can collapse. Internal efficiency has little impact on earnings, which go up and down with external developments in the capital markets. Skandia wanted to change the game and asked: how do we create sustainable earnings?

Our new business strategy centered on generating more value from operations. As a service company, this meant creating greater customer value.

So Skandia decided to focus on customers looking for an alternative to traditional 'life insurance.' How do you create value for a customer who intends to survive and wants to enjoy his retirement? From a sustainable earnings perspective, this means long-term customer relationships.

Skandia made the shift from traditional insurance to a successful financial services company by focusing on intellectual capital (IC). At Skandia, the value of our IC was minimal in the early 1990s; by the year 2000, it had risen to $15 bn. How was this achieved? By developing a number language for communicating the value and status of IC.

Using numbers, we began to make value drivers and the value created or not created (in customer relations, for example) transparent to stakeholders. Both transparency and useful data are crucial for understanding future earnings potential, or 'capital in waiting.' 'Innovation management' focuses on drivers and enablers for a future harvest, contrary to financially oriented management.

The challenge for us was to change from looking at the past to looking into the future. This required a new kind of mental training – we call it 'knowledge navigation.' The overall objective is to cultivate innovation. And innovation normally starts with an analysis of available options. You go for best option before best practice. Openness is crucial. You must ask and listen.

You don't have to be an expert to do this. The important thing is to cultivate a sensibility for events around you and what can be renewed. Innovative business concepts are generally based on a small shift that makes a big difference. In today's competitive world, that small difference might be the whole secret of a company's power of attraction, which is the basis for any economic success. You use facts as rear view mirrors, you don't let them block your view ahead. At Skandia, we used the 'Navigator,' a kind of balanced scorecard, to do this. The Navigator consists of five value-creating fields (see Figure 8.9).

If we picture the domain of IC as a building, our financial focus would be the roof, the top triangle. External customer relations and the internal processes would then serve as the supporting walls. The foundation and basement of the Navigator 'building' is renewal and development. The center of this home is, of course, our human capital. The financial focus is our stored past, our achievements so far. The company's people, customers, and processes are its very

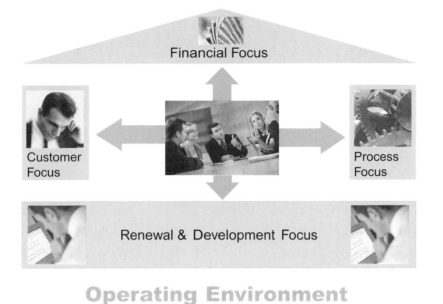

Figure 8.9 *The Skandia Navigator*

existence. Its innovation and development powers form the foundation, its future perspective, the new bottom line.

Along with financial results, the Navigator measures Skandia's IC, such as number of customer contracts, which indicates the value we created for customers, such as number of contracts per employee, which gives us a clue about effectiveness of our processes and organizational effectiveness. Another example is share of premiums from new launches (products), which indicates the success of past product innovation.

The Navigator enabled us to manage IC internally. Then we developed the annual report supplement, to let our investors and stakeholders understand the true value of our company. We said, rather than reporting on the past – the traditional annual report – we will offer a report of the future. Given the rules of the stock exchange, you can't forecast by numbers. Instead, we used narratives about internal renewal processes. Our annual report supplement combines historic and current numbers with information on value drivers for future *results, like actual and historic customer contract numbers, and explanatory stories around them. Visualizing intangibles gives you a feeling for the company's potential.*

Skandia Future Centers (SFC) is a virtual networking organization based in Vaxholm, a small town near Stockholm, in an old villa built in 1860. It is a laboratory for organizational development. It serves as an arena for knowledge safaris, strategic knowledge meetings and simulations concerts. During its first two years, the center had almost 12,000 visitors who came, for example, to test models of innovative knowledge enterprising. Gradually we expanded it by inviting thought leaders, as well as customers, and politicians. Today, it is where history and the future meet.

How can you measure productivity from an IC management point of view? By using a very simple proxy, which I call the IC multiplier. It is structural capital divided by human capital. This ratio shows that structural capital has to be larger than human capital. Otherwise you do not have a multiplier but the opposite, which in turn will lead to an erosion of human capital. If your structural capital is too weak, it will not turn human capital into value and the value of your under-exploited human capital will decrease as well. So the most important components of IC are those which make people more productive. And the financial number to assess this is value added per employee, which opens the eyes for the main value driver today.

There are four phases in the IC management evolution of an organization (see Figure 8.10):

- *Phase 1 is very much about the visualization of intangibles from a reporting perspective. This is what we did at Skandia internally through the Navigator and externally through our supplement IC-report or supplementary accounting, as it is now called by some organizations like the Securities and Exchange Commission (SEC) in the USA.*

- *Phase 2 focuses on human capital injection, often labeled competence adding or knowledge management. This involves both the search for new talent and the implementation of structures, processes and IT systems to increase knowledge sharing.*

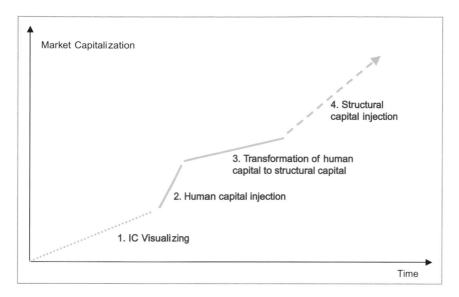

Figure 8.10 *The Four Stages of Intellectual Capital Management Evolution*

- *Phase 3 is the systematic transformation of human capital into structural capital as a multiplier, with much more sustainable earning potential. It is very much focused on packaging knowledge into recipes that can be shared globally and rapidly. We did this at Skandia by packaging knowledge on how to start an operation in a new country: this allowed us to reduce our launch time from five years to five weeks.*

- *Phase 4 is structural capital injection externally. It has a turbo effect on the IC multiplier by combining different types of structural capital for co-creation of new opportunities. One example: Cisco, which combined its own structural capital – its customer relations and the distribution and manu-facturing capabilities it commanded – with the structural capital of smaller acquired companies – their R&D capabilities, with the result that tremendous additional shareholder value was created.*

The challenge for the IC leadership, at a corporate level is to communicate these intangible value creation steps to stakeholders. The old accounting systems focused on financial capital – and, in fact, the double-entry book-keeping was a brilliant social innovation, which coded all economic information in monetary terms. Now it is time for a new generation of tools focused on intellectual capital."

Equally important, increased transparency reduces investor risk. This will lead to lower costs of capital, which will in turn lower the threshold for expected shareholder value added and help a company achieve a higher market valuation. This is especially true for enterprises with significant intangible assets, where performance results in value created, which is usually not reported through traditional accounting and financial statements.

Communicating with a growing number of individual stakeholders on a day-to-day basis represents a major challenge for most investor relations and corporate communications departments. In the future, stakeholders will require more interactive communication with companies via their websites or e-mail. At the same time, the number of information requests will increase. A common data basis makes sure that information for different stakeholder groups is consistent with internally used management information.

With a stakeholder relationship system and portal in place, a company can collect feedback on performance and strategies from investors and other stakeholders via e-mail and website very efficiently. An e-mail link can guide recipients to an electronic questionnaire posted on the company's website, where they can answer questions and make their data entries. As this information is automatically posted in the company's central performance database, it may be used directly for strategic planning.

CFO CHECKLIST

IDENTIFY YOUR HIDDEN ASSETS
What's your value gap? Calculate the difference between your shareholder value and the assets on your balance sheet. Do you fully understand the value potential in the intangible asset base? Conduct an intellectual capital audit. Look for potential missed opportunities for cross-selling and for leveraging assets such as brands, patents, and licenses.

MANAGE INTANGIBLES FOR VALUE CREATION
Are you asset "lite" or asset "rite"? Balance the ratio of tangibles to intangibles. Shed those physical assets which are not part of your value-creating core. Focus your entire corporate culture on exploiting the synergies from your investments in strategically important customers and innovations. Can you track the growth in value of your intangible assets? Put in place those mechanisms for value planning and reporting.

KEEP AN INTANGIBLES SCORECARD
Identify measures for product innovation, customer relationship management, and intellectual property. Extend measures to cover customer and product life cycles. Be sure your measurements are transparent and uniform. Incorporate your integrated strategic and performance management processes.

MAKE CUSTOMERS YOUR MOST PRIZED ASSET
Segment your customers and calculate their lifetime value. Invest in customer analytics and integrated systems, which support your customer-focused strategy. Foster collaboration and sharing across business units – supplement your corporate intranet with portals designed to maximize customer-related synergies.

OPTIMIZE YOUR INNOVATION PORTFOLIO
Marshal your R&D investments into a structured portfolio, identify where they are in the development life cycle and track milestone

achievement. Value the portfolio using suitable techniques such as real options valuation (ROV).

TRANSFORM YOUR VALUE NETWORKS INTO VALUE CENTERS

Identify where in your value chain value is created or destroyed. Define your value centers. Adapt existing planning and reporting processes to accommodate the new value center structure. Be sure that accountabilities and responsibilities are aligned with this new financial management framework.

REPORT ON INTANGIBLES TO STAKEHOLDERS

Prepare an intellectual capital report. Include information on intangible assets, strategic alliances, risk exposures, and unexecuted obligations. Develop a stakeholder relationship management system. Consider the use of portals for a two-way communication flow with investors.

CHAPTER 9

Integrating for Corporate Integrity

BALANCING VISION WITH CAUTION

Thomas Buess, CFO
Zurich Financial Services

Zurich Financial Services, the Swiss-based insurance company, has offices in more than 60 countries, employs more than 70,000 people, and serves more than 38 million customers. Total premium income for last year was US$56 bn and equity market capitalization was approximately US$18 bn.

The priority today for Thomas Buess, CFO, is: "to strengthen our balance sheet." Zurich is not unique – others in the industry have to do the same. Because of the events of Sept 11th and the subsequent decline in stock market values, the company has lost 20% of its capital value. This has weakened both its capital structure and the balance sheet. The CFO and his team will need to raise more capital and consider restructuring the finance function.

The company has grown through a series of mergers – in the late 1990s, it acquired a major asset management business and the financial services business of BAT. This made Zurich a truly global organization. As a result, achieving global integration is a big issue for Zurich.

As Thomas notes: "We have been very decentralized, and are now reorganizing the business into four strong business divisions – one in the UK, two in the Americas, one in Continental Europe.

However, our customers don't really care about how we are organized geo-graphically. Our corporate customers, for example, buy globally – and we have to consolidate customer information from around the world. We no longer see the business as just a range of insurance products, but we focus more on customers. We try to differentiate between retail customers (high-income individuals), the commercial segment, and our corporate customers, the multinationals."

What are the future finance challenges facing Zurich? According to Thomas: focusing on the drivers of shareholder value. The most important thing for us is to provide solutions to our customers, not just products. We are looking for synergies and new ways to price products with higher margins justified by a total solution value proposition.

We need to analyze by business unit what drives shareholder value. In finance, we have established a shareholder value model. Not just to value projects but also to value clients. Our actuaries use real options valuation (ROV) in individual client situations. ROV is very close to what our business is all about – the trade-off between probability, risk, and profitability."

What drives customer value? "The brand, the price, customer acquisition cost, customer retention, and the distribution channel. We treat our customers as an intangible asset and calculate their contribution to shareholder value."

How do you measure the value of a customer? "This varies from customer segment to customer segment. It's easier to measure the value of a corporate customer, more difficult for a private customer. For corporate customers we can allocate risk-based capital and price products on an individually prepared net present value based price. By sharing claims information, we can build strategic partnerships with our corporate clients who participate in the risks to prevent and reduce claims. We give them access to our claims statistics. Some customers can be virtually self-insured using our services and balance sheet while carrying some of the loss risk themselves.

We have shared services for finance, IT and claims (shared across customer segments). Claims are a very high proportion of the costs of some of our products. But, by creating shared services which have the scale and focus, we can save cost and achieve cost leadership."

Clearly, integration is a big issue for Zurich. Customers, business processes, and information – and crucially people – have to be brought together globally through technology. The company is building an information exchange to share data with its customers and respond to transparency requirements.

"There are many problems with having a decentralized organization like ours. First, we have 30 ledgers, so consolidation is a problem. One of our objectives is to improve our closing process. It currently takes too long and involves more than 400 reporting units. The virtual close is top of my agenda with my finance people.

We are changing the character of our finance function. I am getting the message across that we, in finance, are not scorekeepers or policemen, but business advisers. The finance function of the 1980s was large and fat. The finance function of the 1990s was much slimmer and focused more on control and decision support. Our vision for the finance function of the current decade is virtual, with the CFO at the center of a web of relationships, rather than sitting at the top of a corporate headquarters.

Turning to systems, we have an SAP backbone for back-office transaction processing. For the front office, we use different solutions for customer relationship management and for billing. We use technology to treat customers as business partners. So systems integration is important to us.

Procurement was the first support function to go global, with one global instance of SAP running in conjunction with some best-of-breed software. We also have one portal for senior management. With a single sign-on, the senior manager can get all the information he needs at his fingertips – for example, daily information on insurance premiums. We have integrated our ERP with our data warehouse and our portal.

Our management information is quite advanced – we can slice 'n dice in multi-dimensions – by customer segment, by business unit, by business line, by distribution channel. We also have external intelligence feeds – such as competitor market share prices. This information portal is called My Gateway. It brings together financial and non-financial information, the internal world with the external world."

In changing the role of finance, however, I put people top of the agenda. Our skills have to change. We are moving away from number crunching to becoming business partners. I believe the initiative that will bring all these changes together – in processes, in technology, in efficiency, and in skills – is the fast close.

"By making the year-end close a non-event, effectively just pressing the button – we can avoid wasteful reconciliations and error corrections. Instead of just looking at the numbers, we can find out what lies behind them. We won't be looking backwards, we will be looking forwards. Financial discipline will be even tighter, transparency even greater. My job is to balance vision with caution."

Most of the CFOs interviewed for this book have much in common with Thomas Buess of Zurich. He very much sees the role of the CFO as providing the necessary "checks and balances" to counterbalance the more visionary, expansive role of the CEO. On the one hand, it's important to drive the business forward with vision and global ambition. On the other hand, this vision has to be tempered with caution.

Zurich, along with its industry and most of the world's publicly quoted companies, has suffered in the recent stock market collapses. It is having to recapitalize, take stock, and reorganize. Investors are looking to CFOs to provide them with reassurance and confidence – doing the *basics* well. Thankfully, most CFOs have their businesses well under control, but renewed rigor and discipline are priorities. Despite pressure to go "back to basics," CFOs of the world's leading companies are continuing the drive to develop their finance functions to provide better, faster reporting and are determined to play their part in moving the company's performance and strategic positioning to the next level.

We now bring together the underpinning themes throughout this book – integration, reducing complexity, taking advantage of technology, and most crucially, charting a positive vision for the future of the finance function in these uncertain times.

To recap so far. In Chapters 2, 3, and 4, we discussed the *financial supply chain* – leveraging your ERP investment, reducing cost, improving speed, and restructuring. In Chapters 5, 6, and 7, we covered the *information supply chain* – strategic management processes (SEM), analytics, and emerging technologies, such as portals. The previous chapter dealt with the vexed issue of *intangible assets*.

In the wake of the scandals of Enron and World.com, this concluding chapter starts by examining the current debate on accounting standards – and offers some suggestions for rebuilding public trust and promoting the role of the CFO as independent business partner. We introduce a fresh concept – the *corporate reporting supply chain* – which defines stakeholder requirements and offers some proposals for how corporate reporting could be improved to go beyond current limitations and tackle the still largely unresolved issue of how to report the true economic value of your enterprise, *including intangible assets*. This final chapter then offers practical pointers on: how to use the fast close to improve reporting – and how to integrate financial, information, and corporate reporting supply chains.

GLOBAL GAAP AND ACCOUNTABILITY FOR VALUE

Corporations have an obligation to willingly provide shareholders and other stakeholders with information – this is the spirit of transparency. However, for various reasons, management and boards are not consistently making available information that they know investors would want. Too often, this failure is based on the mistaken belief that playing the *earnings game* – managing and beating the market's expectations of the next period's earnings – will increase shareholder value. Consider the recent controversial circumstances:

1. Enron's off-balance-sheet financing and reporting practices

2. Tyco International's acquisition accounting and offshore tax practices

3. The transfer of operating assets to capital assets at World.com.

Just providing the right information is not enough. A firm commitment to accountability is also key. In the end, it all depends on integrity. Rules and regulations alone will not do the job!

The authors of this book believe there should be a global GAAP – a set of accounting standards for reporting a company's financial performance for a defined period. Today, every country that has a capital market either uses a set of local GAAP or a set of national or international standards. Not only the quality of these standards is country-specific but also application and auditing of these country-based standards also vary widely by company.

The big problem with all these GAAPs is that they are generally based on historical accounting and cost conventions. However, capital markets focus on value – and as we have seen in Chapter 8 on intangible assets – value can be substantially different from historical cost. Critics say that existing GAAP:

1. Fosters the earnings "game" played by both management and the markets since earnings have long been the single most important measure of performance.

2. Does not account for or disclose certain types of information about intangible assets.

3. Does not communicate adequate information about value creation because it is a mixed model that includes historical cost, amortized cost, written down cost, and fair value.

So CFOs of global companies face a number of dilemmas. The *first dilemma*: if they are listed in the United States, they have to conform to SEC regulations, rules, and US GAAP. However, if they operate elsewhere in the world, they are more likely to want to adopt International Accounting Standards (IAS).

Implementation of IAS will affect the whole company – not just accounting and IT! Affected companies will have to prepare at least two sets of financial statements, which requires significantly greater time and expense.

The *second dilemma* is how to communicate to stakeholders the underlying economic value of the enterprise which is not covered by the IAS – we refer to this later in this chapter as the information gap.

CASE STUDY
The Importance of Transparency in a Pharmaceutical Company

Not long ago, this was a small country's most valuable company, worth approximately $20 bn. It is now worth a fraction of this amount. The chief executive, who has been the architect of the company's rapid growth over the past seven years, recognizes that the company is facing "the most challenging time" in its history. He says the company is "committed to achieving clarity and transparency by creating a business that is easier to understand and evaluate."

Yet the company's annual report, the document intended to provide accurate data about the company's finance, has raised a host of new doubts. In passages of bewildering complexity, it describes highly unusual transactions in which the company sold the royalties on some leading products to previously unknown companies, seemingly created for this purpose.

Money flows back and forth between the parent and its satellite royalty companies in an almost incomprehensible way. Even though it has sold the royalty rights – perhaps for a total of $360 million, although that is not entirely clear – the company retains an option to buy them back, seemingly at steeply inflated prices. Why? What is the logic of these transactions?

The deals appear to have been driven more by financial engineering than any underlying commercial purpose. The company's pharmaceutical marketing satellite treated royalty revenues as "product revenue," although they appear to have no direct correlation to drug sales. The auditor assures shareholders that the group's financial statement "gives a true and fair view" of company business. True and fair? Maybe. Clear and transparent? Most definitely not.

The chief executive says the company has always made full disclosures of its joint ventures and transactions. He maintains that nothing was hidden and everything was clear. This is hard to reconcile with recent revelations. Investors insist they knew nothing about the royalty deals until recently. These products were important present or future revenue generators. The debt financing of the off-balance sheet vehicles that owned many of its investments in small bio-tech companies was guaranteed by the parent. It was this revelation to investors that prompted the initial collapse in the company's share price, which has damaged its ability to repay loan notes.

Some would say this company used excessive discretion in its accounting. In the current air of suspicion, however, investors are left fearing that published numbers bear little relation to the underlying reality of the business.

Better investor communication should also mean companies become less wary about revealing bad news before they are forced to do so. For example, IAS will change the valuation of company assets, so start explaining this to investors now. Accounting standards also require all previously reported goodwill and intangible assets arising from prior mergers and acquisitions to be tested annually for impairment.

Unexpected revelations of impairments are not a good way to instill confidence among investors. Companies should also use their websites more effectively to explain financial changes. Some argue that firms should disclose new types of information to a far greater extent. CFOs and their finance teams should diversify their expertise to include not only financial measures, but indicators of true future value – their intangible assets. A company's true future value depends on whether its customers, employees, and suppliers will stay loyal, buy more, recommend the company to others, and collaborate with it. Here are some tips for ensuring transparency:

1. *Information* – should be timely, relevant, and in plain language, not accountancy jargon. It should not gloss over the bad news. Accuracy is essential. Remember that non-financial information can be as important as the figures.

2. *Communication* – consider a variety of methods, from press releases, letters to investors, website postings, and open meetings.

3. *Access* – identify who should be able to access this information and ensure that your chosen methods will reach everyone concerned.

REBUILDING PUBLIC TRUST

However your organization defines transparency, it is likely that investors will have more confidence in companies which provide information that they see as accessible and trustworthy. Consider the approach taken by the CFO of the Bridgestone Corporation, headquartered in Japan.

CASE STUDY
Corporate Health at Bridgestone

Bridgestone Corporation is the world's largest manufacturer of tires and other rubber products. Bridgestone and Firestone brand tires are dominant in Formula 1 and in Indy car racing. It has diversified away from tires into various *industrial products, construction materials, sporting goods, and bicycles. Global sales are approx US$20 bn, 43% in the Americas. Although the OEM market is important, the replacement tire market represents a very substantial part of the business.*

Two years ago, Bridgestone had a major problem with quality of its Firestone brand in the USA. These problems are now largely over – American sales of Bridgestone brand tires are surging, powered by new product introductions. Leading the sales recovery in North America are it's 2,200 company-owned stores – the world's largest tire and automotive service network, in conjunction with thousands of independent retailers.

Says Hiroshi Kanai, senior vice president and CFO: "We are a profitable company – with returns on equity of 15% and earnings after tax of 5%. Our market cap is approximately US$12.5 bn. Our four major challenges are:

1. *Full recovery from our US recall problem and rebuilding those customer relationships*

2. *Increasing our market share in Europe from 15 to 20%*

3. *Opening up new markets, e.g. in China and Latin America*

4. *Investing further in our core technology, originated in Japan and adapted for use across the world*

We are essentially a Japanese-headquartered company with a major market focus on North America and extensive international operations. Our corporate philosophy: trust and pride – the trust that we earn from customers and from everyone in the community. And the pride that we feel in earning that trust. Our biggest global customers are General Motors and Toyota. Our fiercest competitors are Michelin (Europe) and Goodyear (USA)."

Bridgestone behaves and acts on an international scale, not only in its approach to technology, but in its relationships with customers and in leveraging their bargaining power with suppliers. It places a strong emphasis on accounting discipline and has a standardized approach to accounting policies and systems. Hiroshi goes on to say: "As a global company with a Japanese base, our integration themes are:

1. *To build on the Japanese accounting standards and culture, conforming to US GAAP where appropriate and IAS elsewhere in the world*

2. *To leverage our global banking relationships, systems, and cash pooling – utilizing our existing local banking relationships, but networking these together on a global scale*

3. *To improve the speed and accuracy of our management information over the Internet*

4. *To leverage our IT investment across the world, particularly our investment in SAP as ERP*

As CFO, the biggest issue for me is RISK. *Our risk prevention measures are:*

1. *Transparency of data – going to the core of what drives performance.*

2. *Global information flows triggered by local incidents (alerts), on an exception basis for headquarters review and possible action – quickly. Having data analytics which provide you, the Corporate CFO, with an accurate judgment of dynamic risk situations, as they unfold.*

3. *Global information on product and service quality –this is* the *most important aspect for any CFO of any global corporation. Maintaining corporate reputation in relation to quality is both the biggest opportunity and potentially the biggest weakness in a worldwide operation of our scale."*

What should the CFO's biggest priority be? "I have no doubts here: corporate health *from a long-term perspective. This is all about* corporate stamina, corporate chemistry. *Anticipating what can go wrong and taking strong counter measures as early as possible. This view is influenced, not only by our recent exposure on the North American market, but also by the recent financial scandals with companies like Enron and World.com."*

CFOs should work on their risk detection and management skills. For example, when closing the books and financial reporting, encourage a corporate mindset that focuses on long-term, sustainable value creation.

Encourage the use of accounting standards, disciplines, and methodologies which give a realistic view of the long-term, rather than short-term illusory perceptions of success.

Today, only certain companies – typically those in financial services – consider risk a key value driver. However, enterprise-wide risk management is slowly being recognized as an important value driver in a broader range of industries. Companies such as Bridgestone are striving to understand more fully the relationship between decisions made and risks thereby entailed.

Externally – stakeholders, regulators, and the general public (as private investors) are increasingly looking for someone in the business they can trust and rely upon. Chief executives are accustomed to signing off accounts – but not to the threat of criminal charges! The US Sarbanes–Oxley Act has been rushed through recently in the wake of the Enron and World.com scandals. Under its core clause, CEOs and CFOs have to certify the company's accounts. This could apply to any director of any company (whether in the US, Europe, or Japan) that either has a listing in, or has raised money on, the American markets.

In the UK and elsewhere, similar corporate governance measures have existed for almost a decade. In contrast to their US counterparts, European directors have signed off their accounts for years. To quote Jan Hommen,[1] Vice Chairman and CFO of Philips, the Dutch electronics manufacturer, "The Sarbanes–Oxley Act is a confirmation of what we have always done. We file under the existing SEC requirements every quarter and I personally sign that everything is correct." But Sarbanes–Oxley adds criminal sanctions – that's the difference. CEOs or CFOs could find themselves facing a long spell in a US jail and this legislation has an impact across the world.

Clearly, the CEO is accountable to stakeholders overall, but the CFO is the executive primarily responsible for timely and accurate financial information.

Today's CFO is looking to exert even greater control and financial discipline[2]:

1. *Producing* financial results, management and forecast information

2. *Reporting* the above results to the business and other parties

3. *Commenting* on past, current and forecast performance

4. *Guardian* of corporate assets

5. *Business partner*, providing financial advice and input into areas such as investment appraisal, operational decisions, scenario analysis, and results interpretation

CFO AS INDEPENDENT BUSINESS PARTNER

None of these roles are new; they have historically formed the bedrock of what the finance function does and will continue to do. What has changed is the emphasis on these roles. The CFO is not just the scorekeeper, not just the business partner inside the business – the CFO now has to play the role of the *independent business partner*. Discussions with CFOs show an appetite for change. Few CFOs want to get "back in their box" as score-keepers. Most see themselves as business partners but, of course, they see their governance role as crucial in protecting shareholder and public interest. They continue to be involved in creating value, but put fresh emphasis on being the external voice of the business.

Being an independent business partner means having to challenge the basis of figures supplied internally with even greater rigor. This challenge process will have a ripple effect through levels of management. Being an independent business partner also means communicating to shareholders – and any other interested stakeholders for that matter – about value and performance (see Figure 9.1).

To quote Walter Steidl, CFO of Generali Insurances, Austria:

> "The CFO is essentially the business conscience of the company. In times like these however pressures for radical change increase dramatically. The CFO must pursue new strategies to sustain and grow corporate value."

The capital markets are demanding more information faster. They want predictability. They want an objective, as well as a commercial view. The CFO and the finance function require a thorough understanding of the business and its performance drivers. In summary, the new role of the finance function has to:

1. Deliver the objective view directly to non-executive directors, shareholders, analysts, regulators, as well as wider external communities. This gives comfort that the facts, figures and opinions being communicated represent a complete and fair view of corporate performance.

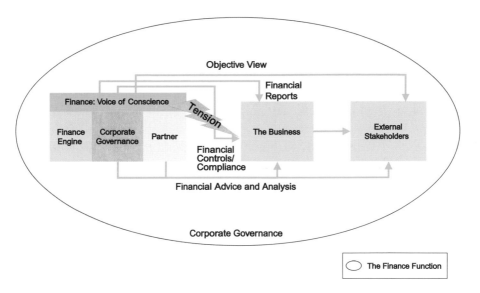

Figure 9.1 *The Voice of Conscience*

2. Challenge and validate business decisions. Business plans and financial projections are tested, accepted, or rejected. Ongoing performance is measured and monitored, with the need for action being flagged. The board can make informed emotional and political decisions based on rational information provided by finance.

As such there has to be a healthy tension between management and the finance function. Increasingly, the CFO will have to say "no" to management decisions and behaviors which run contrary to the interests of investors. As Manfred Gentz, CFO at DaimlerChrysler puts it: "Finance people should have a high degree of integrity and follow moral and ethical standards, even if they are asked not to do so. There have to be *some* rules finance people *have* to follow. This is the only way to regain the confidence of the capital markets."

THE CORPORATE REPORTING SUPPLY CHAIN

Acting as the external voice of the business, the CFO has to ensure that the appropriate information is gained efficiently and distributed effect-

ively. The *corporate reporting supply chain*[3] begins with company executives, who prepare the financial statements that are reported to investors
and other stakeholders. These financial statements are approved by an
independent board of directors, attested to by an independent auditing
firm, analyzed by sell-side analysts, and broadcast by information
distributors, including data vendors and the news media. Investors and
other stakeholders then make their decisions. Standard setters and market
regulators establish the roles and responsibilities of many, although
certainly not all, of the participants in the corporate reporting supply
chain.

The time has come to reexamine how this reporting supply chain works
and how it can be improved. This can only be done by stepping back from
the drama of the moment, yet using recent events as a catalyst for reflec-
tion. Business failure will always exist in free capital markets; even the
best corporate reporting will not make this go away. Improved reporting
can, however, reduce the number and consequences of business failures
when it enables management, the board, and the market to respond more
quickly. Figure 9.2: Finance Under the Spotlight shows the impact of
external pressures on the role of the CFO and finance processes.

Some of the "links" in the chain–company executives and boards of
directors – require no explanation. They have the responsibility for preparing or approving the information that companies report. Other terms
used to describe participants in the supply chain deserve some clarifica-
tion.

1. *Independent auditors* – refers to the firms that provide independent
   audit opinions on the majority of the financial statements issued by
   publicly listed companies worldwide.

2. *Information distributors* – refers to data vendors that consolidate
   reported information and provide it for others to use. This group also
   includes news media, websites, and other communications media.

3. *Analysts* – refers to those who use the information reported by companies, usually in combination with other information and research, to
   evaluate a company's prospects and performance. In this book, the
   term refers most often to sell-side analysts who write research reports
   and issue recommendations on stock purchases to individual and
   institutional investors.

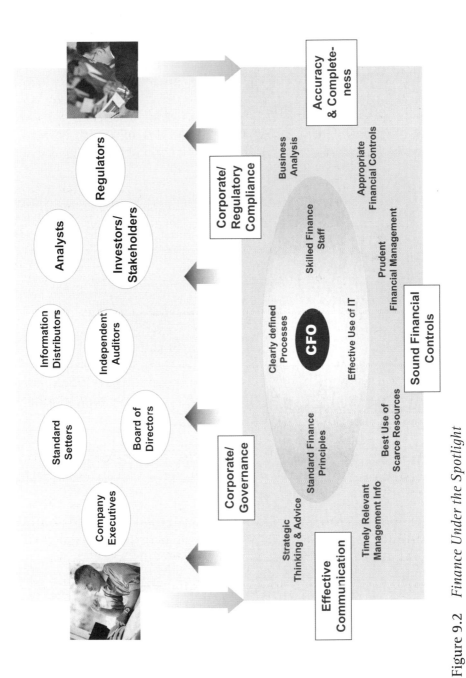

Figure 9.2   *Finance Under the Spotlight*

4. *Investors and stakeholders* – are the ultimate consumers of corporate reporting information. "Stakeholders" refers to the myriad other users of reported information, including company employees, business partners, vendors, and suppliers.

5. *Standard setters* – refers most often to the organizations that set accounting and auditing standards.

6. *Regulators* – includes national governmental agencies, territorial coalitions, transnational bodies, and stock exchanges that set and enforce rules relating to corporate reporting.

The CFO will need to bring together the *information supply chain* referred to in Chapter 1 with the *corporate reporting supply chain* referred to here. The information supply chain – internally oriented – has to provide external investors with flawless information. Other stakeholders must also have information which is complete, accurate, and trustworthy. For capital markets to function effectively, there is a need for more and better information and corporate transparency.

Each interested party represented in the corporate reporting supply chain have their own goals and requirements. Samuel DiPiazza, Jr and Robert Eccles, in their book *Building Public Trust*, suggest a three-tier model for corporate transparency:

- *Tier 1* – a set of truly global and *generally accepted* accounting principles (global GAAP, as referred to earlier in this chapter).

- *Tier 2* – standards for measuring and reporting information that are *industry-specific*, consistently applied, and developed by the industries themselves.

- *Tier 3* – guidelines for *company-specific* information such as strategy, plans, risk management practices, compensation policies, corporate governance, and performance measures unique to the company.

The three-tier model does not mean companies simply report information at three disconnected levels. In common with our theme – the *CFO is the business integrator* – **these three tiers of information have to be integrated**. The historic financial results have to be related first to the economic context of the industry in which the company operates. And, secondly, in relation to its own company specific value-drivers. Stakeholders will then have a view of the company's performance which:

1. Conforms to accounting standards and principles

2. Can be benchmarked against industry specific trends

3. Reflects the intrinsic economic value of the enterprise – the shareholder value

The United States has developed unique and highly specialized rules for accounting for specialized industries. Only in the financial services sector are such rules more widely adopted. Standards for reporting on shareholder value are even less well established. Value reporting is a relatively new concept and many of the reporting requirements are at the company's discretion. There are certain notable exceptions – for example, Denmark's agency for trade and industry has issued guidelines *for intellectual capital statements*. The agency expects improved external reporting to give stakeholders a better grasp of the value of intangible assets.

CLOSING THE INFORMATION GAP

We make the assumption that the CFO and the finance function are fully equipped to satisfy accounting principles and meet accounting standards. However, as discussed in earlier chapters, companies generally are in a state of transition in providing information on value drivers and measures for intangibles at both an industry– and company-specific level. There is a major information gap.

Surveys of various industries show there are information gaps in relation to market share and growth, customer and brand equity, product innovation, and quality of management. Business segment information – for example, analysis of sales and value by customer segment and product segment – is also often lacking and is in fact now a requirement of US and International accounting standards.

CASE STUDY
Value Drivers in the Telecommunications Industry

A telecommunications company wanted to assess exactly how its value would be affected by deregulation. Future revenues would be driven by competition and downward pressure on prices. Creating coefficients of value, management

could see that every 1% loss of market share by 2001 would cause shareholder value to diminish by $227 million. Each 1% drop in annual price tariffs would cost $444 million in value. On the upside, if the company reduced annual operating costs by 1%, or $83 million, it stood to rebuild value by $1 bn. The company now uses coefficients of value to prioritize all proposed change projects. Implementation is monitored via operational and value-creating reporting metrics.

Figure 9.3 illustrates how the company linked telecoms sector specific value drivers to its overall shareholder value model.

In Chapter 5 on strategic enterprise management, we explored how one value driver can be related to another. Value-driver trees can be built which provide linkage all the way through an organization – from the bottom to the top – to a model of shareholder value. The issue for the CFO is first, how to build value-driver trees for internal use, then, how much of this information should be communicated externally. A growing number

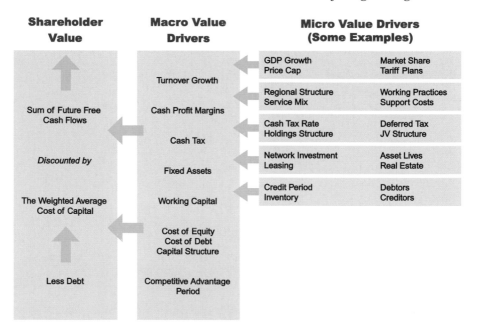

Figure 9.3   *Value Drivers for a Telecommunications Operator*

of companies have begun to adopt value-reporting concepts and produce reports on value drivers.

TIMELY AND ACCURATE FINANCIAL REPORTING

Today the "new" CFO of a globally acting company has to communicate additional information, such as market share and growth, customer and brand equity, product innovation and quality of management. He also has to ensure flawless and trustworthy legal information according to legal regulations, such as the Sarbanes-Oxley Act. The combination of these requirements may easily bring the corporate reporting supply chain to a deadlock. It is therefore vitally important that an efficient reporting concept is developed.

Fast, accurate financial reporting has always been a high priority. At the beginning of this chapter, the CFO of Zurich Financial Services focuses on the *fast close* as the heart of his finance transformation program. Closing the books is a simple task . . . in theory! In practice, the closing process often becomes extremely complex and very demanding. Why? Because organizations today are larger and more complex. Businesses change more rapidly – products change, structure changes, new distributions channels emerge. Accounting standards are becoming more complex and in many industries (such as banking) regulation and reporting requirements are increasing. Many of the CFOs interviewed for this book believe there are benefits to a faster close. This view is reinforced by a research study carried out by KPMG in 2000 citing the following reasons for a faster close:

1. Faster publication for benefit of shareholders
2. Board demands faster publication of internal information
3. Demonstrate professionalism of reporting
4. Capital market demands earlier publication
5. Time gained is used for analyses that bring value added
6. Competitors publish their figures earlier

The same study showed that companies experienced the following problems (in order of priority) in achieving a speedy close and a high standard of annual reporting:

1. Poor quality of figures

2. Insufficient integration of data processing systems

3. "Surprise" during annual close

4. Large number of reporting levels

5. Insufficient checks, unclear reporting process

6. Auditors need too much time

7. Insufficient IT support for the reporting process

8. Difference in accounting principles

A faster close is not just a matter of reducing the cycle time with new technology. It's about analyzing underlying problems that are causing the time delays and then fixing them, one by one. Ultimately it's about changing business processes. This requires strong leadership and sustained commitment by the CFO.

A finance spokesman from Motorola commented on the impact of the faster close and more streamlined reporting at Motorola: "the internal audit department measurements showed that quality has improved substantially as a result of our fast-close project, there has been a 33% reduction in management and clerical staff time involved, and an improvement in audit staff productivity of at least 25%." Motorola achieves a monthly close in one and a half days and a year-end close in five days. Initiatives that helped them achieve this include:

1. Evaluation of performance and variances from plan are monitored on an ongoing basis

2. Corporate adjustments are discussed and processed one week before the cut-off

3. All submissions are in base currency (USD), which provides a consistent view of the results

4. A third-party inter-company billing process leverages EDI systems for invoices, payments, and receipts. Minimal time is spent at month-end on inter-company account analysis

A faster close can eliminate nonvalue-added activities and enable staff to spend more time on productive analysis. A faster close should also give you better, more comprehensive and transparent data – making decision-making easier and supporting successful stakeholder communications. A faster close requires increased standardization in accounting practices and better coordinated, more streamlined business processes.

There are particular issues to be resolved between subsidiaries and the group accounting center. Such issues range from inter-company account reconciliation, and translation of data from local GAAP to your consolidated reporting GAAP, to the requirement for manual input of data by subsidiaries into group reporting format. Figure 9.4 shows that the quickest benefits achieved by a faster close are usually obtained just by better management; further benefits can be obtained by changes in business processes; ultimately new technology has to be implemented to achieve the rest.

Most companies who achieve the fast close use consolidation software which is integrated with their ERP transactional systems. In an ideal world, there is a single chart of accounts, one standard consolidation system, and every affiliate reports to the center using one international GAAP.

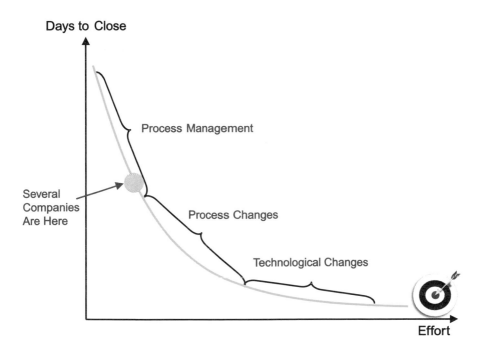

Figure 9.4 *Achieving Quick Wins with a Fast Close*

CASE STUDY
The Integrated Benefits of a Faster Close

This company was only able to close its books within 12 days of the month end – this was too long and the CFO initiated a project to cut the time taken down to 5 days. The first step was business process reengineering – bottlenecks were found in data coding, inefficiencies in month-end procedures resulting in higher levels of journal postings, significant manual intervention, and disputed inter-group recharges.

The new revised closing processes involved the following:

1. *Increased automation – for example, online daily posting of subledgers were integrated with sales and costing reports.*

2. *Reduced errors – accounts code validation was done at source, removing extensive error correction at the month end.*

3. *Discipline – strict cut-off procedures enforced at affiliates.*

4. *Reporting – the consolidation of results, the production of monthly management accounts, and the production of management information were carried out using integrated software, removing the need for spreadsheets and manual interventions.*

The affiliates were the initial focus of attention and saw improvements early on in the project. The group had to adopt a single chart of accounts and quick wins were also achieved by closing prior to the month end and rolling forward. But the burden of delivering improved closing performance also fell on the group head office. The head office part of the project covered not only statutory reporting but the interfaces with treasury, tax, and budgeting functions. The project was further extended at a later stage to include management reporting at board level which also covered non-financial data.

*Having achieved the benefits of a **hard close** – accurately recording transactions at source, aligning the chart of accounts and reducing reconciliations – the company went on to achieve the benefit's of a **soft close**. This meant finding an effective balance between timeliness and accuracy. Initiatives included* *reduced allocations, a materiality guide for adjustments, automated accruals, and weekly rather than monthly reporting cycles.*

*The **fast close** involves automatic interfaces between financial and operational systems, the use of portals and very little, if any, manual processing, full online review and real time reporting.*

Focus was achieved by using highly visible performance indicators for measuring in both quantitative and qualitative terms the progress the company was making in achieving its fast close objectives. Special attention was paid to the change process. A main board member took an active role as project sponsor; a special effort was made to gain the buy-in of key personnel involved in the closing process; organizational changes were communicated to staff affected as early as possible to eliminate uncertainty.

Most organizations assume that high-quality information cannot be delivered quickly. Manfred Gentz (DaimlerChrysler) disagrees: "when we shortened the process the quality didn't suffer, in fact quality has improved with the fast close." Quite often organizations that spend too long on the closing process incur a higher marginal cost with very little benefit in materiality terms in additional accuracy. Many of the benefits of a fast close are not fully realized until the end of an improvement project.

INTEGRATING PROCESSES, PEOPLE, AND TECHNOLOGY

Earlier in this chapter we mentioned the importance of integrating the *financial supply chain*, the *information supply chain* and the *corporate reporting supply chain*.

In the following case study the mySAP Financials solution is presented for integrating processes, people and technology to meet the requirements of today's high performance and adaptive enterprise.

CASE STUDY
mySAP Financials, Value Proposition

Hans-Dieter Scheuermann, Senior Vice President of General Business Unit Financials at SAP AG, describes SAP's strategic approach to developing the

mySAP Financials solution: "In the traditional ERP world organizational structures and their relationships are represented in a uniform process concept, database and system. Today's business models create many complex intra- and inter-company relationships and the classic ERP world is too limiting.
   There is a need for:

- *Adaptability: for solving complex business issues and for managing the unexpected*

- *Usability: role-based user interaction across the enterprise*

- *Scalability: to benefit from the economies of sharing IT and processes across the enterprise*

CFOs often find that organizational complexity gets in the way of transparency and harmonization. Integrated systems like SAP's, where interoperability is achieved through standards implemented in technology, are a necessary prerequisite to making changes happen. So standardized enterprise processes have to be built on an IT platform which is integrated – linking processes with technology. SAP's approach to this technical platform involves integrating process networks, application architecture and process communication standards. This three-tier platform is illustrated in Figure 9.5.
   SAP decided to go for a Web service architecture to implement this integrated IT platform and provide enterprise flexibility and scalability through these building blocks:

- *Exchange technology to provide intra- and inter-enterprise integration*

- *Process modeling and monitoring tools to ensure consistency*

- *System landscape management tools to allow transparency and control*

- *Portals to deliver people-centric information*

- *Applications to guarantee semantic integration and offer encapsulated web services on the level of process steps and functions (for example, Web service "actual currency rate" from Reuters).*

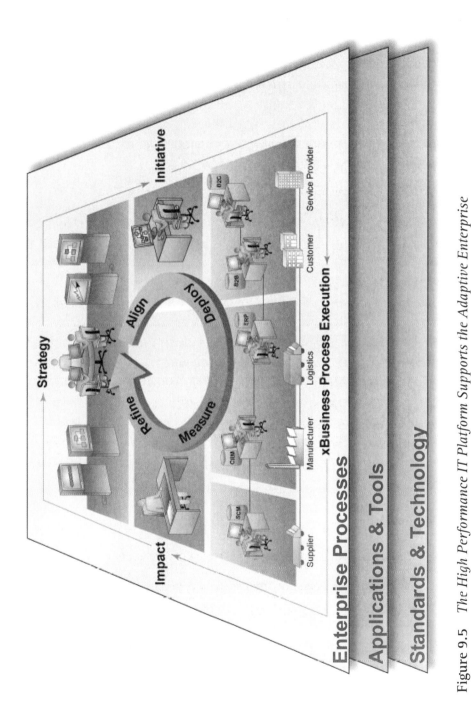

Figure 9.5   *The High Performance IT Platform Supports the Adaptive Enterprise*

Hans-Dieter says "Our development plans are evolutionary. We build upon a solid foundation from the past and a vision of what will be required in the future. Figure 9.6 illustrates the evolution of these three levels in our integrated platform.

We have always expanded and adapted our solution according to current finance demands – for example, changes in reporting, the application of IAS and conformance to US GAAP. Increasingly, financial statements and valuation standards are based on shareholder value instead of only on creditor protection and caution as prescribed by the German GAAP (HGB).

The requirement to report according to segments leads to a convergence of external and internal accounting. This convergence is desirable for inter-company communication and could lead to a reduction in cost while increasing the speed and quality of financial statements. To satisfy the requirements of the capital markets only real-time data offers the required company control and cost reduction.

The fast close is a great motivator for change – heightening the importance of speed, materiality and transparency. Our accounting solution supports these trends through extensive automated functions for the reorganization and restatement of data. There are also new factors influencing external financial statements. In addition to data on actuals, for example, we incorporate intangible assets (for goodwill impairment tests), auditable plan figures (for the SEC requirement for forward-looking statements), rolling forecasts and comprehensive risk reporting. Fast close delivers better data quality for external, as well as for internal, decision-making and therefore is a valid contribution to strategic enterprise management.

In the past software solutions were designed to reflect integrated transaction processes. Nowadays the focus is on integrated decision support:

- *Analysis and retrieval of external data*
- *Strategic decision-making at corporate and business unit level*
- *Analytics for optimizing operational processes*

One of the reasons for the worldwide success of the SAP solutions at more than 28,000 customer sites is the integration and process know-how in our solution. Increasingly, changing organizational models mean that in the future, **processes**

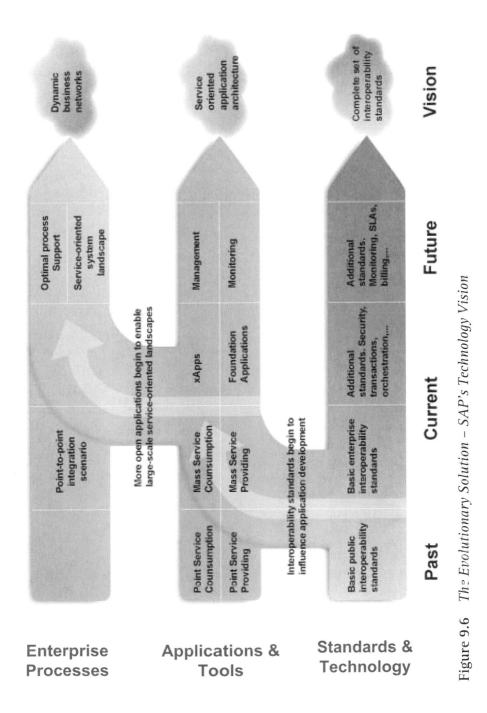

Figure 9.6   *The Evolutionary Solution – SAP's Technology Vision*

and **data** will have to be adapted quickly and flexibly for the **user** in ever-changing system landscapes.

Today, as a result of increased empowerment, through the use of technology and the growing trend toward self-service, each employee has to process more information than ever before – and make decisions more quickly. Fortunately technology is available today for integrating business processes and making information available to users, reducing this potential overload. The vision for the finance function must take advantage of user-centric technologies – such as portals – as well as process-centric integrating technologies such as exchange infrastructure for B2B and A2A (application to application)."

The links between portals, applications and exchanges is illustrated in Figure 9.7.

Hans-Dieter goes on to say: "Portals provide made-to-measure, user-specific interfaces. This improves efficiency and increases acceptance by the end user.

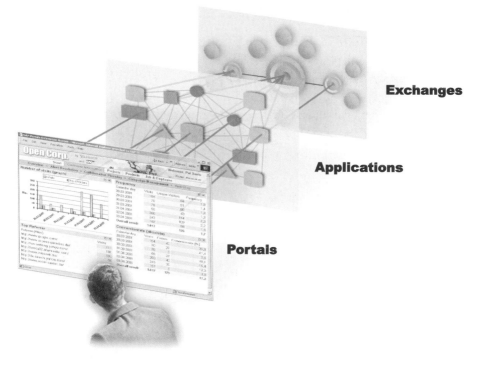

Figure 9.7 *User-centric and Process-centric Integration*

The enterprise portal offers centralized access to all existing applications; where the applications originate is irrelevant – in the portals these applications are integrated seamlessly. The exchange infrastructure connects all these system landscapes in an organized way, reducing the complexity created by too many interfaces between the applications of different external suppliers, external customers, and internal users. Such integration is very important to our customers today – that is why we in SAP have made it readily accessible."

The mySAP Financials team has created three key functional areas for its accounting solutions:

1. *Financial Supply Chain Management is the financials part of the value chain required for collaborative processing with suppliers, customers and financial institutions.*

2. *Business Accounting is the financials link that enables process integration and information integration in a heterogeneous environment via, for example, uniform valuation methods.*

3. *Strategic Enterprise Management and Business Analytics covers both the comprehensive functions for SEM of the corporation or a business unit and the analytical applications to control and optimize the business processes.*

Figure 9.8 shows how the business processes can be brought together to provide a holistic solution. The CFO and the finance function can use this as a starting point in developing their vision for the future.

To quote an established SAP customer in integrating processes and technology, Hitachi's Executive Vice President and Representative Director, Yoshiki Yagi says: "We unified the accounting system for the whole company. Based on SAP R/3 we implemented and expanded shared services (for payment, settlement, fixed-assets and closing). We use the business warehouse (SAP BW) for KPI management. Of course, there are still challenges to overcome, for example the data transfer between the new consolidation system and our "hi-Fronts" (Hitachi financial real-time operation network systems), but the concentration and standardization will have an enormous impact on our operational power."

Hans-Dieter goes on to point out: "we bring together processes, information and the role of the user in application scenarios to demonstate how all this

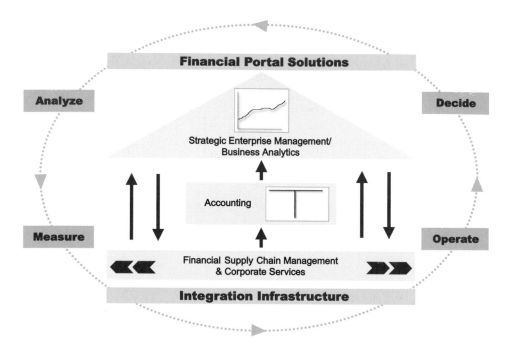

Figure 9.8 *Integrating Processes and Technology*

technology can enable the finance function to cut costs and collaborate more closely with business partners. The order-to-cash and period-end closing scenarios are good examples of what can be achieved in transaction processing and reporting. Our scenarios for decision support cover costing and results simulation, as well as risk identification, risk measurement and risk reporting.'

The mySAP Financials' vision for finance unites three key elements: business insight, operational efficiency and collaborative models. In Figure 9.9 these elements are related to the modules within the mySAP Financials suite.

So, mySAP Financials – embedded in the framework of mySAP technology – is a clear extension Beyond ERP. Financial supply chain, information supply chain and now, the newly identified, corporate reporting supply chain request new flexibility and adaptability of systems. We at SAP are committed to this in an evolutionary roll-out process, cross-industry and worldwide."

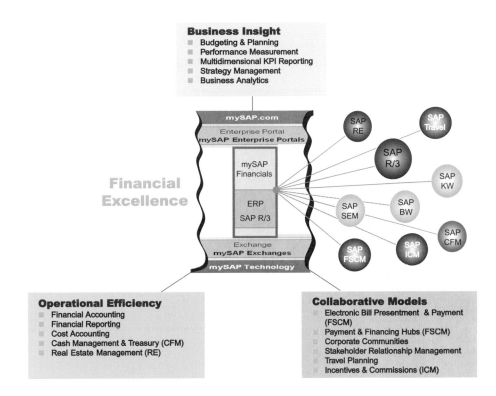

Figure 9.9   *mySAP Financials: Supporting New-Age Finance*

Throughout this chapter, we have discussed how the CFO is becoming more accountable for enterprise business performance; previously, compliance with accounting standards was enough. Today, more information is required for external reporting. The CFO is increasingly involved in both internal and external discussions on what information to disclose, in anticipating the questions that investors and their analysts will ask, and in helping to avoid, wherever possible, unwelcome surprises. Capital markets today are less tolerant and more demanding of the CFO. In the United States and elsewhere in the world, CFOs are now seen to be responsible and legally accountable for corporate decisions.

This book has covered the landscape today facing CFOs and their finance functions. It started with the issue of complexity and how integration can help the drive to achieving simplicity. As we've seen, integration isn't just about technology. It's about processes, organizational change and culture too. While we were writing this book, this landscape for the finance professional was in turmoil due to the notable failures in corporate accounting discipline which rapidly escalated into issues of global concern.

However, overreaction to crises which are short-lived is often inappropriate. Following your professional instincts is always the best approach. As always with change it is important to be realistic about where you are today and about how you benchmark against your peer group. But having a vision of where you want to go is even more important. And so is keeping it up to date!

Our approach as authors has been to bring together in one place what we see happening in the finance functions of some of the world's most influential enterprises. We provide a balance between what's working in practice and aspiration. We hope that you, the CFO, and your finance function will find this book useful as a starting point in moulding your corporation's aspirations to what is both a practical and robust solution for the future.

CFO CHECKLIST

TEST YOUR CORPORATE INTEGRITY
Challenge management at all levels to validate financial data for external reporting. Audit for completeness, compliance, and consistency. Consider your three-tier model for corporate transparency: GAAP, industry-based standards, company-specific standards.

BECOME THE INDEPENDENT BUSINESS PARTNER
Demonstrate to stakeholders the links between marketplace opportunities and strategy – between value drivers and measured results. Work with your CEO to ensure your organization complies with best practices. Take advantage of opportunities to present to stakeholders – be visible and inspire confidence. Build trust by presenting real results and issues.

MAP YOUR CORPORATE REPORTING SUPPLY CHAIN
Survey your stakeholders – ensure communications clearly reflect the true value and performance of the enterprise. Provide a commentary on risks and uncertainties.

CLOSE THE INFORMATION GAP
Identify the value drivers. What's missing? Develop a strategy for measuring, interlinking, and modeling value drivers throughout the enterprise. Integrate with your processes for planning, forecasting, and reporting on financial performance. Link your stakeholder communication channels.

GO FOR A FASTER CLOSE
Benchmark your performance for timely and accurate reporting. Evaluate the advantages of moving from a faster hard close, to a soft close and ultimately, a virtual close. Measure and track the benefits.

INTEGRATE THE FINANCE SYSTEMS LANDSCAPE
Map your financial supply chain and your information supply chain – identify the weak links and improvement opportunities. Take advantage of the latest technology for portals, exchanges, and application integration.

FRAME YOUR VISION FOR FINANCE IN 2010
Evaluate today's finance initiatives against the requirements of the organization tomorrow. Against the backdrop of changing technology, develop a future finance vision. Consider the finance function becoming a *business* in its own right. Anticipate new skills for *valuing the value chain*, resource integration, and enterprise risk.

Epilogue

In this final part of the book we stray beyond today's realities into an imaginary future. Many of the CFOs we've interviewed are interested in exploring the possibilities raised by the following questions:

What is the finance function of the future going to look like? Will the job of the CFO exist as we know it in, say the year 2010? What skills will be required? How will the power of technology be harnessed? Will the role of the CFO and the CIO be merged? Consider a vision for the finance function of 2010, based on a fictional but realistic, leap forward in time.

A FINANCE VISION FOR 2010

The year is 2003...... The CEO of ConsumerCo – a global branded products company with operations all over the world – presents a strategy to the board of directors: "Today our organization is country and supply-chain based; tomorrow it will be globally based on brands. We will have a renewed focus on innovation. Our year-on-year growth will be 4% and we will standardize our business processes world-wide to improve efficiency."

The CFO has a number of finance initiatives already under way. He is implementing shared services, going for a faster close, and even considering outsourcing the finance function. As he listens to the CEO, he worries about his ability to control the organization since he does not have the information to run the business on a global brand basis. Transparency and accountability for global accounting standards are foremost in his mind.

The CIO has been successful in implementing ERP and now sees the opportunities for reducing the number of instances and going for one global process model. She has a number of ideas for using technology for on-line retailing, but in the present economic climate, making the case based on ROI will prove difficult.

The Chief Marketing Officer (CMO) is fighting for his company's survival in the market place. Increased spending on advertising and trade promotions will be crucial to sustaining market share. He needs information globally on customer segments and advertising effectiveness to make his case for further discretionary spending. Inevitably, his relationships with both the CFO and CIO are strained.

It's 2005....Based on his strategy presentation, the CEO encourages his board executives to work together on a series of initiatives aimed at taking advantage of the latest technologies – portals, exchanges, and Web-based services. The CIO is delighted! By working together with the CMO, initiatives are launched for *smart items and agents* – the new technology for unique product identification based on radio frequency. This radically reduces supply-chain inefficiencies. Automatic replenishment, automatic invoicing, and new controls against pilfering are introduced. Linkages among manufacturer, retailer, and consumer get closer!

When the CMO retires, the CIO takes over his role. She introduces voice recognition and translation technology for sales order taking and management reporting – with *push alert* information. Communication is now based more on voice than on text.

The CFO has a number of new projects under way, including:

1. The transparency project in which he works with the CMO to introduce real-time analytics for customer segmentation. The goal is to adapt transaction processes to match the requirements of information processes. Handling huge amounts of data in real time requires new technology investment – intelligent search engines, sophisticated analytical tools, and new predictive rules based languages are introduced. The CMO can now learn from experience how customer behaviors are likely to develop and respond rapidly with targeted campaigns.

2. The ERP 2 project – he works with the CIO, suppliers and customers, to iron out remaining inefficiencies in the global supply chain infrastructure. Remaining opportunities for outsourcing in both front and back office are fully exploited. The business case is made for further investment in exchange and portal technology. The company is well on its way to achieving a virtual finance function.

Looking ahead to 2007....., the company has been transformed! It is now operating with only 20% of the products it had five years ago and is currently enjoying 8% per annum compound growth, with only 30% of the people. The supply chain is now fully outsourced; the company even partners with its competitors on non-competitive product projects. Many of the back-office and front-office processes are shared with business partners and there is a truly virtual global organization for managing each of the remaining brands. Staff members are located in parts of the world where the taxes and employment costs are low. For example, data centers are based in India and the finance shared services operates in Costa Rica.

The finance function has changed beyond all recognition! Transaction processing is virtual and seamless. Finance and marketing specialists are virtually indistinguishable and there is no such thing as an IT department anymore. Everyone is an IT "expert"!

The CFO is the primary deal maker and considers himself to be an *internal venture capitalist* funding new projects whose key role is evaluating their risks and returns. The CFO is legally accountable for conformance to the new global enterprise-wide GAAP. He focuses on value reporting, not accounting. It's his job to educate internally, to re-skill based on technology, and to make certain that the business function takes advantage of the fully integrated information supply chain. Since there is no physical supply chain anymore inside the business, there is no need for a COO. The CFO has the integration role and manages the value chain economics.

The CMO, on the other hand, is preoccupied with maximizing the value of the company's intangible assets, the source of the value creation – its brands and innovation pipeline. She is responsible for the global brand organization. For the first time in her career, she feels that she has the right valuation mechanisms, the right processes, the right systems, and the right measures! She is not reliant on the CFO, since historic accounting is a thing of the past. She also has no need for a CIO, since technology is an integral part of the product marketing and supply chain process.

The CFO is busy framing his finance initiatives for the year 2007 – 2010:

1. Finance is to become a business in its own right. A virtual control room manages the few exceptions remaining in the seamless transaction processing environment. Finance collaborates with external business partners via shared services.

2. The new global corporate governance model is to be implemented. Enterprise-wide integrity is the name of the game. This will require new processes and fresh skills to ensure compliance.

3. The new business model is on the drawing board – yet again! Consumer behavior changes so rapidly that the CFO seems to be constantly planning new scenarios and preparing predictive models based on the shape and character of the market. New value chain economic techniques are to be tested for more rapid, more comprehensive decision making.

The new finance organizational model for 2010 has only three specific roles:

1. The business economics manager (focused on searching for unique value creation opportunity)

2. The resource integrator (focused on people productivity from technology)

3. The enterprise risk manager (focused on stakeholder investment and security).

What is the organization like in 2010? It is ever changing, flat and non-hierarchical. It is cross functional and process driven. Silo-free and transparent. Corporate boundaries are a thing of the past, since the success of the extended enterprise is the ultimate goal. The only barriers are legal and regulatory.

Jobs are not defined by specific roles any more; everyone works in teams, sharing knowledge freely and using their knowledge to feed the global corporate learning base. These teams are not static; they are constantly changing to meet work-flow demands where there are discontinuities, bottle-necks, and problems to be resolved by human intervention. The lights-out era has arrived – for example, intervention is only required where exceptions to the norm arise.

How will people function in this organization of 2010? They feel confident in handling customers as well as suppliers and feel a deep empathy for their own consumers. They work outside normal corporate boundaries, moving freely between components of the extended enterprise. They use technology intuitively, as if it was second nature, to make transactions happen, to cut new deals, and to make difficult and often complex decisions. Such decisions are made on their own authority, without recourse to hierarchy. Individual rewards and incentives are unnecessary: the success of the extended enterprise is regarded as personal success!

Biographies

CHAPTER 2: LEVERAGING YOUR ERP INVESTMENT

Michael Sylvester was born and raised in Houston, Texas. He holds a B.S. in Foreign Service from Georgetown University and an M.S. in Accounting from Northeastern University, and is a Certified Public Accountant. After starting in the international tax practice of an international accounting firm, Michael worked in industry in the U.S. and Europe for a number of years before coming to SAP AG in 1999. He has been Product Manager for Accounting since that time, participating in development and software architecture projects as well as dealing with various implementation issues with regard to international accounting standards.

CHAPTER 3: STREAMLINING THE FINANCIAL SUPPLY CHAIN

Reiner Wallmeier has been at SAP since 1987 as a developer, project manager, and development manager, being one of the founders of R/3 development. He is now Director of Product Management in Financials. Over the past few years he has focused on the architecture of a new business accounting model. Prior to joining SAP he was head of accounting and controlling at a Japanese trading company.

CHAPTER 4: MOVING FROM "SHARED" TO "MANAGED" SERVICES

Stephen Burns is a management consultant with a global business background. His particular areas of expertise are shared services and business process outsourcing. His background includes work with both "global 1000" corporations (Exxon Mobil, STMicroelectronics) and "tier one" consulting organizations (PricewaterhouseCoopers, SAP). His published writings span a variety of topics ranging from internal audit to expatriate life in Asia. Stephen has a degree in physics from Swarthmore College and an MBA from The Wharton School.

CHAPTER 5: CONNECTING STRATEGY WITH OPERATIONS

Dr. Karsten Oehler is Director of Program Management for mySAP Financials. Prior to joining SAP, he spent more than ten years at several international companies as a product manager and consultant for managerial accounting software. He has published books on IT systems for financial applications and OLAP, as well as other publications on software systems for managerial accounting. He is a frequent speaker at conferences and seminars.

Marcus Wefers is Director of Product Management for SAP SEM. He started at SAP in 1990 developing software applications for operational and strategic enterprise management. He also developed interfaces for operational R/3 applications. During his time as development manager, he had a major influence on the development of SAP SEM. Marcus has led numerous international development projects in the United States, Asia, and Europe.

CHAPTER 6: CONVERTING DATA INTO ACTION

Jochen Mayerle holds a graduate degree in Business Informatics and joined SAP AG in 2001 as a member of the mySAP Financials Product Management team. He has more than 10 years' experience in designing, developing, and implementing cost accounting solutions. Jochen is an expert in the area of financial analytics.

CHAPTER 7: COLLABORATION VIA THE ENTERPRISE PORTAL

Markus Kuppe joined SAP AG in 1997 and has since headed various development projects for cost management applications and enterprise portals. He is now Director of Product Management for the mySAP Financials Portal Solutions, creating new collaborative financial applications with and for customers. Markus holds a graduate degree in Mathematics from the University of Darmstadt.

Ariane Skutela is a product manager at SAP AG in Germany. Currently focused on mySAP Financials Portal Solutions, she works with customers to determine their product needs and requirements for product planning and development. Ariane has several years experience in logistics and IT controlling, involving the development of concepts, software training, and management consulting. She is a frequent speaker at SAP conferences. Ariane holds a graduate degree in business economics.

CHAPTER 8: MANAGING INTANGIBLES

Jürgen Daum is a senior business consultant at SAP AG and is an internationally recognized expert in enterprise management systems and finance. His previous position at SAP was Director of Program Management, in which capacity he was responsible for the strategic positioning of mySAP Financials. Before joining SAP he was CFO of a German IT company. He is the author of the book Intangible Assets and Value Creation.

CHAPTER 9: INTEGRATING FOR CORPORATE INTEGRITY

Kraig Haberer is responsible for developing product, marketing, and sales strategies worldwide for SAP's financial solutions, and is Director of Product Marketing for mySAP Financials. Prior to joining SAP, Kraig held several senior marketing and product management positions with leading financial application software companies including FiNetrics, Inc. and Computer Associates. Additionally, Kraig practiced as a certified public accountant with PricewaterhouseCoopers in the Audit and Business Advisory Services group as well as served as a financial controller in the private sector. Kraig holds a B.S. in Accountancy from the University of Illinois and is a Certified Public Accountant (CPA).

Barbara Dörr is a member of the product management team for mySAP Financials, and was the project director for this book. Her main activities lie in generic financial topics such as Fast Close. She joined SAP AG in 1990 as an instructor for customer courses in financials, focusing on integration, closing activities, and consolidation.

Support Team

Stephanie Eger is a management assistant in the mySAP Financials team and was involved in the writing sessions of this book. Stephanie joined SAP AG in 1998 after her European secretary studies in Mannheim.

Sue Bishop is a research analyst with CCR Partners Limited and was involved in the writing and editing sessions of this publication. Prior to joining CCR Partners, Sue worked in the financial services industry.

Notes

Chapter 1

1. PricewaterhouseCoopers Financial and Cost Management Team (1997/1999) *CFO: Architect of the Corporation's Future*, Wiley.
2. PricewaterhouseCoopers Financial and Cost Management Team (2001): *eCFO: Sustaining Value in the New Corporation*, Wiley.

Chapter 2

1. SAP (2001) *e-Business Solutions help Colgate clean up*, Annual Report.
2. SAP (2001) *Exchange Infrastructure: Process-centric Collaboration*, Whitepaper, Version 1.1.
3. Paul Stedman, (November 2001): *Global Deployment Strategies in the Pharmaceutical Industry for open e-Business Integration*, SAP UK.

Chapter 3

1. The Aberdeen Group.
2. Killen & Associates, Inc. (October 2000) *Optimizing the Financial Supply Chain*.
3. Dun & Bradstreet.
4. Killen & Associates, Inc. (November 2001) *Renewed Focus on Cash/ Opportunities for CFOs and Treasurers in the FSC*.
5. SAP (2001) *mySAP Financials Corporate Finance Management*, Whitepaper.
6. mySAP Financials (2001) *Electronic Financing and Settlement with Orbian*, Solution Brief.

Chapter 4

1. Andersen/Akris.com (2001) *Shared Services Extend their Reach.*
2. *CFO Architect of the Corporation's Future*, op.cit.
3. Institute for Strategic Change (2002) *Accenture: Integrating Enterprise Outsourced Solutions*, Research Note.
4. *Information Week* (July 2002) *Osram Case Study.*
5. Case studies provided by Atos Origin, a leading vendor of managed services and applications management.
6. Ken Kenjale and Arnie Phatah, (June 2002) *Avoiding Past Mistakes*, Syntel, TexYard Case Study.
7. Dan Jankowska, (May 2002) *Covisint Presentation*, Society of Information Management.
8. KPMG/SAP (July 2002): *Web Services – the Hype-Free Guide*, Whitepaper.
9. Web Methods (2002) *Enterprise Web Services in the Financial Services Industry.*

Chapter 5

1. SAP (June 1999) *Strategic Enterprise Management – Enabling Value Based Management*, Whitepaper.
2. Brian Lever and David Ketchin (April 2002) *The Performance Management Proposition*, Atos KPMG Consulting.
3. *CFO: Architect of the Corporation's Future,* op.cit.
4. SAP (2001) *Beyond Budgeting* Whitepaper prepared in collaboration with the Consortium for Advanced Manufacturing International (CAM-I) Beyond Budgeting Round Table.

Chapter 6

1. Henry Morris and Robert Blumstein, (2001) *Analytical Applications, Market Forecast and Analytics 2001 to 2005*, IDC.
2. Douglas Dorrat, CEO of VisionCube Plc. *Customer Value Management*, Whitepaper.
3. Neill Adams *Perspectives on Creating Value*, Jonova, Inc.
4. Aberdeen Group, Inc. (April 2002) *Financial Analytics Software – User Observations.*

5. Interview with Michael D. Capellas, Chairman and CEO of Compaq Computer Corporation, SAP Info Publication, Article No. 2097, 15 May 2002.
6. Paul Bhui *HR Analytics Presentation*, Atos KPMG Consulting.
7. W.H. Inmon (March 2002) *Analytics: 10 Critical Success Factors*.

Chapter 7

1. eCFO: Sustaining Value in the New Corporation. op.cit.
2. Drs Steffens, Dorrhuer, and Zlender (November 2000): *Portals: Usability Test of Selected Business Processes*, University of Mannheim.
3. SAP (2001) *Portal Infrastructure: People-centric Collaboration*, Whitepaper.
4. Pricewaterhouse Coopers and SAP (2001) *The e-Business Workplace – Discovering the Power of Enterprise Portals*. Whitepaper.
5. META Group (2002) *Generating Value from Enterprise Financial Applications*.

Chapter 8

1. David Aboody and Baruch Lev (March 2001) *R&D Productivity in the Chemical Industry*.
2. PricewaterhouseCoopers (February 2000) *Innovation and Growth: Thriving Beyond 2000*.
3. Alfred Rappaport (1986) *Creating Shareholder Value*, New York: The Free Press revised and updated edition 1998.
4. Jürgen H. Daum, Senior Business Consultant with SAP AG: *Intangible Assets and Value Creation* (published in 2002); much of the material in this chapter is based on his original research and insights.
5. Both case studies, ABB and Cisco, are reported under this aspect in Daum, *Intangible Assets and Value Creation*, op.cit.
6. Baruch Lev (2001) *Intangibles: Management, Measurement and Reporting*.
7. Conceptual framework for a Tableau de Bord is introduced and described in Daum: *Intangible Assets and Value Creation*.
8. Skandia case study, interview with Leif Edvinsson originally published in *Intangible Assets and Value Creation*, Jürgen Daum.

Chapter 9

1. *Financial Times* September 2002.
2. Graham Harvey (October 2002) *Delivering Business Promises*, Atos KPMG Consulting, Whitepapter.
3. Samual A. DiPiazza, Jr (PricewaterhouseCoopers) and Robert G. Eccles (Advisory Capital Partners), (2002) *Building Public Trust*, Wiley.

Index

Index compiled by Annette Musker